Praise for *Dudley Carter: Tales of the Legendary Wood Sculptor*

"Lambert and Sikkema's tribute to Dudley Carter is a lively and loving portrait of the great Northwest master, capturing the life and work of an artist as powerful as the ancient forests from which he drew his strength and inspiration. More than biography, more than anthology, *Dudley Carter* is a tapestry woven of many voices and stories, richly illustrated with the works of Carter and brought vividly to life through the memories of family, friends and fellow artists (many themselves Northwest legends).

Dudley Carter reminds us that Carter's gift lies not just in his monumental sculpture or graceful carvings, but also in his singular ability to capture in physical form the enduring and ethereal spirit of the Northwest itself. *Dudley Carter: Tales of the Legendary Wood Sculptor* is the perfect coda to a revered Northwest original, whose work uniquely connected ancient traditions, modern cultures, and personal visions in a legacy that has no equal."

Leonard Garfield, Executive Director
Museum of History & Industry, Seattle

"With this deep and broad depiction of the life, works, and working milieu of sculptor Dudley Carter, the authors open up that world to a new generation of readers of art history and Pacific Northwest history. Lambert and Sikkema combine photographs, family reminiscences and letters, and the memories of Carter's large coterie of apprentices and others to build an extraordinarily fascinating study of a man whose life spanned most of the twentieth century."

Margaret Rockenbeck
Redmond Historical Society Programs Chair

Dudley Carter

Tales of the Legendary Wood Sculptor

'Lyn Fleury Lambert and H. Mary Sikkema

Foreword by Daphne K. Morris

NW Wood Words
USA

Dudley Carter: Tales of the Legendary Wood Sculptor
Copyright © 2020 NW Woods Words, LLC

Published by NW Wood Words, LLC, USA
www.nwwoodwords.com

All rights reserved. No part of this book may be reproduced or transmitted in any form or by any means, electronic or mechanical, including photocopying, recording, or by any information storage and retrieval system, without the written permission of the publisher, except by a reviewer who may quote brief passages in a critical article or review to be printed in a magazine or newspaper, or electronically transmitted on radio, television, or the internet.

Verifying the dimensions, dates, and titles of Dudley Carter's works was an important but challenging aspect of this book. The authors discovered discrepancies even in Dudley's own records, but they have done their best to corroborate the information. Measurements are listed by height, width, and depth.

ISBN: 978-1-7345006-0-8

FIRST PRINTING

Designed by Tim Young
Edited by Lisa Lambert

Front Cover: *Forest Deity*, 1947, red cedar, 14′ × 9′ × 4′
Dudley at work on *Forest Deity* outside Granite Falls, Washington. The artist carved the twenty-foot-high stump still rooted in terra firma where the tree had grown for many years. *Forest Deity* has been displayed outdoors at Bellevue Square in Bellevue, Washington, for over seventy years.
Photograph AP/Paul Wagner

Back Cover: Detail of *Celestial Adventure*, 1991, red cedar, 8′3″ × 16′ × 6′10″
Photograph Ronald Holden

To Anna, Dudley's granddaughter and preeminent protégé

A few years after her grandfather died, Anna was awarded two prestigious public commissions in Bellevue and Redmond, Washington, which afforded us the opportunity to get to know her, to be captivated by her sunny outlook on life, and to be immensely impressed by her extraordinary talent. Anna greatly enhanced this book by sharing with us many memories of her grandfather and photographs of his works. We are ever so grateful.

Contents

FOREWORD — xi
    By Daphne K. Morris

PREFACE — xiii
    By 'Lyn Lambert

INTRODUCTION: *Once upon a time…* — xv
    By 'Lyn Lambert

I ROOTS OF THE TREE CARVER

  1 *In the Beginning…* — 2
    From the notes of Dudley Carter, his brothers Stanley and Darwin, and their father, Foster

  2 *Pioneers of the Lumber Industry* — 11
    From a conversation with Ted Nelson

  3 *Futures Found in Bars of Soap* — 16
    From a conversation with George Tsutakawa

  4 *Legacies and Liberties* — 19
    From a conversation with Bill Holm

  5 *Carving Out an Art Career* — 24
    From a conversation with Jane Oestreich

6	*Working through the Depression* From a conversation with Evelyn Balko	30
7	*Legend of North Wind and Storm Wind* Adapted by David M. Buerge	33

II CARVING HIS OWN NICHE

8	*Zen of the Axe* Reminiscences of Geordie Tocher	38
9	*Illusions and Reality* Reminiscences of Philip R. Wood	40
	No Bad Bear Days From the memories of Lex Hanson	48
10	*Condor* By 'Lyn Lambert and Mary Sikkema	52
11	*Legend of Wek Wek and the Holukmeyumko* Compiled by 'Lyn Lambert and Mary Sikkema	54
12	*An Infusion of Geniuses* By 'Lyn Lambert	57
13	*Craftsman or Artist?* From a conversation with Everett DuPen	62
14	*A Lumberjack in the Halls of Ivy* From an interview with Duane Hanson by Liza Kirwin	65
15	*An Original* From a conversation with Thomas Dunstan	68
16	*Reviving History* From the writing of Albert H. Culverwell	73
17	*A Masterpiece* From a conversation with Kemper Freeman, Jr.	77

III TOTEMIC PRINCIPLES

18	*Totem of Lake Wilderness* By 'Lyn Lambert	82
19	*The Northgate Connection* From conversations with Marvin Boys	85
20	*Mink and Wolf Totem* By 'Lyn Lambert	93
21	*Spiritual Perceptions* From a conversation with James Washington, Jr.	96
22	*Transitions and Transformations* Reminiscences of Geordie Tocher	102

23	*Legend of Moon the Transformer* Adapted by David M. Buerge	106
24	*A Tribute for Two* By 'Lyn Lambert	109
25	*Little Orphan Alder* By Don Clark	112
26	*A Grand Totem for a Prairie School* From the writing of Ann McLeod	114

IV THE MASTER CARVER

27	*At Home in the House of the Master* From a conversation with Bill McNae	118
	At Play in the House of the Master By Anna Vaughan Hanson	124
28	*Secrets Revealed* From a conversation with Donald McAusland	126
29	*Forest Reflections* From a conversation with Robert Chervenak	130
30	*Desert Studio* From a conversation with Earl J. Neel	132
31	*Great Expectations, Diminished Actualities—Fine Art Forthcoming Nonetheless* A memo from Dudley Carter	135
32	*Beyond Expectations* By Abby Sher	138
	Attitude is Everything By Ron Sher	143
33	*A Timely Request* From a conversation with Ted Nelson	145
34	*Delivering Three Big Cedars* By Jesse Wilt	147
35	*Spirit of the Northwest* From the writing of James C. Michaelsen	153
36	*A Most Decent Proposal* From the writing of Nancy Crozier	159
37	*Garland of Earthly Delights* Perceptions of Jon Kraft	163
38	*Meeting the Man in the Mural* Reminiscences of Masha Zakheim	165
39	*Restoration and Reward* From a conversation with Roger Baird	171

40	*A Sanctuary for Sanctuary* From a conversation with Dick Cooley	178
41	*Yes, Dudley, there is a Santa Claus* From conversations with Bertil Valley	184

V LEGACY

42	*The Washington Centennial Hall of Honor* By 'Lyn Lambert	192
43	*Transcending the Wave* Reminiscences of Geordie Tocher	194
44	*An Emerging Vision* From the writing of David L. Vaughan	198
45	*The Maid of the Woods Tree* From the notes of Dudley Carter	201
46	*Art and Moralizing* From the writing of Richard S. Beyer	205
47	*Life in the Fasting Lane* From the writing of Steve Johnston	208
48	*Healing Art* From a conversation with Kathy Conner	212
	Catch the Wind By Kathy Conner	218
	Legend of the Sea By 'Lyn Lambert	219
49	*As Light Illuminates the Darkness* From a conversation with Dean Fredrickson	220
50	*Windsong* Excerpted from "A Patient Hand" by Ronald Holden	228
51	*Ingrained Difference* From the writing of David Marshall	230
52	*"It would be better if…"* From conversations with Michael Vaughan	232
53	*A Sister Remembers* From the writing of Aene Carter Ferguson	240
54	*Voices of the Spirit* From conversations with Ralph Bennett	242
55	*Legend of How Raven Put the Light in its Right Place* A version of the legend told by Ralph Bennett	246
56	*And the Story of Memaloosa Sam* By Dudley C. Carter, edited by 'Lyn Lambert	250

57 River of Life 254
    By Anna Vaughan Hanson

EPILOGUE: *Never Say Never* 259
    By 'Lyn Lambert

AFTERWORD: *To Preserve and Protect* 265
    From a conversation with Mayumi Tsutakawa

AFTER PHOTOGRAPHS 267

ACKNOWLEDGEMENTS 280

CHRONOLOGY OF DUDLEY C. CARTER SCULPTURES 282

ABOUT THE AUTHORS 294

Foreword

Dudley Carter was one of the best known and most prolific wood sculptors on the West Coast. He grew up in British Columbia logging camps operated by his family in the early part of the twentieth century. His early experiences and his proximity to timber led him on a lifelong career in carving. Another early influence in his life was his interest in Haida and Kwakwaka'wakw (Kwakiutl) monumental art. He produced his own first monumental work in 1932 and was an active sculptor until he died just short of his 101st birthday.

His work is a notable sixty-year achievement and is for much of the public their most prominently encountered experience of monumental art with Native American derivation by a single artist in western Washington. His prodigious output and its similarities as well as its differences from Northwest Coast Native art invite a spectator to appreciate it from many viewpoints.

Bill Holm, one of the leading scholars and teachers in the field of Northwest Coast Native arts, worked with Carter and knew him well. Holm stated that Carter thought of his work simply as wood sculptures rather than as totem poles in the traditional sense. Although in their monumental and sculptural character, and sometimes their themes, they resemble poles of the Northwest Coast, Carter was clearly not trying to mimic the Northern tradition. In fact, his style was closer to the Southern tradition of the Coast Salish and Nuu-chah-nulth nations, which had no indigenous tradition of monumental totemic art and in which the artists often created their own visual language. Indeed, the figures that appear on Carter's poles are often idiosyncratic rather than reflecting a standard iconography. Another deviation from an established motif is Carter's insertion of a signature pineapple crosshatching pattern. It is quite a reliable clue in the identification of his carved pieces.

In another sense, too, Carter's work resembles the Southern artists' work: like theirs, his poles are primarily designed to recount a myth or legend with broad significance rather than to display inherited crests having significance for the owner's family. And, as with some of the Southern poles, the meaning of Carter's poles is at least partly private—possessed in the mind of the artist and not available to the casual observer. Dudley Carter's work will best be appreciated when the viewer recognizes the ways in which it both is and is not Native-style art.

Carter was generous in sharing his carving techniques, and his enthusiasm was contagious. Although many awards were bestowed upon him, as one of his students pointed out to me, a most prized honor for Dudley Carter was to have a former student return to his studio with a new Carter-influenced carving in hand.

Daphne K. Morris

Daphne K. Morris is a past board member of the Seattle Art Museum's Native Arts of the Americas and Oceania Council and co-author with Lloyd J. Averill of the guidebook *Northwest Coast Native and Native-Style Art*.

A portion of this foreword was previously published in *Northwest Coast Native and Native-Style art: A Guidebook for Western Washington*, 1995, reprinted with permission of the University of Washington Press.

Preface

 Compilation of this book has been a decades-long effort, not long considering the efforts expended by the subject of these chronicles covered an entire century. Dudley Carter's work and his life were truly monumental, so it stands to reason that a comprehensive book about such a man would be a monumental task.

 In 1991 when Dudley Carter was one hundred years old and I was serving as his secretary, Dudley showed me the handwritten beginnings of his autobiography. In his steady, ever-so-legible longhand, he had composed several pages. It was eloquent writing—fascinating reading—but it covered only the first four years of his life. Unless Dudley quit sculpting and settled down to write full-time he might not get the autobiography finished—ever.

 Dudley certainly wasn't ready to quit sculpting, but he was eager to get his autobiography out. I suggested that we might find a writer who could help speed up the process and Dudley was agreeable. I had a particular writer in mind. My friend Mary Sikkema was an accomplished writer with a strong desire to publish a book. I knew Mary to be, like Dudley, a person deep into her Christian faith. She was bright. She was insightful. I introduced the two, and soon the three of us began meeting regularly. Mary posed questions, Dudley responded, and I recorded the sessions and acted as "interpreter," as Dudley liked to call me. Dudley's hearing was seriously impaired, but he could hear my voice better than most. Also, his speech was rather indistinct, but I managed to understand him somewhat more readily than could many people.

 We met once a week, but soon Dudley suggested twice-weekly meetings. He may have known something that Mary and I didn't. We could see that his health was failing, but we didn't expect his time with us would end any time soon. Dudley welcomed us, sharing his stories, until just days before he died.

 After Dudley's death, his family discouraged us from attempting to complete his biography. Mary was decidedly disappointed. She very much wanted to see the Dudley Carter project through.

I began to envision another type of book—a collection of stories about Dudley combined with photographs of his works. As Dudley's secretary, I had helped him with his Christmas cards and expected that I could connect with a number of his friends and family who might be interested in sharing some Dudley Carter stories. Mary liked the idea, and to our delight almost everyone I contacted was enthusiastic about contributing to such a book. We also reached out to other people who had been influenced in some way by their connection with the artist or his works. Mary and I interviewed some storytellers. Other storytellers wrote out their remembrances or tape-recorded them. We wrote and polished each story, endeavoring to keep them in their tellers' voices, and sent our draft manuscripts to each storyteller for approval or refinement.

The experience was enriching and enjoyable beyond our expectations. The people in Dudley's life were as delightful, as varied, and as surprising as is his art. The Dudley Carter stories celebrate not only Dudley and his art but also the lives and works of numerous notable artists and interesting characters.

The enjoyment wasn't without sadness. Many of our contributors passed away before they could see their stories in print. And very regrettably, a few years into our collaboration, Mary's health began to fail, and she was no longer able to write. Her illness proved to be terminal. Mary died in the fall of 2015. I could not let the book drop. Dudley Carter's art was too important, his stories too interesting and inspirational. The photographs of his work could be invaluable and crucial to preserving Dudley's contribution to the world of art. I resolved to see Dudley's book published. Working on my own proved to be rather capricious, but providentially, Lisa Lambert offered to join me in the project. With Lisa's genius in the mix, Dudley Carter's book is indeed a new and improved product.

I hope Dudley, his family, and all of the storytellers will be pleased with these chronicles. I hope Mary will be pleased. And I hope countless readers will be pleased too.

'Lyn Fleury Lambert, 2020

Introduction

Once upon a time...

Once upon a time, not so very long ago, in a land not so far away, there lived a man, weatherworn, wiry, and wise, who at the age of forty literally hewed his way out of the forest primeval and into the sophisticated world of art.

After working for decades deep in the Northwest Coast's woods at the behest of lumber industry giants, the mini Paul Bunyan found himself in the center court of the country's newest major art museum, acclaimed for his first monumental axe-hewn wood sculpture. The prolific woodsman-cum-artist combined two remarkably long, lucrative, and demanding careers—timber cruising and sculpting. When not working in the woods, he was creating countless art works in wood, the likes of which had never been seen before and—until nature can revive her old-growth forests—may never be seen again.

Dudley Carter's life itself was a work of art spanning a full century at a time when such longevity was rare. He overcame numerous deadly diseases and disasters, any one of which could have cut his life short. And it was a life that, in spite of considerable commercial success and critical acclaim, brought none of the vagaries that can often accompany life in the limelight.

During the Great Depression of the 1930s, American monumental sculpture seemed to be root-bound. Statues and monuments typically took the form of idealized likenesses, and to Dudley Carter they lacked spirit, lacked energy. So, this enterprising man, inspired by the indigenous peoples of the Northwest among whom he had lived as a youth, took his double-bladed axe and single-handedly enlivened sculpture by elevating the craft of wood carving to a true art form.

Dudley Carter was a top-notch timber cruiser, a profession that required him to trek through dense forests seeking out and mapping harvestable building materials. The artist in him envisioned the majestic trees not only as planks and posts, beams and boards, but also as a medium for his own artistic expression. Dudley determined that he could illustrate wondrous tales, myths, and legends much like generations of West Coast Indians had done with their totem poles. Native works generally proclaimed pride in the history or accomplishment of a man, his family, or clan; Dudley's creations would convey conflict, love, the power and beauty of nature, and the origin of the world and universe.

To Dudley Carter realism did not make a piece of sculpture a work of art; the beauty of representational sculpture was not in the accuracy of its portrayal. A sculptor too concerned with superficial details could conceal the natural pattern—the character—of his medium. From Dudley Carter's perspective, the medium is much of the message.

The very nature of his medium destined much of Dudley's art to limited longevity. Without adequate care, wood yields to the forces of nature. Fortunately, private collectors, museums, and other institutions preserve many of Dudley's fine artistic compositions. But nature has had her way with too many others, and they have succumbed to weather and vermin. Providentially, pictures can speak quite eloquently of sculptures that have been forgotten or have returned to nature. And stories told by those who remember him can keep alive the spirit of the artist. So within the pages of this book, readers may find enjoyment in the works of a very fine artist, and perhaps, even inspiration in the example of a life well lived.

When asked to name what he considered to be his finest work, Dudley always deferred, saying that he hadn't done it yet. That was likely true. His monumental works are marvelous indeed, but his finest accomplishment may have been his remarkable life. That was completed on April 7, 1992—a century-long commission. No doubt the Commissioner would say it was a work well done.

'Lyn Fleury Lambert, 2020

The sculptor's shingle
Photograph 'Lyn Lambert

Part I
ROOTS OF A TREE CARVER

"To understand my work,
you must know where I came from."

Dudley Carter

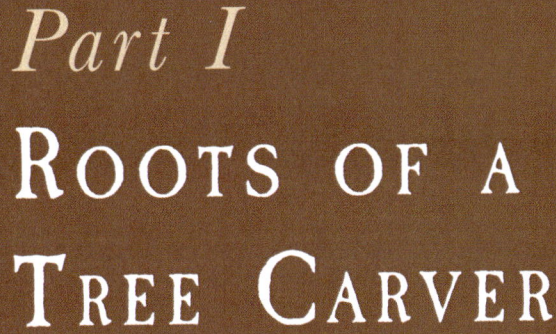

Carter Brothers' Logging Operation, Stave Falls, 1902, by Dudley Carter
Sketch courtesy Abby Sher

Chapter 1

In the Beginning

From the notes of Dudley Carter, his brothers Stanley and Darwin, and their father, Foster

Michelangelo was said to have suckled his passion for marble with his foster mother's milk in the quarries of Settignano. Dudley Carter, labeled by some Michelangelo with an axe, acquired his ardor for wood in the virgin forests of British Columbia.

On prominent display in the pioneering Carter family's rustic cedar home stood a world globe, not of manufactured origin, but one carefully crafted by young Dudley and his two older brothers under the guidance of their father, Foster Carter. The boys cut cedar rounds from a log, clamped them firmly, bore a hole through their centers, and joined them together with a bolt running between the North and South Poles. The saw cuts of the rounds formed the lines of latitude. After trimming it smooth and painting the lines of longitude, the boys were instructed by their father in painting a map of the world on the globe. They delineated the continents, major bodies

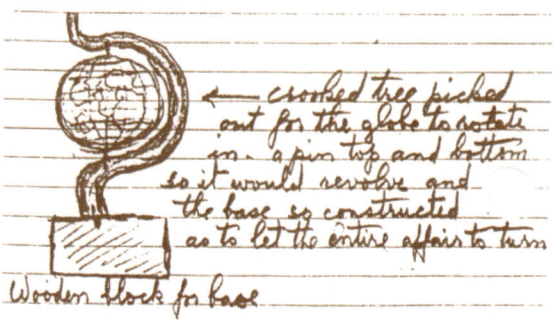

Sketch of handcrafted globe, by Stanley Carter, constructed by the young Carter boys under the guidance of their father
From the papers of Stanley Carter, courtesy Clarence Carter

of water, countries, provinces, and states. A crooked tree branch supported the eighteen-inch orb on a

Stanley, Darwin, and Dudley (left to right) on the banks of Devil's Creek, which ran through much of the Carter homestead. Foster's old Indian dugout canoe is to the left. Fred Easthope took this photo as a gift to the boys' mother for her birthday, February 14, 1894. Photograph courtesy Eltheen Carter King

wooden block base, allowing the globe to rotate on its axis.

Foster's purpose in directing his sons to make such a globe was not solely to teach them wood craftsmanship; the globe served as a teaching aid. In spite of the absence of schools in the backwoods of British Columbia, he was determined that his sons would be educated. Having benefited from formal schooling in the British West Indies and later in England, Foster saw to it that his young ones would grow in knowledge. Each evening he would set out the next day's studies, emphasizing the three Rs, natural science, health, and geography. Early geography lessons focused on places central to Foster's own life, starting with Barbados in the West Indies, where he was born some thirty years previous.

When Foster was in his late teens, his father's successful Caribbean sugar cane plantation came upon hard times. In 1882 the entire family—Mr. and Mrs. Christopher Blackett Carter, three sons, and a daughter—made their way to a new life in Eastern Canada. Though Foster was the classically educated eldest son from a privileged family, once in Canada he found he enjoyed manual labor. He first settled in Montreal, where he worked at several physically demanding jobs. Later he moved to North Bay, Ontario, taking up farming with his brother Edwin.

In September of 1886 Foster Carter married the lovely Sophia Amelia Miller, who had been born seventeen years earlier in Cambridgeshire, England. Sophia had spent much of her young life in a convent school in Eastern Canada. A year after their marriage a son was born to the young couple. Foster, enamored of science and evolution, named the child after the famed evolutionist Darwin. Another son, Stanley, arrived in April 1889.

Foster's brother Edwin found Ontario's weather too harsh, and in 1889, after the completion of the Canadian Pacific Railway in 1885, he headed for the milder climate of British Columbia. He homesteaded 160 acres on the Stave River. Within a year his parents, his brother Norton, and his sister, Meta, followed, beginning yet another new way of life in Western Canada. It wasn't long before

In the Beginning

Foster and Sophia determined that their future also could be better fulfilled in Western Canada, and in December 1890 the young Carter clan boarded a westbound train.

Arriving at Whonnock Station, some three miles west of the junction of the Stave and Fraser Rivers, they were warmly welcomed by Edwin. A difficult uphill journey of seven miles on foot faced the weary travelers, for no wagon road, not even so much as a horse trail, linked the railway and Edwin's homestead. Foster tucked the tots into a gunnysack, cut holes in the bottom so their legs could protrude, hoisted them to his back, and the family set forth. Sophia followed the men, carrying such necessities as she could manage. Sophia, it so happened, also bore an especially precious bundle, for she was in the early stages of pregnancy with Dudley Christopher.

A crudely blazed path led them through dense virgin forest. Canopies of thick evergreens turned daylight to darkness as the Carters made their way, often crawling over wind-felled trees—some as large as ten feet in diameter—notched with toeholds by earlier adventurers. Nothing much grew in the shadow of the trees, and the forest floor held only wet mosses and loose, slippery duff. The constant roar of the Stave River, as it tumbled toward its confluence with the Fraser, told of the power of nature in their new land.

The safe arrival at Edwin's homestead was a joyous reunion of three generations of Carters. Foster, Sophia, and their boys settled in with Edwin,

The Old Carter Homestead, Stave River Valley, 1892,
by Dudley Carter
Sketch courtesy Sharlene Nelson

Grandfather and Grandmother Carter, Norton, and Meta in Edwin's large two-story home. Over a period of time, Foster cleared his own land and constructed a log house five miles further up the west bank of the Stave River.

In the spring of 1891 Foster took Sophia to New Westminster, then the capital of British Columbia, to await the arrival of their third child. They stayed in a small cabin on the site where a monument to the British explorer Simon Fraser was later erected. On the sixth of May Dudley Christopher Carter, a healthy child, was born. Bishop Sillitoe officiated at the baby's christening with a Salvation Army man serving as his godfather, even though Foster was a declared atheist at the time. While in New Westminster the Carters became acquainted with the Easthopes, recent immigrants from England and the family from which Dudley would later choose his wife.

Foster moved his expanded family to their completed sixteen-by-sixteen-foot cedar log home. The entire house—roof, floor, fixtures, and furniture—was hand-split cedar. Joints between the logs were chinked with moss to prevent drafts. There was no shortage of building material; the land produced a bonanza of arboreal giants—real believe-it-or-not trees. One measured fifty-three feet in circumference at four feet above the ground and divided into five trunks about sixty feet up. Nearby lay a red cedar windfall sixteen feet in diameter. On top of the windfall grew another cedar estimated to have been five hundred years old. Its roots had started in the moss of the nurse log and worked their way to the ground. The Carters surmised the big fallen tree could have dated to the time of Noah, but the wood was still sound.

The ancient forests grew healthy and sound, but staying alive was a challenge for pioneer families. A cholera epidemic swept through the area, and Dudley, at sixteen months of age, contracted the disease. His mother carried him around on a pillow for months, for he was scarcely more than a little bag of bones. Few infant victims of cholera lived, but Dudley was a survivor. His constitution was again put to the test when he developed rheumatic fever a few years later, triggering hearing problems and arthritis that would plague him for the rest of his life.

In spite of his ailments, Dudley enjoyed a vigorous childhood. He and his brothers, as each reached the age of six, went to work in the logging operation the family established in 1893. The entry-level job for the young boys was skid greaser. Dudley described himself as a little brat of six or seven feeling he was performing a very important job. Toting a can of grease in one hand and wielding a stick with a rag tied to one end in the other, he slopped grease on every skid as powerful oxen snorted and pounded at his heels. In 1898 the Carter Brothers purchased a team of horses, and hauling timber out of the woods became a little easier. The old ox team became corned beef.

It was far from all work and no play for the youngsters. With no toys, no organized games of any sort, nature entertained them. In the summer when the bracken ferns were tender, the boys would get kitchen knives and cut the ferns into miniature logs, the way the men did with the trees. Capturing a large grasshopper and looping a piece of sewing thread over its neck, they would have it haul the little logs. Nature fascinated them—brooks and ponds filled with fish, frogs, and water insects, and fields alive with meadow mice making their runways. Foster, a student of the physical world and evolution, encouraged his sons' interest in their environment.

Nature also provided many special, edible treats. The boys developed a fondness for the tender shoots of sweet and flavorful licorice ferns growing on the trunks of the maples. They gathered wild berries with their mother, often coming upon a bear helping

In the Beginning

Skid Greaser and Ox Team, by Dudley Carter. Sketch courtesy Sharlene Nelson

himself to the bounty. The boys fished for brook trout with a line of common string, a bent pin for a hook, and a worm, grasshopper, or piece of red yarn for bait. With red wool they could fish all day without bothering to change lures. They became expert at harpooning trout with a long piece of wood sharpened to a point. They could catch more fish in an hour than they could carry home. Some were Dolly Vardens almost three feet long.

Sophia baked bread in round cans and often presented her sons with a slice of warm bread slathered with thick condensed milk or butter the boys had made by shaking cream from the lumber camp's cow in a quart bottle. The brothers would run down to the meadow and pick tender grass and clover shoots to top off the treat.

The boys were not permitted to carry guns before they were ten years of age. Until then they were encouraged to challenge the mountain lions and other predators with their tin can parade—dishpans and oilcans vigorously pounded upon to drive away the beasts of prey that had an appetite for their mother's chickens.

The family also raised a few sheep and pigs. When there was more meat than they required, they packed the extra lamb and pork into parcels, and the three little fellows hiked seven miles downstream to the socialist commune of Ruskin to sell the meat from house to house.

The Carter brothers frequently moved their

Roots of the Tree Carver

logging operations to other camps, and Sophia cooked and baked for the workers. The young Carter boys did kitchen patrol—washing dishes, peeling potatoes and apples, and carrying firewood and water. As the boys matured they took on ever more demanding jobs in the family business. By their early teens they were regarded as expert tree fallers. They got a thrill out of felling big timber, watching the forest giants come crashing down. The boys also got a rush from challenging the rapids at night or running their canoe as near as possible to the thundering fifty-foot Stave River waterfall and catching the backflow to avoid being swept over. Life was far from dull.

For a time, the family moved to the homestead of a man named William Matheson to carry out a logging project. Matheson was a member of the Christadelphians, "Brethren in Christ," a religious body founded by John Thomas in the United States in 1848. Foster Carter, an avid evolutionist who placed his faith in science, enjoyed spirited conversations with Matheson. William Matheson proved to be a convincing evangelist, and Foster grew to appreciate the Bible's teachings. From then on he made a lifetime study of Biblical truths, particularly prophesies, which he found very stimulating. Eventually, most of the Carter family, including Dudley Christopher, became and remained devoted to the Christadelphian faith. To this day the Christadelphians, a relatively small and quiet branch of Christianity, believe they have revived the practices of the church of the first century.

The homesteading Carters enjoyed frequent synergistic experiences with the Indians in the area. Some Natives were employed in the logging operations and were impressive workers. The daughter of an Indian chief at Langley instructed the boys in constructing a spinning machine so they could make use of the wool they sheared from their sheep. In the fall, Indians travelling on foot to Pemberton Meadows for the winter would often call at the Carter home in need of a needle and thread or some other small thing.

The Stave Falls area revealed many signs of earlier Indian encampments. The Carters found stone hammers, spears, and arrowheads. Rough carvings of Indian origin were often found lodged in log booms. Ancient trees holding the remains of crude burial boxes in their uppermost parts were not uncommon sights. One day when Darwin and Dudley explored the river a short way above the falls, they came across an abandoned fifteen-foot Indian dugout canoe that apparently had been there for years. Bullet holes in its side suggested its occupants had been engaged in battle in days gone by.

In 1906 Foster Carter accepted the job of trades instructor at the Indian School at Alert Bay, a Kwakiutl (now known as Kwakwaka'wakw) village tucked away on Cormorant Island opposite the mouth of the Nimpkish River on the northern end of Vancouver Island. The family now numbered seven boys—Eden, Erchron, Nathan, and Eschatol had joined the clan. Darwin, Stanley, and Dudley, in their late and middle teens, now had their first opportunity for a public school experience. Perhaps more important to their training was the work experience they gained at Alert Bay Sawmill. Also, immersion into the rich Kwakiutl culture—with its powerful totems and moving potlatch ceremonies—had a profound effect on them, particularly on Dudley, who always had an artistic nature.

The time at Alert Bay, while interesting, proved arduous. It is a bleak place in winter. With the birth of their eighth child imminent, Foster moved Sophia to Vancouver where she gave birth to Aene, a daughter at last! Back at Alert Bay, a serious strain of measles ran through the native population, hitting the Carter family as well. Eden, known as Edie, died of pneumonia, a complication of the measles. The rest of the boys also became ill. Darwin spent nearly five months in Vancouver General Hospital being treated for an abdominal abscess caused by the measles. While Darwin remained confined to the hospital, Dudley was brought in suffering from double pneumonia that progressed to pleurisy and empyema. Doctors removed portions of six of his ribs, which Dudley said grew back as a solid plate. It was touch and go, but after lengthy hospital stays both boys recovered. In 1909 the family left Alert Bay and moved to Vancouver before returning to Stave Falls, only to find their log house ransacked and most of their treasured possessions, including the handcrafted globe, gone.

Foster and his three eldest sons purchased twenty acres of bush land in Haney, BC, sixteen

Dudley and Teresa on their wedding day, 1919
Photograph courtesy Eltheen Carter King

miles from Stave Falls. There they built a home and a barn, cleared more land, and planted a garden and fruit trees.

The death of Edie at Alert Bay left a gap of seven years between the first three sons and the younger children. A second daughter and ninth child, Eltheen, was born in 1912. Darwin commented in his writing, "When we three were younger, people used to remark to Mother as to our behavior when she took us visiting. We did not interfere with other people's things and generally behaved well. Here at Haney, the younger ones attended public school and the change that came over them was amazing. They would talk back to Father and Mother, tell lies, and be disobedient. This was the result of the public environment. But still some of them grew out of this condition, all of them more or less, when they reached adult years. This was because of the upbringing they had before attending public school."

After settling in Haney, Foster and his three eldest sons went to work for a large hydroelectric plant in Stave Falls. From 1909 until 1917 Dudley

Building the Skidroad 1899 to 1902, by Dudley Carter
Sketch courtesy Sharlene Nelson

remained employed with the power company, which operated under such names as BC Electric, Western Canada Power Company, and BC Hydro. Dudley served in a number of capacities, such as canoe man, guide, tree faller, stump and rock blaster, trestle builder, draftsman, surveyor, and even foreman of railroad construction. He began studying engineering and was soon employed by the engineering staff. Fellow engineers encouraged Dudley to continue his studies at McGill University, but his appendix ruptured, disrupting those plans.

By 1917 construction for the power company

Dudley, Teresa, and their daughter, Mavis. Photograph courtesy Eltheen Carter King

In the Beginning

Communion of the Souls, 1930, sketch of plaster cast
by Dudley Carter
Sketch courtesy Abby Sher

was completed, and Dudley was hired by Clark & Lyford to do stadia topography, surveying, and timber cruising. A cruiser received the highest compensation in the timber business due to the hazardous nature of the work, the technical knowledge and experience it required, and its exigent physical demands. His life depended on his wits, on his ability to navigate a canoe through raging rapids, his fortitude in climbing precipitous mountains, and his aptitude at outsmarting the native inhabitants of the forests and seas—grizzly bears, wolves, mountain lions, and killer whales. Dudley remarked, "Killer whales are playful, but they play rough!"

In 1918 Dudley was again hospitalized. The cause this time was the influenza pandemic, said to be the most destructive epidemic of modern times and estimated to have caused twenty million to forty million deaths worldwide. Not only did Dudley nearly succumb to pneumonia as a result of the disease, he was further jeopardized when a delirious patient in the hospital attacked him with a knife, almost succeeding in taking his life.

Dudley recovered from the flu and married Teresa Easthope in 1919. The couple established residency in the Grandview area of Vancouver, where their only child, Mavis, was born in 1922. Dudley continued to work for the firm of Clark & Lyford, but in 1924 he suffered a complete physical breakdown. Scurvy—brought on by the poor diet and severe hardships that were the lot of the timber cruiser—put him out of work for two years. Always known to have a bent for drawing, he began to study art, spending the summers in British Columbia and winters in California and Mexico. By 1926 he had regained his strength and returned to work for Clark & Lyford until 1928, when he resigned and took a position with Porteous & Company in Seattle. Again, he was in charge of field operations and timber cruising—not only in Washington but also in Idaho, Oregon, California, and Canada. The following year the Great Depression struck, and Dudley—with a Bunyanesque intensity—turned his attention to the world of art.

The spirits of the forests and the early peoples of the Northwest woods would begin to speak through the art of Dudley Christopher Carter.

NOTE: "In the Beginning" was compiled, edited, and abridged by the authors from papers provided courtesy of Clarence Carter, son of Stanley Carter, and the Mission Community Archives, Mission, BC.

Chapter 2

Pioneers of the Lumber Industry

From a conversation with Ted Nelson

The lumber industry of yesterday was an institution truly North American in character; it required strength, skill, alertness, endurance, teamwork, and boundless resourcefulness. Dudley Carter and I were fortunate to experience much of that character firsthand, for we both spent a large part of our lives working in the midst of the greatest stands of big timber on the face of the earth.

Dudley was a true pioneer in the industry. I came along later, beginning my career as a timber cruiser and forester in California's pine region. Then I enjoyed a long career with Weyerhaeuser in the Douglas fir region of the Pacific Northwest. My wife, Sharlene, and I have written a book for children on logging in the Old West.

Dudley Carter wrote his own epic about logging in the Old West, but he carved his story in cedar and published it in the form of an impressive panel, *Pioneers of the Lumber Industry*. It is a powerful representation of the Northwest lumber business in its early days. His montage is, in many ways, autobiographical, as it portrays much of Dudley's own pioneering experience in the woods.

The Schafer Brothers Logging Company of Aberdeen, Washington, commissioned Dudley to do that panel and a companion piece—a larger-than-life portrait of the three Schafer brothers themselves. The works commemorated the brothers' fifty years

Dudley Carter with *Pioneers of the Lumber Industry*, 1949
Photograph courtesy Anna Vaughan Hanson

in the timber business. At the peak of their operation, the Schafers were running one of the largest logging, milling, and shipping concerns in the industry.

A study of *Pioneers of the Lumber Industry* begins at the bottom of the panel. The viewer notes a large tall stump in the left foreground. In the early days trees were cut high— generally four or five feet above the ground—because the wood at the butt of the tree was unusable and logs that flared at the end were hard to move.

Next to the stump Dudley portrays an ox team. Loggers called them bull teams. The big, wheezing, grunting beasts pulling huge logs—up to eight feet in diameter and forty feet long—are driven over the skid road by a bull whacker. He walked along near the lead yoke, now and then using a prod—a nail on a rod—sticking the oxen in their hindquarters to urge them on. According to Dudley, the Carter family drivers preferred a more humane approach.

Three Schafer Brothers, 1949, red cedar, 8′ × 5.5′
Companion panel to *Pioneers of the Lumber Industry*, collection of Hedda Schafer Shepherd, Fremont, California. Below, from left: Peter, Hubert, and Albert Schafer
Photographs Hedda Schafer Shepherd

12   *Roots of the Tree Carver*

Pioneers of the Lumber Industry, 1949, red cedar, 7′10″ × 5.5′. Collection of Hedda Schafer Shepherd, Fremont, California
Photograph Hedda Schafer Shepherd

Details of *Pioneers of the Lumber Industry,* 1949
Photographs Hedda Schafer Shepherd

Their bellowing voices could be heard a mile or more away cajoling, praising, flattering, and sometimes profaning the bulls into a little more pull. Occasionally they resorted to a switch.

In front of the bull team, leading the slow but steady drive, Dudley shows the skid greaser, who was usually the youngest member of the crew. His job was to daub grease on the cross-skids to relieve friction as the tons of wood groaned over them. Dudley did this job when he was six years old. Usually the skid greaser followed behind the last bulls and ahead of the first log. Here Dudley has the fellow out front and he's barefoot!

Just above the skid greaser is a tree faller or chopper, as they are called in the California redwoods. To reach the point where the tree could best be cut, the fallers cut notches into the trunk. Springboards, wooden planks about five feet long with a metal clip on the business end, were anchored into the notches. Sometimes the springboards were placed two or three notches up the tree. The fallers would balance on their springboards while felling the tree with axes and a long crosscut saw. Dudley said he learned to dance on a springboard.

Three husky hand loggers appear beside the undercut in the tree. They are working with peaveys, heavy wooden levers with pointed metal tips and hinged hooks near the ends that were used to roll logs onto the skids or into the waterways.

Above the hand loggers Dudley has carved a donkey puncher operating a stationary steam engine called a donkey. The donkey was a drum with a length of steel cable used for yarding—hauling the log from the stump to a collection point. The engine's boiler with its smokestack is above the head of the donkey puncher. Early logging with steam donkeys was termed ground lead, meaning the logs were pulled along the ground.

On a tree to the right of the donkey puncher is a high-climber about to go between one hundred and two hundred feet above the ground. He is wielding his razor-sharp axe and straining against his safety belt. His task is to sever the top of a forest giant while bracing himself against the swaying trunk. The shock of the falling crest sends the trunk, and the climber on it, gyrating dizzily in great and sudden arcs.

To the left of the donkey, Dudley shows a tug, a locomotive, logging trucks, a sawmill, and a steamship—all illustrating the magnitude of the Schafer operation. The Schafer brothers did skookum or large-scale logging, buying their first of eighteen locomotives in 1913. In subsequent years they had five sawmills in operation. During the Depression, the brothers formed Schafer Brothers Steamship Lines. For many years they controlled their product from stump to the yard of the retail lumber dealer.

Dudley's carving also portrays life in the logging camps. He shows a camp bunkhouse above the second pair of bulls. A logging camp was a world

Fallers Cutting Big Timber,
by Dudley Carter
Sketch courtesy Sharlene Nelson

My first timber cruising jobs were for the Diamond Match Company in California. I generally cruised with a partner; Dudley usually cruised alone. He was such a good pacer he could do everything himself. With a handheld compass and his tally book, he'd go it alone. One important aspect of timber cruising: you're required to be observant, looking for indications of defects in the trees that are often obscure. A little conk high in a tree signaled that the wood was unsound. And, of course, you are identifying species, estimating heights and diameters, and determining the value of the logs that could be produced. Dudley's timber cruising skills supplemented his artistic skill and vice versa. Here in this panel he put them all together. It is a wonderful trip down memory lane for anyone associated with the lumber industry. This is quite a work of art.

NOTE: In "A Timely Request" on page 145, Ted Nelson explains how he came to be associated with Dudley Carter.

all its own. Most camps were just bachelor camps—big meals, hard work. I considered it a really neat experience. In a 1927 issue of *Industrial Worker*, a newspaper published by a radical union commonly called the Wobblies, a job report concerning Schafer camps read, "Conditions poor and board fair." This was really high praise if not out and out flattery. When a Wobbly delegate admitted that conditions were merely "poor" and that board was "fair," anyone familiar with Wobbly reporting understood that the Schafers, at least at that time, had the finest board and conditions imaginable.

Dudley spent a lot of his time following the logging camps, and as a timber cruiser he'd be out in what we called spike camps weeks at a time—cruising every day of the week, sunrise to sunset, fair weather or foul, wearing tin pants and tin coats. This foul weather gear was heavy and stiff, in no way like the high tech garments of today. They weighed a ton.

Ted W. Nelson (1931–2010), longtime friend of Dudley Carter, retired after many years as a vice president of Weyerhaeuser Company. With his wife, Sharlene, he authored books on the subjects of North American lighthouses, sailboat cruising, and a book for children on the logging industry.
Photograph Mary Sikkema

Pioneers of the Lumber Industry

Chapter 3

Futures Found in Bars of Soap

From a conversation with George Tsutakawa

When we first met, Dudley Carter and I discovered we had a number of commonalities. To begin with, we found that we both had won awards for carving soap.

Though born in Seattle, I was taken at age seven to live in Japan. My grandfather introduced me to ancient Oriental art traditions in my early years. I also heard talk of the great modern artists of Europe and admired examples of their work. One day I announced that I would be an artist. This displeased my father, who expected me to be an obedient son and take over his business. So he disowned me. "You go to Seattle," he said. And he put me on a steamship at the age of eighteen, all alone. Having been away from America so long, I was no longer able to speak English very well. This was in 1928.

After I arrived in Seattle I learned about a soap-carving contest being sponsored by the *Seattle Times*. I carved a bar of soap, regular Ivory soap, entered the contest, and won second prize. I received a scholarship that enabled me to study under the noted sculptor Dudley Pratt, who introduced me to other artists and students in Seattle. I met Dudley Carter in that way. He also received instruction from Dudley Pratt through winning the soap-carving contest.

By 1932 I was studying art at the University of Washington. The following year, the big art event in town was the opening of the new Seattle Art Museum. No art student would miss it. I was impressed to see a huge

George Tsutakawa's 1928 award-winning soap carving
Photograph 'Lyn Lambert

Prominently displayed at the east end of the garden court of the Seattle Art Museum at the opening of the new museum in 1933 is Dudley Carter's *Rivalry of the Winds*, surrounded by a collection of ancient Chinese sculptures. Photograph the Seattle Art Museum

wood sculpture by Dudley Carter prominently displayed. Small bronze animal forms by our teacher, Dudley Pratt, trimmed the rim of the base that supported the sculpture.

The next time I saw Dudley Carter was in 1940 at the Golden Gate International Exposition in San Francisco. He was carving a huge log on Treasure Island during the Art in Action part of the fair. The exposition celebrated Pacific unity, the hopeful expression of a new spirit of cooperation in trade and friendship among the Pacific nations. Then came Pearl Harbor. I was inducted into the US Army to teach Japanese at the US Army Intelligence School in California. For imagined national security reasons, the government interned my uncles, who owned Tsutakawa Company in Seattle. I visited them at the internment camp at Tule Lake, California, and there I met Ayame Iwasa, who was also interned with her family. Ayame later became my wife.

After I left the service and returned to Seattle, I heard from Dudley Pratt that Dudley Carter had taken a position as instructor of sculpture at the University of Washington during the war. Carter left at the end of the war; Everett DuPen came to set up a department of sculpture in the art department;

Futures Found in Bars of Soap

> "Admitting an interest in drawing since childhood, Mr. Carter asserts that his participation in The Times Soap-Carving Contest a year ago first caused him to take his artistic endeavors seriously. As a result of his work at the Art Institute, he has created a number of pieces of sculpture which have won generous praise from his instructors.
>
> Several of these are handsomely executed figures of women, one in particular which reveals a fluidity of pose in which undoubted technical excellence is subordinated by the finished beauty of the work."
>
> Dorothy Neighbors, "Former Winner In Contest Has Unusual Talent," *Seattle Times*, 1930.

and I became a full-time instructor there in 1947.

I visited the studio Carter established on Bel-Red Road, and we discussed wood carving. Dudley encouraged me to try that medium. He told me he had access to good wood through his years working for lumber companies. In the late 1940s I experimented with wood, and I think some of that wood I worked came from Dudley's collection of cedar burls and planks. I created my first obos from wood. Obos are a form of art inspired by stacks of rocks Himalayan people pile at crests of high passes to thank the gods for safe passage.

In 1962 Everett DuPen, Glen Alps, Ray Jensen, Dudley Carter, and I all received awards at a meeting of the Past Presidents' Assembly. It was the first time that rather prestigious group of Seattle women chose to honor men only. We were selected as representative of the beginning of a renaissance in public art, as we were all doing public commissions, including work for the Seattle World's Fair.

As public artists we had to transcend individual limits. It is very different from making art in the privacy of a studio, where one creative mind fabricates the work. A public artist must work with engineers and architects to create art that lives in harmony with the public place. This fundamentally transforms every way of thinking for an artist.

In addition to having the soap award and the Past Presidents' honor in common, Dudley Carter and I were two of the few artists among the one hundred citizens the State of Washington chose to honor for its Centennial Celebration in 1989.

I've kept my soap carving all these years. One could spend much time meditating on that little work. It shows a human figure struggling desperately to break out of a box filled with skulls and gruesome faces. However hard it may be, whatever the obstacles there may be, one must break out of confining boxes and follow one's dreams. Dudley did just that.

George Tsutakawa (1910–1997), prolific sculptor, painter, and esteemed teacher of several generations of art students at the University of Washington, Seattle. Internationally renowned, most especially for his metal fountain sculptures. His work expresses profoundly his beliefs about our human relationship with nature. Deeply influenced by the natural beauty of the Pacific Northwest, Tsutakawa became concerned that our Western worldview has long been intent on separating humans from nature and destroying nature in order to build an artificial dream world. He suspected that modern art reflected this attitude. Photograph 'Lyn Lambert

Chapter 4

Legacies and Liberties

From a conversation with Bill Holm

It's fair to say that Dudley Carter played a part in reviving interest in Northwest Coast art. Dudley utilized Indian themes, was influenced by Indian forms, and his work was accepted as art and visible in art settings.

However, it is interesting that while the powers that be in the Seattle Art Museum accepted Dudley's work, they were not interested in acquiring traditional Northwest Coast Indian material for their collection. The Gerber collection of Native art, procured by the Burke Museum in 1968, had previously been offered to the Seattle Art Museum but was rejected. Of course, that attitude on the part of most art museums has changed—witness the Seattle Art Museum's later acquisition of the extensive John H. Hauberg collection of coastal Indian artifacts.

Although Dudley Carter's work is very much his own, it shows the influence of many of the Northwest Coast Indian culture groups. His enchantment with the Kwakwaka'wakw art and culture at Alert Bay is especially evident in much of the art he later came to create. When Dudley lived among them, the Kwakwaka'wakw were known as Kwakiutl. Many of their attitudes about life, as well as their art, had a profound effect on Dudley.

It was much the same with me. I spent my boyhood in Montana, impressed by the ways of the Plains Indians. I never lost my enthusiasm for them. When my family moved to Washington State, my interest grew to include the Northwest Coast Indians. I attended the University of Washington and had the good fortune to study under Dr. Erna

Gunther, an anthropologist and noted authority on the Northwest Coast Indians.

By the beginning of the twentieth century, many ancient traditions and artistic expressions of the Native Northwest peoples were virtually extinguished. Governmental prohibitions of certain customs and the rapidly accelerated acculturation and proselytizing of the Indians were largely responsible for that decline. The governments did all they could to discourage ceremonies such as the Kwakiutl potlatch, even outlawing them. Christian missionaries brought upon the Natives great pressure to abandon all customs deemed to be pagan. Having lost the major purpose for creating their artistic display, they soon lost the ability to produce it.

The Kwakiutl, a little more assertive in their character than other tribes, were the least disrupted by the prohibition. They resolutely but covertly defied the anti-ceremonial laws, and Dudley Carter witnessed a number of important and festive potlatch ceremonies. The potlatch was a public validation of an individual's privileges and status. It was a time of feasting, gift-giving, dancing, and dramatic storytelling. Potlatches often featured the dedication of a new totem pole. Unlike other tribes, the Kwakiutl never did stop carving their totems. There were, in fact, several impressive totem poles at Alert Bay when Dudley lived there. A fine stand of poles showing Kwakiutl art in all its grandeur can still be seen at Alert Bay.

Burial customs of the Kwakiutl also made quite an impression on Dudley. Imagine a young teen finding remnants of a human skeleton at his feet, the remains having fallen from the high branches of a giant evergreen. Dudley experienced that. One of the Kwakiutl burial customs involved placing the deceased in a box, either an Oriental tea chest—a standard trade item—or a burial box artfully constructed of cedar. The extremities of the departed were folded up to fit the container. The box was then wrapped in cloth, frequently blankets, and raised to the highest sturdy boughs of an ancient tree. The lower limbs of the tree were usually removed as a way of protecting the remains. As years went by, the blankets or cloth

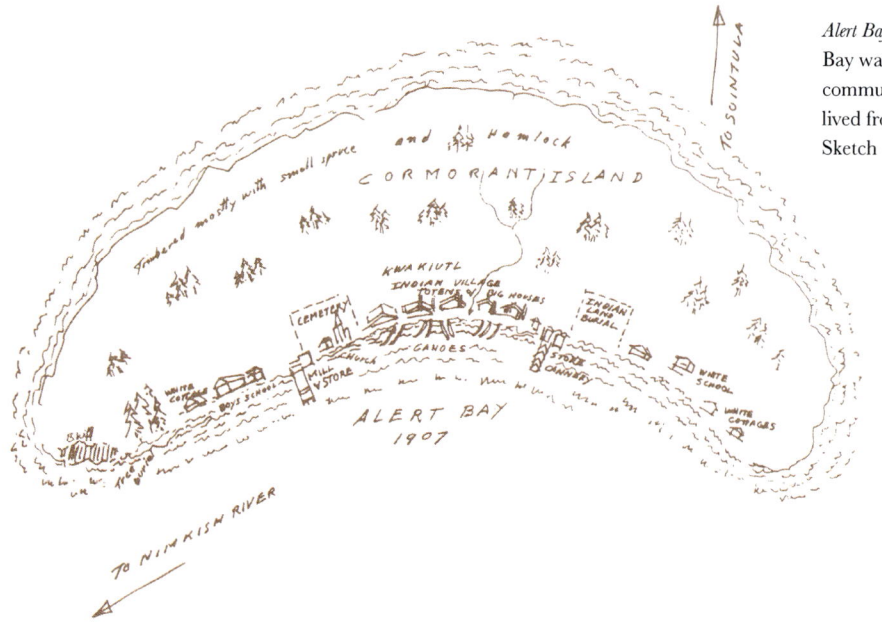

Alert Bay, by Dudley Carter. Alert Bay was the site of the Kwakiutl community where the Carter family lived from 1906 to 1909. Sketch courtesy Abby Sher

Rear view of *Northgate Totem*, 1952, red cedar, 59′ × 7′ × 7′, *Canoe*, red cedar, 32′ long, at Northgate Shopping Center, Seattle, Washington When the photograph was taken in 1991, the pole had been repainted. The colors are not as originally applied by Bill Holm, but designs as incised by Dudley Carter show clearly. Photograph 'Lyn Lambert

Legacies and Liberties   21

coverings would be reduced to tatters; the box would deteriorate; and down would come the skeleton of the long-departed soul. To a sensitive young Dudley, whose brother died at Alert Bay, bones lying at the base of a tree would further impress upon him that death happens. It's very much a part of life.

My initial contact with Dudley came about in 1953. I received a master of fine arts degree in 1951 and was teaching art in the Seattle public schools while continuing to expand my study of Northwest Coast Indian art material. Dudley was working on *Northgate Totem* and contacted me to see if I would paint the pole. The possibility was intriguing, but when I saw what he wanted done, I wasn't sure I could deal with the forms he had worked into the carving. They did not meet with my understanding of traditional designs. Though clearly based on Indian schema, Dudley's way of using these designs departed from the Indian formline system beginning to settle in my mind. We talked this over and Dudley decided he didn't want the figures themselves painted. We agreed that I would paint only the decorations he carved on the back of the pole and the giant letters that formed the Northgate Shopping Center sign.

Dudley must have liked what I'd done, because in 1955 he asked me to assist him with the *Wolf and Mink Totem*, a commission for the Shell Oil Company refinery east of Anacortes, Washington. My job was to add a series of small painted formline elements on either side of the shallow relief figures he incised on the back of the pole.

A few years later I had occasion to call upon Dudley for help. I was working with a group of people building a Kwakiutl-style house for a children's camp, which later became Camp Nor'wester on Lopez Island. The house called for large split cedar planks, and Dudley's good-natured expertise in splitting cedar was invaluable.

Dudley expressed the opinion that the more northerly peoples, those residing north of the Euclataw Narrows, produced the best art. I think he may have had a rather narrow view of what the best art is. It is true that the northern tribes were more prolific in their art, and perhaps it was more complex. However, the styles of the northern Natives and the lower Coast Salish are quite different, so it is difficult to compare them.

There is a commonly held belief that Northwest Coast Natives produced great art because the people had an easy life. Food was abundant and the image is that "when the tide goes out, the table is set." In fact, what we might call more sophisticated art was produced in the North where life was the hardest. So perhaps in that regard, Dudley was right. In the south, the Puget Sound and Strait of Georgia territory, subsistence was easier and families could make their living with less organization. Further north, life was more of a struggle. It was necessary to organize things. The northern peoples established a hierarchy of chiefs and rank. With rank and privilege established, the people had to have display, hence the creation of art in the form of complex totem poles, masks, and ceremonial paraphernalia. Bill Reid, a noted Native carver of recent times, called these "objects of bright pride."

Northwest Coast Indian art and culture is often termed primitive. If used to mean preexistent or ancient, the term is appropriate. However, considering the aesthetic aspects of the art, the cerebral and spiritual concepts of the culture from which it sprang, and the technical skills involved in the execution of the work, it is actually highly sophisticated. Dudley Carter obviously appreciated our sophisticated legacy from the primitive Indian masters, and he did much to preserve it.

It is clear to me that Dudley Carter was not and did not want to be known as Dudley Carter the totem pole carver. He was, and wanted to be recog-

> "A formline is the characteristic swelling and diminishing linelike figure delineating design units. These formlines merge and divide to make a continuous flowing grid over the whole decorated area, establishing the principal forms of the design."
>
> Bill Holm
> *Northwest Coast Indian Art: An Analysis of Form*

nized as, Dudley Carter, sculptor. Dudley was not a copyist. He was an artist. As a student of Northwest Coast art, it is interesting to me to examine the manner in which Dudley worked respectfully within the Indian configurations, but interpreted them freely. That might bother some. It doesn't bother me. Dudley Carter did not do "Indian totem poles." Dudley Carter did Dudley Carter sculptures. Dudley remarked that the great Indian carvers were creative. He was right about that, but the Indian carvers worked within the rules or canons of the art. Dudley worked creatively, using the rules when they suited him.

He definitely departed from tradition in his propensity to carve a pole upright. I've never known another carver who carved a pole while it stood upright. It adds to the work immeasurably because wood has a grain that runs in the tree vertically. When you carve it you have to carve it sloping down the grain. With the pole vertical, half the chops have to be directed up, which is enormously difficult. It takes extraordinary effort. Dudley had great control of his axes, so he could do that. But it makes no sense.

Dudley felt free to take liberties with the indigenous art because he held a healthy appreciation of its source. His appreciation was evident in his earliest publicly recognized work. *Passing of a Race*, Dudley's first entry in the 1930 *Seattle Times* soap-carving contest, depicted an Indian maiden kneeling before an empty cradle at the base of a totem pole. It expressed his concern for a vanishing society, perhaps a society we cannot or should not try to duplicate, but one from which we might borrow and gain much.

NOTE: Renovations to the Northgate Mall in the fall of 2007 required the five-story-tall totem, a fixture at the mall for over fifty-five years, to be removed. Rather than see the totem destroyed, Northgate Mall executives graciously donated the pole to the Suquamish Tribe, who, in conjunction with their tribally owned business corporation, Port Madison Enterprises, paid for its removal, transportation, and restoration. The *Northgate Totem* has stood proudly at the Suquamish Clearwater Casino, overlooking Agate Passage in Puget Sound, since February 2008.

The carved canoe that accompanied the totem now rests in front of the resort's Angeline Spa.

(More on the *Northgate Totem* can be found in "The Northgate Connection" on page 85.)

 **Bill Holm**, curator-emeritus of Northwest Coast Indian art at the Burke Museum, professor emertus of art history at the University of Washington, author of numerous books on Northwest Coast Indian art, including the classic *Northwest Coast Indian Art: An Analysis of Form* (University of Washington Press, 1965). Admired for his many fine examples of traditional carving as well as his paintings, drawings, and prints depicting the Coast, Plateau, and Plains Indians. In 2003 the Burke Museum established the Bill Holm Center for the Study of Northwest Art to continue his legacy.
Photograph 'Lyn Lambert

Legacies and Liberties

Chapter 5

Carving Out an Art Career

From a conversation with Jane Oestreich

The Northwest lumber industry collapsed in the winter of 1929 putting thousands out of work, including Dudley Carter. He confronted this potentially disastrous turn of events by responding to a newspaper ad placed by my father, Arnold Stahmer. Father hired Dudley as an assistant in his commercial art business, unaware that he would be instrumental in launching this woodsman on a whole new career.

I believe Dudley saw the downturn in the lumber business as an opportunity to advance his interest in art and sought employment with my father to expand his knowledge of fine art as well as commercial art. Dudley did lettering, photo layouts, touchups for display ads, and so forth. Much of the company's business came from the Miller Freeman publishing company. Freeman heirs later developed Bellevue Square.

Dudley's talent so impressed Father that he encouraged his protégé in artistry beyond the commercial work he had hired Dudley to render. Always known as A.J., my father earned a reputation as a fine artist for his watercolors and oil paintings. He knew the fledgling art community of Seattle very well. In fact, he helped organize the Puget Sound Group of Northwest Painters and at one time served as its president. He introduced Dudley to others who could further his venture into the world of art.

It's an understatement to say that Dudley's

Dudley Carter cuts a dashing figure in his early days as a timber cruiser
Photograph courtesy Eltheen Carter King

talent captured the attention of important people in the community. Three years after Father hired him, Dudley Carter's first attempt at monumental art, *Rivalry of the Winds*, joined the collection of the Seattle Art Museum.

When I attended the world's fair in San Francisco in 1940, I discovered to my surprise that California had also noticed the Northwest's Dudley Carter. My girlfriend and I had just two days to take in the fair, and as we scooted around trying to cover it all, we paused on a balcony that provided an overview of the first floor of an immense building. I looked down and saw an axe carver at work on a huge log—Dudley Carter! The woodsman my father helped launch into art now stood on a precarious-looking scaffolding creating an enormous totem-style sculpture. Dudley had captured attention beyond even my father's imagination.

With the entry of the United States into World War II, the lumber industry was propelled into a period of unequalled prosperity. Dudley was again in demand as a timber cruiser. He returned to Washington State as he said, "a wanted man." He and my father had remained great pals, and Dudley mentioned he was in need of someone to type his cruise reports. My father recommended me. I'd been trained at Wilson's Modern Business College, was married, and had two small children by that time. The extra remuneration came in handy.

The Carters were renting an old ranch house in the middle of a large hazelnut orchard just south of Sacred Heart Catholic Church on Main Street in Bellevue. That old orchard site later became the Surrey Downs neighborhood.

According to a 1932 article in the *Seattle Times*, although Dudley was a professional forest engineer maintaining offices in the Liggett Building in downtown Seattle, his "avocation is sculpture."

"Indian Group," Seattle Times, 1932.

Carving Out an Art Career

I hadn't really known Dudley until I had the opportunity to work with him. Typing those timber cruise reports proved to me that he was by no means an uneducated woodsman. He knew intimately all the timber types and could accurately estimate the volume of lumber in a forest. He drew maps locating lakes, streams, roads, changes of tree species, and topography and often had to determine and indicate where a railroad or road system might be built in order to remove the timber.

Dudley's cruise reports consisted of page after page of measurements—often hundreds of pages. He wrote them out longhand, and for over sixteen years, I typed them, including carbon copies. I can't recall how many carbon copies, but I suppose as many as my manual typewriter would allow. Dudley would add his hand-drawn, hand-colored maps to each and every copy.

We became very good friends. When Dudley and Teresa would leave town, I would check on their home. At Christmastime Dudley would often provide a tree for us. He once brought us a lemon tree from the Earl Neel Nursery in Palm Springs. Mr. Neel convinced him to use the nursery as his winter studio. Dudley always enjoyed working in public, and the nursery gave him an opportunity to do that. He delighted in getting to know people like Walter Annenberg and Bob Hope, who often stopped by to watch him at work.

The Carters owned property in Gibsons on the Sunshine Coast, a ferry ride north of Vancouver, British Columbia. They had a cabin

The Carters' beach cabin and studio in Gibsons, British Columbia. Teresa Carter and the Oestreich children, Mark and Daniel, enjoy the beach amidst driftwood, a ready source of carving material for Dudley. Photograph courtesy Jane and Kurt Oestreich

Above: David Vaughan holding son Michael, Mavis Carter Vaughan, Mark, Jane, Daniel Oestreich, and Teresa Carter at Gibsons, British Columbia. Top and bottom, right: Dudley Carter hosting a cookout. Below: Mark Oestreich at foot of *Maid of the Woods* near Verlot, Washington. Photographs courtesy Jane and Kurt Oestreich

there that served as their home and Dudley's studio—they called it their summer camp. It stood just above the high tidemark on the beach. My husband, Kurt, and I and our small children stayed overnight there in the 1950s. We had wonderful beach picnics with the Carters and their daughter, Mavis Vaughan, and her family who lived nearby.

In the mid-fifties Dudley and Teresa moved to Bellevue-Redmond Road where he built a residence and studio. They were just up the hill from our home in Redmond. Microsoft sits on his property now. I don't think the Carters ever furnished a home like you or I would. I remember they had a screened-in porch and they slept out there in sleeping bags. They had a stove outside and did most of their cooking there. That lifestyle seemed quite natural even for Teresa. I don't think she had much of a social life of her own. Dudley couldn't hear well and Teresa handled his telephone contacts and other social things for him.

Carving Out an Art Career

After I had worked for Dudley for a while, our family moved to a home in Redmond proper. It had a handsome fireplace wall—just the place for a work by Dudley Carter. Kurt and I visited Dudley's studio hoping to choose a sculpture. Most of his work was huge, but we found the perfect piece, *Bird Carrying Message*—a beautiful bird in flight carved from sugar pine. Like many of his carvings, it's Dudley's interpretation of the Northwest Native-style of carving. The message is represented by a stylized eye. Dudley offered to come to our home to help hang the piece. He wanted to be certain it was positioned just so, at the correct angle of flight, something he must have seen so often in the wilds. It's a beautiful piece and we are fortunate to have it. We paid seventy-five dollars for it in 1963.

Dudley pauses to chat with Jane Oestreich while working on a carving shortly after his one-hundredth birthday.
Photograph courtesy Jane and Kurt Oestreich

One time Dudley invited our family to go along with him to see *Maid of the Woods*, the carving he did on a living tree near Verlot, Washington. We drove west of Granite Falls and worked our way on foot through dense brush and difficult overgrowth, as there was no trail to the site. We finally reached the enormous old tree, towering some 120-feet high with a thirty-foot nymph carved on its trunk. *Life* magazine published a photographic article of Dudley at work on the tree, and Paramount Pictures filmed him and the *Maid of the Woods* for a newsreel feature story. Ripley's ran it as a *Believe It or Not!* newspaper item. Dudley intended the maiden to be the main figure of a composition that would involve the entire tree trunk. He never completed the project because plans for a park in the area were abandoned. Years later the tree was struck by lightning—twice. So much for the old theory that lightning never strikes in the same place twice.

In the 1960s the timber industry found a better way to determine the volume of a forest than by sending out a cruise party. With Dudley no longer timber cruising our business relationship ended, but we kept up our friendship.

After my husband retired in the late 1970s, Dudley asked him to go to Oregon with him. He wanted Kurt to help him build wagons and other things, which as I recall were to be part of the Centennial of the Oregon Trail. Kurt declined the offer. Having just retired, he was tired. Dudley just kept on working, although he was much older than Kurt.

The last time we visited with Dudley he happily told us he had recently celebrated his one-hundredth birthday with a number of large parties and ceremonies. He was still working but took time to chat. He gave us a tour of the park grounds where he was living and showed us the sculptures he had on display. Our daughter-in-law and Kurt's sister from Germany were with us, and they marveled at the beautiful, expressive faces his carvings wore. Our daughter-in-law longed to buy one of his works. She knew just where she would place it. Dudley's asking prices had gone up over the years, however, and the $5,000 price was much more than a little beyond her budget.

It was getting close to lunchtime and Dudley invited us into his home. He told us what he planned to have for lunch that day, basically nuts and fruit—very frugal, very simple. But that is the type of life he always lived. More or less a vegetarian, he didn't eat meat and potatoes as we did but rather nuts, apples, and raisins. As long as I knew him he ate that way. And he always worked, never felt the need for a vacation.

Dudley was never one to worry about what anybody thought of him. I have to mention his garb. In his later years he generally wore a plaid shirt and a knit hat as his carving attire. He had a way of wearing his hat that gave him a charming gnome-like appearance. He just lived his life as he wanted. He was a genuine, one-of-a-kind, human being.

Jane Oestreich and husband, Kurt, with *Bird Carrying Message*, 1960, sugar pine, 20″ × 4′. Jane Oestreich worked many years performing secretarial services for accounting and insurance companies and for Dudley, typing timber cruise reports.
Photograph 'Lyn Lambert

Carving Out an Art Career

Chapter 6

Working through the Depression

From a conversation with Evelyn Balko

In the early 1930s I lived next door to Dudley Carter and his family in Everett, Washington. Dudley, Teresa, and their daughter, Mavis, shared a modest home with Teresa's brother, Ernie Easthope. There was always something in the works at that house. Dudley appeared to be a master of, maybe not all, but many trades, ceaselessly busy. Ernie was a marvelously clever inventor, great with gas engines.

The Easthope family gained quite a reputation for their engines in those early years. An old twenty-five-foot Indian dugout canoe with an Easthope engine is said to have been the first gas-powered fishing boat in the British Columbia fishing industry.

Power alone wasn't enough for Ernie. He seemed hooked on speed. He souped up an Italian airplane engine, put it on an old boat he had, and gave the world its first 100-mph boat, or so the Easthopes claimed—the forerunner of the hydroplanes.

Everett flourished in the twenties and came to be known as the lumber capital of the world. Then the Great Depression set in and most of the working men in Everett were idled. What jobs there were paid very poorly.

Not only was the economy depressed, I faced my own depressing situation. Not yet eighteen, I'd married my high school sweetheart, a young man with a promising future as a professional baseball player. But a mill accident dashed our hopes. His

Marine engines produced by the Easthope brothers were considered the best to be had on the West Coast. Ernest Easthope built a hydroplane that was clocked at one hundred miles an hour on Green Lake in Seattle. In addition to building boat motors, Ernest Easthope operated a gasoline stump puller company in Everett.

injuries destined him to live his life in a wheelchair instead of playing out his dreams on the baseball field.

Dudley and his family were very supportive of me while my husband was confined to the hospital. Often, when I returned from visiting my husband, Teresa invited me to dine with them. She was kind and gracious, a lovely woman. Dudley saw her as the most beautiful woman in the world. And he delighted in Mavis, their daughter, who was about eight years old at this time and very thin, with dark brown hair and ebony eyes. The Carters named her after an English bird. I recall all the Carters playing tennis together, a happy family.

My life was not so happy. My husband began to drink heavily and became abusive. Caring for him kept me housebound and I spent hours gazing out the window. One day I saw Dudley, a dashing figure with dark, wavy hair and flashing, fiery eyes, tackling a huge block of cedar he had somehow acquired, and my spirits began to lift. Dudley, like many others, lost his job in the forestry industry. But there he was, attired in rugged jodhpurs and laced-up knee-high lumberman's boots, swinging his double-bitted axe. I remember at times he wore a white artist's smock—a vision in white!

One day I went over to get a closer look at Dudley's work and a Scandinavian fellow came ambling by. Everett was pretty much a Scandinavian community. The fellow watched Dudley for a time, shook his head, and proclaimed, "That looks like an awful lot of work just to make chips!" That's all he could see. Chips. I could see the beauty of it all. I told Dudley he would be famous someday. He told me I gave him inspiration to continue with that first carving.

Dudley showed me his photographs of bathing-suit-clad models posed to represent the figures in the sculpture he envisioned. He told me the Northwest Native legend that inspired the work, a tale of harsh North Wind and warm Chinook Wind vying for the affection of an Indian princess. Chinook Wind prevailed, of course, for he found a bounty of berries in the icy world and brought them to the princess. North Wind had nothing but cold and more cold to offer her and she rejected him. I could relate to that.

I was not the only one to appreciate Dudley's work. Shortly after he finished his carving, which he called *Rivalry of the Winds*, the Northwest Federation of American Indians held their convention in Everett. Native leaders, representatives of thirteen tribes in the federation, asked Dudley to enter his sculpture in their parade and display it at the convention. The chief organizer of the convention, Joseph Hillaire, a Native carver himself, stayed at the Carters' home for the duration of the event.

A short time after the Indian convention, Dr. Richard Fuller and his mother visited Dudley. They were in the process of building the new Seattle Art Museum in Volunteer Park. Recognizing Dudley's talent, they purchased *Rivalry of the Winds*. They paid $1,500 for it, about half the price of an average home in those days. Dudley never said much, but when he told me of that sale he just glowed. He'd taken the Depression's difficulties and created an opportunity. I took courage from his resourcefulness. As difficult as it was, I divorced my husband and

Mavis Carter, left, with her friends and the unfinished *Rivalry of the Winds*. Photograph courtesy Eltheen Carter King

made a life for myself.

I lost track of the Carters for a number of years and finally caught up with Dudley again about 1960. I learned he was working on a huge totem pole right in downtown Seattle. I'd remarried and told my new husband I wanted him to meet my old flame.

After meeting Dudley, my husband remarked, "I understood he was your old flame, but I didn't know how old that flame was!" My second husband was a prince—my Chinook Wind.

After I reconnected with Dudley we remained good friends. He visited my husband and me at our home in Fauntleroy and loved our view of Puget Sound. Not far from us, according to Duwamish legend, is the center of the universe, the spot where Chinook Wind and North Wind vied for the hand of the Indian princess.

In 1976, the year Dudley's wife Teresa died, I suffered a stroke. Now it appears that I, like my first husband, shall finish my days in a wheelchair. Dudley and I continued to visit often. I could hardly speak and he could barely hear—but still we managed to communicate. I was widowed in 1986 and Dudley remained a source of inspiration. He introduced me to his friend Bertil Valley. Bertil too is a stroke survivor and has been a great encouragement to me.

I will always miss Dudley Carter, but my heart is full of fond memories of him. Those memories often come to mind and help me through the difficult days that life seems to thrust upon us. Life can be tough. We have to be tougher. As Dudley would put it, we have to "keep on keepin' on."

Evelyn Balko (1910–2002), pictured with Dudley Carter and her friend Caroline Payne at Dudley's one-hundredth birthday celebration at a Bellevue mall, was born in Edmonds, Washington. Following her graduation from high school, Balko taught young Japanese students to read and write in a little village in the Cascade Mountains. She was particularly proud to have served as a Rosie the Riveter at the Boeing Airplane Company during WWII. Shortly before her death, Balko received a plaque from the US Department of Labor Women's Bureau acknowledging her patriotic effort. Following her work at Boeing, she was employed for many years at a Seattle jewelry store.

Photograph courtesy Evelyn Balko

Chapter 7

Legend of North Wind and Storm Wind

Adapted by David M. Buerge
This Duwamish story inspired Dudley Carter to create *Rivalry of the Winds*.

Down on the Duwamish River, near where the ancients divided the world in the beginning, lived old Mountain Beaver with his wife and daughter.

Mountain Beaver's daughter was a beautiful young woman, and the head men of two neighboring villages, Chinook Wind and North Wind, wanted to marry her. North Wind was a cold man, cold as winter, and when he came courting he brought only gifts of ice, snow, and a cold, cold wind. Chinook Wind brought gifts of food when he visited—choice berries, the fruits of the earth. Mountain Beaver and his wife chose Chinook Wind for their son-in-law and gave their lovely daughter to him.

North Wind's rejection kindled a raging anger within him. He slaughtered Chinook Wind and his people, all except Chinook Wind's grandmother, a powerful old woman who fled to a hill above the riverbank. Mountain Beaver's daughter escaped North Wind's fury by digging a tunnel all the way back to her parents' house. There, in secret, she bore Chinook Wind's child, a boy who became known as Storm Wind, "The wind that tears the trees up."

Burning with resentment, North Wind built a fish weir of ice across the river to bar salmon from migrating upstream. Hiding in her hilltop hut, Chinook Wind's grandmother had no food except what her two slaves, Pocket Gopher and Mole, could steal for her. North Wind added to her torment by sending his slave, Raven, to defecate on her, making

Rivalry of the Winds **was featured at the convention of the Northwest Federation of American Indians held in Everett in 1932. A** ***Seattle Times*** **article noted that, "It is remarkable for the manner in which the sculptor, while preserving the stolidity characteristic of the Indian, has given the figures life and expression."**

"Indian Group," *Seattle Times*, 1932.

her impure and unable to exercise her power. The poor fire she made from cattail stalks could not melt the mask of filth and frozen tears covering her face.

Back at Mountain Beaver's house, Storm Wind grew into a strong young man. When he became old enough to hunt, his grandmother warned him not to go to the hill across the river, the dangerous place that held the secret of his past. Of course, once he became a man that is exactly what he did.

As he approached the forbidden hill, he heard singing. "I am growing warm; my young relative comes," the old woman sang, and when she opened her door, there stood young Storm Wind. "Look at me," she pleaded, "see how Raven has used me."

She told him who she was; she told him all about his father and his murdered people, and together they plotted revenge. Before he left he tore up great fir trees for her to put on her fire, commanding them to be light and easy for her to handle, and he

---

Opposite page:
Rivalry of the Winds, 1931
Red cedar, 14' × 4' × 4'
Purchased by the founders of the Seattle Art Museum for display in the museum's Garden Court, later displayed outdoors in Volunteer Park. Restored in 1997 and moved to the museum's Arcade Building, downtown Seattle. Later it was moved to the King County Public Library in Redmond, Washington.
Photograph courtesy Dudley Carter

gave her an arrow pointed with bone to jab Raven when he came to her. As the fire's heat melted the mask from her face, purifying her, she became stronger. When Raven showed up she stabbed him, and he flew off to his master, crying that the old woman's grandson must have come back to her. As her power returned, the old woman began weaving baskets.

Down at the river, logs of yew that Storm Wind threw into the current pressed against the icy weir, threatening to break it. As North Wind struggled unsuccessfully to lift them out, Storm Wind came by and tossed them easily over the weir. Remembering Raven's story, North Wind surmised who this powerful stranger was and tried to conciliate Storm Wind by dressing up his daughter with icy ornaments and offering her as a bride.

Storm Wind went back to the hill where his great grandmother had finished weaving her baskets. He blew a strong warm wind and brought Chinook Wind and his people back to life. He blew again, tearing up trees and hurling them into the river. Then Great Grandmother demonstrated her power by pouring rain water from her baskets, making the river rise behind the straining fish weir. Desperate, North Wind told his daughter to go to Storm Wind, but every time she approached, more of her icy ornaments melted, adding to the flood. At last the weir gave way; the river ran free; and once again salmon could pass upstream. North Wind fled away down the valley, but Storm Wind let him return for awhile every year to visit his people. When he does, he brings no gifts except ice and snow and a cold, cold wind. We call his visits winter.

Legend of North Wind and Storm Wind

NOTES: The legend of North Wind and Storm Wind should not be characterized as a Duwamish creation story. That is too Western a category; most Puget Salish myths are creation stories to some extent. It is rather a myth about the origin of the seasons and a basis for rain-calling ceremonies carried out during the coldest period of the year. Duwamish women would take baskets of water and wash the face of Great Grandmother's hill to bring on the spring rains, while boys swung bullroarers, imitating the sound of Storm Wind to hurry his coming.

David Buerge's adaptation is based upon the version of the North Wind and Storm Wind myth narrated to Arthur Ballard by Anne Jack (born 1855), a Muckleshoot Indian from the Green River valley in Washington State, and upon other versions of the same myth that appear in Arthur Ballard's "Mythology of Southern Puget Sound," *University of Washington Publications in Anthropology* 3, no.2 (1929): 55–64.

David M. Buerge, historian, student of Duwamish history and mythology, widely read freelance writer, and author of the book, *Chief Seattle and the Town That Took His Name: The Change of Worlds for the Native People and Settlers on Puget Sound* (Sasquatch Books, 2017). Buerge further indulged his interest in history by teaching Washington State history to middle school students.
Photograph 'Lyn Lambert

Part II
Carving His Own Niche

"It is convenient to have different shapes of axes: some very narrow; some broad; some rounded and others square; some short handles and some long handles."

Dudley Carter

From an interview by Julia Hobby, September 1973, transcript, Archives of Northwest Art, University of Washington, Seattle, Washington

Dudley arranged a sampling of his axes and adzes specifically for this photograph.
Photograph Eddie Davis

Chapter 8

Zen of the Axe

Reminiscences of Geordie Tocher

The double-bitted axe—now there's a Zen trip. There it is, the tempered steel blade about three feet away from you, doing its work. And you're directing it with your mind, over and over again, each chop an extension of your thoughts and your body and your creativity. It's quite a deal—a magical feeling.

No wonder Dudley Carter chose this axe as his trademark. He knew it well, having used it from the time he was a kid. With that tool in his hand he'd go over to the right brain and lose track of time and the rest of the world. He would be tremendously creative and do strong, powerful sculpting.

There's a metronome effect at work with a double-bitted axe. A single-bladed axe can scallop and bounce, but not the double-bitted axe. With the other blade hanging out behind like a metronome, it's got to be pushed out way beyond its apparent dimensions. It cuts truer. I know. I carved with it and loved it too.

There's a duller and sharper side to that axe. If Dudley was chopping through a knot, he'd spin the axe in his hand and take the duller side. He turned that technique into a flashy move, a bit of razzle-dazzle show biz, twisting the axe just before he'd take another blow with it.

Dudley said, "When you're carving with an axe, go into the deep pockets first. Get way in and then work your way back out." To me that was an important lesson from a man I consider to be a prime artist on the Pacific Coast—a supreme practitioner of the Zen of the axe. But Dudley Carter wielded his axe to express his true nature, not to arrive at enlightenment. I think perhaps he had achieved that state.

Geordie Tocher (1927–2007) and Dudley Carter in the summer of 1991 at Slough House Park, Redmond, Washington. Geordie was a lifelong adventurer, woodsman, accomplished artist, artists' agent, entrepreneur, and as Dudley described him, "Strongest man I ever knew—built a canoe and sailed it to Hawaii!"
Photograph 'Lyn Lambert

Dudley Carter in a Zen moment, 1980
Photograph Sue Winters, courtesy Anna Vaughan Hanson

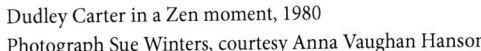

Zen of the Axe

Chapter 9

Illusions and Reality

Reminiscences of Philip R. Wood

In the late 1930s or early 1940s Dudley Carter carved a remarkable bas-relief of a nude for us that we displayed in our ranch home. In preparing this story, I measured the work and was absolutely amazed. Sharing space with the lady for some sixty years, I assumed she was at least twelve to fourteen inches wide, but I discovered she is only eight inches wide! Dudley shaped a thirty-eight-inch-tall female form, appearing a foot or so wide, within the narrow width of eight inches—and her proportions please the eye. He created an illusion. That is art—true art.

San Francisco Beginning

It was through his close friendship with Gottardo Piazzoni that I met Dudley. In the 1930s Piazzoni, who was known as the Dean of San Francisco painters, taught at the California School of Fine Arts. I attended that school and so did Gottardo's daughter Mireille. I fell in love with Mireille and first visited the old Piazzoni ranch in 1933. Dudley began visiting the ranch about that time. Gottardo had befriended him as a budding artist new to the San Francisco area.

A wilderness area in the Chupines Canyon hides the old Gottardo Piazzoni ranch in the hills of California's Carmel Valley. Gottardo was almost twenty years older than Dudley, and Dudley almost twenty years my senior. Age was of no consideration—artists are at home with artists and we were all artists in this wonderful setting.

Gottardo, famous for his murals of California landscapes that graced the grand staircase of the main branch of the San Francisco Library, was a marvelous, understanding person. He encouraged Dudley to enter one of his sculptures in an art show for which Gottardo would be a juror.

Dudley loaded *Condor*, a huge wood sculpture, on a trailer, hitched the trailer to his car, and drove through the hilly streets of San Francisco. Heading down a steep hill in the Italian district with that heavy thing behind him, the inevitable happened—the hitch broke. The only reason the trailer and the treasured tree trunk didn't go plunging to the bottom of the hill was that Dudley had learned from an earlier mishap when he moved from Canada to California. Telling me the story of that incident, he said he saw something go sailing past him and wondered what in blazes it was before he realized it was his trailer. After that he always rigged a safety hitch when trailering anything.

That safety hitch prevented a catastrophe this time, and Dudley managed to get the rig parked at the curb. He determined he needed a tow truck, but that would have to wait until morning. In his usual methodical manner, he lit kerosene lamps, hung them on the trailer, and went to sleep in the car. Young hoodlums came out during the night and threw rocks at the lamps, breaking them. Nonetheless, Dudley got the sculpture to the show on time.

Gottardo couldn't believe his eyes. "Dudley," he said, "You didn't have to bring that big thing down here. A picture of the work is all we need to do our judging!" For the rest of his life Dudley always chuckled whenever that story came up.

An early 1930s Seattle newspaper clipping from Dudley's files, undated and untitled, heralded Dudley's move to California, reporting that "Dudley Carter, whose monumental wood carving, 'Rivalry of the Winds,' towers above the fountain court of the Seattle Art Museum, is a Seattle wood-carver who has made good in the City of San Francisco." According to the news item, on a visit to Seattle Dr. Heil, Director of the Legion of Honor Palace and De Young Museum, declared *Rivalry of the Winds* **to be "the finest woodcarving he had seen in the West." The article went on to say, "And now, Mr. Carter is in San Francisco with several important commissions awarded him there."**

Bas-Relief of Nude, ca. 1930s or 1940s, 38.5″ × 8″ × 1″
Photograph Thomas P. Wood

Illusions and Reality

But important people in the San Francisco art world saw this remarkable sculpture. As a result, at the grand opening of the San Francisco Art Museum in 1935, there stood *Condor*, a provocative work of art at home in the company of many other fine works. And Dudley, who very much enjoyed the company of Piazzoni, became a regular visitor to the ranch. He and Gottardo became close friends, and Mireille and I became husband and wife.

The old Piazzoni ranch house is situated four miles from the Carmel Valley highway—four miles of true dirt road filled with ruts and hollows and rocks. One must ford a creek six times and open six big cattle gates before arriving at the house. The cattle own the road, and travelers must obtain their permission to proceed, honking horns and hollering incessantly until the cattle let them pass.

Another charm of the ranch was that there was no electricity. We cooked on a wood stove and used kerosene lamps for illumination. Dudley liked that. It took him back to the rugged reality he enjoyed in his youth.

At that time the area teemed with animals—deer, mountain lions, eagles, badgers, raccoons, and coyotes. There were even Bavarian pigs. According to local legend, a man of questionable heritage—

Piazzoni Ranch, Carmel, California
Photographs Thomas P. Wood

Carving His Own Niche

thought to be the son of a British royal—owned a huge spread known as the Moore Ranch and imported the Bavarian porkers. Years later the pigs' descendants ran wild in the lower Carmel Valley. Dudley loved that area. It didn't offer the giant trees he knew in British Columbia; it was primarily scrub brush with just a few oak and sycamore. Still, Dudley loved it. He simply loved nature.

There were hundreds of cottontail rabbits. We found they were excellent for the table during the Depression years, and occasionally Dudley and I would hunt them. Deer hunting, on the other hand, entailed much time and equipment—too big an operation for a couple of artists merely passing time together.

Dudley and I took many walks together. He would talk about surviving in the wilderness and show me plants and berries that could be safely eaten. Dudley was always a practical man, often regarding the landscape in a manner more scientific than artistic. We discussed water, earth formations, plants, and animals. Our friendship was cemented through a mutual interest in nature, but there was also our mutual interest in art, particularly sculpture and painting. I believe Dudley was always carrying a mental image of a future sculpture—always had a piece of wood on his mind.

He understood the loving regard that Gottardo, Mireille, and I had for the landscape. He understood our work as landscape painters—the basics of form and design are fundamental, primordial—like a mountain. There are many calling themselves artists who play with fundamentals and violate truths. Dudley was not one of those. He held the same simple and direct conception of art as we did.

Dudley Carter is known primarily as an axe sculptor, but the nude he did for us is rather delicate—quite unlike his huge choppings. Her figure, with its remarkable illusionary quality, is distorted to fill the space. Dudley likely learned this technique from the Natives and he did it well. But he didn't simply copy them. He always put his own touch on his works. His sense of form, simplicity, and restraint gave great power to his art, be it small or monumental.

But this man who loved living in the great outdoors lived with his family for a year or so in a small apartment in the city of Carmel. I occasionally visited the Carters there and remember Teresa, his wife, darning socks as we talked. Dudley always wore cashmere socks and Teresa was always darning them. I suggested she could buy him socks not made of cashmere, which wouldn't need to be darned so darned often. "Yes," she said, "I could buy them, but Dudley wouldn't wear them."

Wek Wek and the Holukmeyumko

When Dudley was living in the Carmel apartment, I went with him into the Big Sur country to bring out a log for a project at the outdoor Forest Theater in Carmel. We drove into a rugged canyon with steep hillsides heavily populated with redwoods, parked the car, and trudged down a logging road—more of a trail carved into the hillside than a road. Dudley pointed down the hill to a donkey engine. I'd seen donkey engines used in the redwood forests of Sonoma County, but never thought I'd be expected to work with one. I mentioned this to Dudley, but he passed it off as though there was nothing to it. For him it was old stuff.

Further down the hill lay the object of our expedition, a section of a huge redwood tree. The lumber company working the area had given Dudley the massive log, at least eight feet in diameter and twenty feet long. We went to work.

Dudley took a length of steel cable and tied the donkey engine to an uphill tree. After affixing a cable around the log, he fired up the engine and the donkey pulled the log up to itself. The donkey then tugged itself and the log uphill to the tree to which

Illusions and Reality

it was tied. This process was repeated over and over until, at last, the log lay alongside the logging road. Our work was finished—the logging company would later haul the log to the Forest Theater. There Dudley, with his woodsman's axe, would transform it into *Wek Wek and the Holukmeyumko*. The Forest Theater was home to that fine sculpture for many years.

Dudley's First Haida House

Dudley's work came to the attention of Samuel F. B. Morse. Sam, a relative and namesake of the inventor of the telegraph, was an artist himself and a successful entrepreneur. He owned Del Monte Foods and developed the Monterey Peninsula into a playground for the rich and famous. Dudley did work for Sam in exchange for the use of a piece of property on the Carmel River where he built a home and studio. He fashioned it after a type of Northwest Coast Haida dwelling with which he was enamored. Dudley constructed, carved, and erected the building in the Native manner, using no nails or hardware, at a cost of just $7.50.

On one of my visits to the Carters', a huge black bird came strutting towards me. As it came closer I could see that it was a turkey buzzard. It seemed to want to get to know me, and I appealed to Dudley, "What in the world is this?"

Dudley Carter teaching his daughter Mavis to shoot
Photograph courtesy Eltheen Carter King

He replied, "That's my friend, Buzzy."

I'd never been introduced to a tame buzzard before—such a wild creature is the buzzard. For several months Dudley fed his feathered friend and made many drawings of the bird. Buzzy was free to go, but he seemed to know a good setup when he found it. Eventually, however, the buzzard did fly off and never returned. Dudley hoped fate was kind to his buzzard buddy. Over the years Dudley worked many images of the big birds with their huge wingspans into his carvings, perhaps reminiscent of Buzzy.

The Carters' cabin was totally secluded—nobody lived anywhere nearby. It sat under the cover of big redwood trees. I remember Mavis playing there, and Teresa hand washing and hanging all the laundry on a line. In later years Dudley would

> The home and garden magazine *Sunset* ran an article (June 1936) about Dudley working at the Forest Theater at Carmel-by-the-Sea. They pictured him with the "gigantic" *Wek Wek*, describing him as "the Paul Bunyan sculptor." They also noted that "The United States Coat of Arms, which hangs above Col. Troup Miller's desk in the Persidio of Monterey, is surprising proof that Dudley Carter can turn from hewing large surfaces to the carving of delicate detail."

44   Carving His Own Niche

remark that he hated living under the redwood trees, saying, "It was always so damp."

At that time Dudley contracted an ailment, and Piazzoni sent him to Dr. Leo Eloesser, a famous medical doctor who treated numerous artists. Dr. Eloesser was a patron of the arts and an accomplished violinist himself. He not only treated artists compassionately and expertly, he did so at no charge. Dr. Eloesser was recognized for his surgical technique for treating chronic empyema, a condition that in his teens had cost Dudley six ribs and nearly his life. Dudley carved *Running the Rapids* for Dr. Eloesser.

1939 Golden Gate International Exposition and *Goddess of the Forest*

By the time Mireille and I returned from eight months in Europe absorbing art and history after our marriage, many artists were busy preparing for the 1939 Golden Gate International Exposition on Treasure Island. Dudley was one of those artists—he carved the façade of the Shasta-Cascade Building for the exposition. In 1940 Dudley and many other artists worked in the Art in Action area. I would occasionally stop by and say hello on my way to and from my own work at another part of the fair. Dudley attracted a lot of attention carving *The Ram* and the giant *Goddess of the Forest*.

Obtaining the log that became the *Goddess* is a story in itself. Dudley sent me a sketch he drew showing how the colossal sixty-ton redwood log went tumbling to the depths of a canyon, along with the two engines it took to pull it on the lumber company track. The log was irretrievable and finding another log to measure up to the original

Sculptured Table, 1932
Red cedar, 3.5′ × 5′
Top is one piece, carved on all sides with Northwest animals, supported by four cougars. Loaned to Shasta-Cascade Building in 1939–1940 for the Golden Gate International Exposition. Photograph courtesy Philip R. Wood

Shasta-Cascade Building Façade, 1939
Sugar Pine, 32′ × 26′
Designed and executed for the Golden Gate International Exposition, represents industry, wildlife, and native people of Northern California. Most likely destroyed. Photograph courtesy Philip R. Wood

The *Modesto Bee and News-Herald,* January 3, 1939, reported, "The completed Shasta-Cascade building typifies the modern trend in architecture, harmonizing with the exposition theme, and is ornamented on the façade by interesting wood carvings executed by Dudley C. Carter, widely known sculptor and woodsman."

Illusions and Reality

Result of first effort to deliver timber for Goddess of the Forest to San Francisco International World's Fair, 1940
Sketch by Dudley Carter
Courtesy Philip R. Wood

was impossible. The lumber company substituted a thirty-ton log and managed to get it to the fair just thirty-one days before the windup of the exposition. Completing a work of such magnitude in so short a time seemed inconceivable. Dudley took it as a challenge, completing the task one day before the fair ended. He spent the final day delighting fairgoers by autographing wood chips as souvenirs of the exposition.

After the Fair

Then came World War II and everything became disjointed. The Carters decided to return to Washington State, and Dudley sold his Haida house in Carmel to S.F.B. Morse. Sam and Dudley moved it to land that Sam owned on Big Creek in Big Sur country. Sam eventually deeded that property to University of California, Santa Cruz, keeping a ninety-nine-year lease on it.

I spent two of the war years as a personnel manager of war-related construction projects in Canada, travelling as far north as the Northwest Territories. As I flew over the ancient forests of Canada, I was reminded of the unbelievable tales that Dudley used to spin. He talked of rivers where uprooted trees, three hundred feet tall, could

An art critic at the *San Francisco Chronicle* wrote that the Shasta-Cascade building façade "cries vehemently for preservation," but following the fair, Dudley could find no trace of it or of the nine eagles he carved for the court of the same building. Regrettably, some of the fair's statuary and other art were destroyed. When the exposition closed in September 1940, Treasure Island, where the fair was held, was taken over by the US Navy in support of the war effort. Dudley's Shasta-Cascade works were likely among the works destroyed.

Dudley Carter and *Replica of a Haida House #1*, 1935
Redwood and native oak, 12' × 24'
This was the Carter family home from 1935 to 1941. S.F.B. Morse purchased the structure from Dudley. Used by Morse family heirs as a private cabin, it was most recently situated at Devil's Creek Flat in the University of California, Santa Cruz, Landels-Hill Big Creek Reserve. Photograph courtesy Dudley Carter

Top right: Dudley Carter in 1974 pausing during the reconstruction of *Replica of a Haida House #1*. Bottom right: Dudley with Philip Wood on left and Emmanuel Montoya on right. Photographs courtesy Philip R. Wood

disappear over and under a waterfall. I realized his fascinating stories were true, not embellished or exaggerated. The country of Dudley Carter's origin was a giant country, filled with giants.

Those flights over the forests brought to mind a tale Dudley once told me about a grizzly he encountered in the Canadian wilderness. He and two other cruisers were hiking along a narrow trail on the side of a rock cliff with an unscalable rock wall on one side and a deadly drop-off on the other. Dudley was in the lead with the others following, about twenty feet separating each of them, when a rumbling that grew ominously louder stopped them in their tracks. They turned and saw a huge bear bounding up the trail behind them. The three men flattened themselves against the wall of the cliff, hoping the grizzly would pass without incident. The bear ran past the first man without pausing. As he approached the middle man, he paused, raised one paw, and took a swipe at the top of the man's head—a mighty swipe! Then the bear started running again, thundering on, right past Dudley. Dudley explained that the man in the middle had red hair and concluded that grizzlies must not like red hair. The man sustained only superficial injuries and finished the timber cruise mission.

After the war, we reconnected with Dudley and

Illusions and Reality

Teresa. They would use our home in San Francisco as a sort of halfway house when en route from the Northwest to do some work in Monterey or Palm Springs. I think Dudley enjoyed working in the desert. He enjoyed the art he was able to accomplish and the money it brought in, as well as the desert air, pleasant surroundings, and his patrons.

When Dudley and Teresa stopped over they always brought along wine Teresa had made. Mireille and I assumed that all wine came from grapes. We were surprised to learn that Teresa made her wines from carrots or almost any vegetable or fruit one could name. That may be stretching it a bit, but her wines were definitely different.

Whether we were enjoying grape, carrot, or pear wine, we had many pleasant dinners together. Whenever Dudley came alone to stay with us, he'd enjoy spending time sitting in the kitchen reading. Sometimes he would talk with Mireille about food and would explain what foods were best. He frequently would help Mireille prepare meals. He himself ate very little, like a grape for breakfast. And he never failed to dextrinize almonds before eating them. Dextrinizing, as I understand it, is the process of toasting the almonds in an oven until they turn brown. I believe it's a word coined by Dr. Frank McCoy who wrote *The Fast Way to Health*, which Dudley regarded as his nutritional bible. Dudley copied sections of Dr. McCoy's book by hand and gave them to Mireille and me.

Dudley advocated fasting. As I reflect on his vigor and longevity, he had the right idea. Mireille and I had always tried to eat the right foods, eating less of them too. Dudley carried it many steps further. He never spoke much about his diet and nutritional beliefs when Teresa was with him, but when he was on his own we got an education!

Dudley's constitution demanded exercise. When staying with us he was not able to chop away at a large sculpture, so he needed other exercise to stay

No Bad Bear Days
From the memories of Lex Hanson, Dudley's grandson-in-law

Dudley experienced much real-life drama in the decades he spent as a timber cruiser among forests from Alaska to California. He counted thirty-three times in his career when, alone in the wilderness, he was charged by black or grizzly bears. Amazingly, each one ended on a positive note.

The first three times a bear charged him, nature conveniently provided him with climbable trees as a means of escape. The next three times burly bears came at him, Dudley found himself in timber too large to scale, and he was forced to face them off. His last line of defense was his axe, and he had supreme confidence with it. Coming out unscathed from those six encounters with bears, Dudley knew he could stand his ground. And so he did—twenty-seven more times.

Dudley Carter had no bad bear days.

Yet he had learned when he ought not to push his luck. Dudley related a story from his early timber-cruising experience that occurred near a small stream just south of the Canadian border when he came upon a pack of wolves that had just pulled down a deer. They were so aggressive in ravaging and guarding their prey that Dudley determined it was one time when it would be best for him to move off his compass line—not the time to stand his ground.

in shape. He thought a good walk to be the best exercise, but he also worked his arms, legs, and whole body while indoors. When he got into bed at night, he would raise each leg one hundred times—up and down. During the day I might find him in the living room moving his arms or his legs in a repetitive exercise pattern, oblivious to all else.

Oblivious. This applied to Dudley most of the time. One reason for this was his hearing. I don't think he ever used a hearing aid, and I never asked him about it because that was his own business. I just spoke loudly to him and that did the job. When he sat and read, or was drawing or writing, I could pass right in front of him, making noises or other distractions, and he would not look up nor acknowledge my presence. This attitude definitely was in his favor, whether caused by his deafness or fostered by his intensity of interest.

Restoration of *The Ram*

Dudley was ninety-two when he came to San Francisco to restore *The Ram* at City College. It took him two weeks, working with a chisel, to remove layers of paint that vandals had applied to the sculpture. Toward the end of that project, he stayed at our home and I asked him why he didn't use paint remover or a blowtorch. He explained, "It would darken the wood."

An art student named Emmanuel Montoya helped Dudley restore *The Ram*. Emmanuel also acted as Dudley's chauffeur on occasion. Upon completion of the restoration project, he brought Dudley, his luggage, and all his paraphernalia to our house. Before unloading his station wagon, Emmanuel confided, "Dudley has this big box he thinks he can sneak on the plane."

"Sneak?" I exclaimed when I saw it. The box was over five feet long, two feet high, and two feet wide—it looked like a coffin. It was all Emmanuel and I could do to lift and maneuver it into my basement. Dudley had constructed the box in Santa Cruz to keep his tools secured while he and Dick Cooley, a professor at University of California, Santa Cruz, were working on a wood sculpture outdoors.

When it came time for Dudley's return home, he decided to go to the airport by shuttle bus, as Mireille and I were unable to take him. I telephoned a few shuttle services and inquired about the box. Transporting a box that size was questionable and the prices were outlandish. I decided to attack the box. Inside were five or six axes, a chain saw, a handsaw, a wad of old clothes, a pair of leather moccasins, chisels, hammers, cans of oil, and some fuel! I thought his lunch might be in there someplace too. Dudley told me he had been to a flea market and bought the handsaw for one dollar and the shoes for fifty cents. He always had an eye for a bargain.

After talking things over with Dudley, he agreed to a new and smaller box. I was able to whittle down the dimensions to about three feet in length and less than twelve inches high. The slimmed down plywood box—wrapped in muslin sheeting, tied with a rope, and holding all Dudley's tools—flew back to Seattle, minus the oil and fuel. Dudley left the coffin with me—said he'd pick it up the next time he came down to San Francisco.

Restoration of the *Goddess of the Forest*

Dudley returned to San Francisco and stayed with us for a couple of weeks while he fussed with the restoration of the *Goddess of the Forest*, which had spent many years in Golden Gate Park. He had made some drawings and wanted copies of them. Some aspects of the sketches were quite faint, so I went clear downtown to a lithograph place to obtain quality copies. After they were done Dudley looked at the lithographs and said, "I'm going to the

Illusions and Reality 49

business district to make the copies." He made them himself for a nickel apiece and never did pay me for the lithographs. Not that he was miserly or stingy—far from it. He was simply so engrossed in his work that the thought of paying for the lithographs just never occurred to him.

The Evolution of a Feast Bowl

When the Carter's daughter, Mavis, was getting married, Dudley said he wanted to buy one of my watercolors as a wedding present. He selected a beauty, a scene of the ranch house when it still had the beautiful color of the original three-foot redwood shakes on the roof. When Dudley asked the price, I told him to forget it—that I was happy to give it to him and I hoped Mavis and David would enjoy it. Dudley insisted on paying, though, so we argued. Finally, Dudley said, "I'll make you something you want—a carved chair or a canoe paddle? Maybe you'd rather have a feast bowl for the table?"

I thought a chair was too much for him to do and I had canoe paddles I liked. I agreed to the feast bowl, which was good for us and a nice easy job for him. Dudley made a sketch indicating how he would carve it, with frogs and lizards and other life forms, and we settled on the trade. Years passed. I would see Dudley, but no bowl. At first I didn't ask about it, but finally I worked up the courage to inquire, "What ever happened to that feast bowl you were going to carve for me?" He was extremely apologetic and assured me he would get around to it. I knew he had been truly busy and was not pressing him, only asking, but I wanted that feast bowl!

I cannot say how many years passed before Dudley showed up at our front door with the feast bowl—ten years would not be exaggerating. Finally, the bowl arrived and it was, and is, a beautiful bowl. But there were no frogs or lizards or anything, for that matter, carved on it. "I didn't have time to carve the rest of it, but you can do it," he said, pointing out where the frogs should go. "Here you can put a lizard and so forth."

We laughed, looked at each other, and laughed and laughed. We understood.

I took the bowl to the ranch expecting to work on it there, but the unadorned bowl was used for many purposes, including a bird bath. Years later I carved the frogs and lizards, snakes and salamanders, and leaves and berries, until the bowl was finished.

The feast bowl was sitting on a table in our living room in plain sight the next time Dudley came to visit. As Dudley entered the room, he stopped and

Feast Bowl, 35″ long and 14″ wide
Carved by Dudley Carter, ornamentation by Philip Wood
Photograph Thomas P. Wood

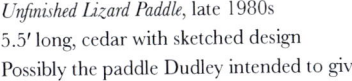

Unfinished Lizard Paddle, late 1980s
5.5′ long, cedar with sketched design
Possibly the paddle Dudley intended to give to Philip Wood, "for old times' sake." The lizard figures prominently in Miwok mythology.
Photograph Lisa Lambert

stared at the bowl. Standing beside him I casually remarked, "Do you recognize that bowl, Dudley?"

He did not answer, so I said, "It's the bowl you made for me. You made the bowl and told me to carve the frogs and things."

"I didn't think I did those," he said, pointing at my lizards. Then he laughed. We both laughed. We both understood, again.

"Busier than ever!!"

The last time Dudley visited us in San Francisco he offered to make a paddle for me for old times' sake. I tried to talk him out of it, but he insisted and made sketches of what it should be like. I still have the drawings, though I never saw the paddle. Maybe he was working on it. Maybe he was planning to bring me the paddle expecting me to carve on it—I will never know.

Four months before he died, just short of his 101st birthday, Dudley wrote on his 1991 Christmas card to us, "Busier than ever!! Have to find some short cuts. Here is for the Merriest Christmas and the Greatest New Year to you all. Love, Dudley. Hope to find time for a visit."

Philip R. Wood (1913–2002) with Dudley Carter and Mireille. Born in Oakland, Wood was a noted painter and muralist. Recognized as equally fluent with oils and watercolors, he specialized in landscapes of northern California. He studied for a five-year period at the California School of Fine Arts and was greatly influenced by Gottardo Piazzoni, who was well known as a master interpreter of California landscape and the father of Wood's artist wife, Mireille. Wood was also a jazz pianist. Dudley referred to the Woods as his "oldest, closest friends."
Photograph courtesy Emmanuel Montoya

Oil portrait of Dudley Carter, 1983, by Mireille Piazzoni Wood
12″ × 16″
Photograph courtesy Philip R. Wood

Illusions and Reality

Chapter 10

Condor

By 'Lyn Lambert and Mary Sikkema

Condor is a lament, much in the manner of the writings of Californian John Steinbeck, who expressed so well the ceaseless struggle of people who depend on the land. Many of Steinbeck's books, notably *The Grapes of Wrath* and *Tortilla Flat*, tell of the human exploitation and suffering in California during Dudley's early years there.

Carter himself was a dispossessed worker; although never did he agonize over his situation. When the Depression caused a halt in his work as a timber cruiser, he moved with his family from British Columbia, Canada, to California to pursue a career in art. Although acclaimed by a few influential people in the art community, Carter, as an outsider, was not welcomed by many local artists. Dudley believed they wanted to keep the market to themselves.

In 1935, while searching along a narrow roadway by a tributary of the Carmel River for discarded wood to sculpt, Dudley spotted a large redwood stump and his mind's eye inverted it, envisioning *Condor*. Thoughts of this remarkable bird often came to the artist's mind. He admired the creatures—with their nine-foot wingspans—as they soared over the coastal ranges from Monterey to Southern California. Prior to coming across the redwood remnant, Dudley had learned of a condor that had been shot, wounded, and abandoned by a thoughtless individual. Realizing that their numbers were on the decline, he carved his concern for the plight of the California condor into the stump. Almost hidden in the collapsing wings of the wounded bird are grotesque, anguished human faces reminiscent of the downtrodden, dispossessed workers of the Dirty Thirties.

He transformed the stump where he found it, leaving the big bird to roost by the side of the road until Gottardo Piazzoni invited Carter to enter one of his works in an adjudicated show. Dudley loaded his creation into a box trailer, hitched it to his Ford Model T, toted it to San Francisco, and launched his California art career.

Condor captured the interest of many. It was the first work seen by visitors entering the new San Francisco Art Museum when it opened in 1935. At the close of the museum's opening celebrations, *Condor* was moved into the gardens of the Carmel Art Association, whose membership Dudley felt had previously shunned him. After a time, the work came back to its creator, who kept watch over the bird until 1975 when Allied Stores bought it and fifteen other Carter works. In 1995 Marvin Boys, an art patron and great friend of Dudley's, acquired the work intending to display it for the public's appreciation.

Condor, 1935
Redwood, 6′ × 5′ × 2.5′
Pictured in Marymoor Park, Redmond, Washington. Acquired in 1995 by Marvin Boys for public display. Currently owned by King County Parks, Washington.
Photograph Lisa Lambert

Chapter 11

Legend of Wek Wek and the Holukmeyumko

A myth from the Miwok, indigenous to Northern California, compiled by 'Lyn Lambert and Mary Sikkema

At sacred time, when the hoop of the earth was not complete and people were learning the ways of all things, Wek Wek the Falcon Man, son of Molok the Condor and grandson of Coyote the Wise One, was sorrowful. His eyes swam in pools of water for he saw that his people were becoming more and more dispirited.

On the sea side of the mountains, home of the Miwok, the land offered up nothing with which the people could make music, and without music there can be no harmony. Without music the Miwok were unable to enact the spiritual ceremonies attending birth and death and the healing rituals of life. The people were so dispirited that their voices had no song, their hands and feet no dance. Having lost the harmony of the power songs that were sung at the very creation of the world, each generation grew increasingly disheartened. Pessimism and fatalism blanketed their world. Wek Wek the Falcon Man feared that without music what once was a beautiful, enlightened world would dissolve further into chaos,

Dudley Carter with *Wek Wek and the Holukmeyumko* at Carmel, 1935, redwood, 12′ × 5.5′ × 5.5′
Photograph courtesy Dudley Carter

Dudley Carter carved *Wek Wek and the Holukmeyumko* on the grounds of the Forest Theater in Carmel, California, in 1935 when the Depression had silenced the music for so many. He hoped people would find strength and encouragement in his legendary work. Following the totem principles of design, Carter carved Wek Wek's genealogy on the reverse side of the sculpture. *Wek Wek and the Holukmeyumko* remained on the grounds of the Forest Theater for many years and graced the Palace of Fine Arts during the Golden Gate International Exposition of 1939 and 1940. It was one of sixteen works purchased from Carter in 1975 by Allied Stores for a planned, but never developed, shopping center in Redmond, Washington. In 1995 Marvin Boys, a patron of the arts, acquired this sculpture and a number of other fine Dudley Carter works with the hope of displaying them permanently in a King County park to be established to commemorate the artist. King County Parks situated the work in the Pet Memorial Garden in Marymoor Park, Redmond Washington.

Legend of Wek Wek and the Holukmeyumko

like other worlds before it.

Wek Wek sought the wisdom of his grandfather, Coyote. Coyote, creator and jokester, teacher and keeper of magic, is associated with all things magical. His magic does not always appear to work, but Wek Wek knew that it always serves a purpose. There is hidden wisdom in the advice of Coyote. Coyote teaches the balance of wisdom and folly and how they go hand in hand.

Wek Wek told Coyote that his heart was insisting he travel east, beyond the mountains where there was known to be a special reedy-stemmed plant with which beautiful music could be made. Coyote affirmed that there was such a plant to be found east of the mountains, but he warned his grandson of the dangers that would confront him should he attempt such a mission.

"Rattlesnakes guard the blue elderberry plants of which you speak, but even more menacing are the Holukmeyumko," cautioned Coyote. "The desirable Holukmeyumko, Keepers of the Stars, will play beautiful music on their elderberry flutes. They will use their womanly wiles to persuade you to stay with them."

Weighing his grandfather's advice, the Falcon Man was undaunted and further determined. He flew off, over the distant mountains. Overcoming the rattlesnakes, he gathered the precious seeds of the elderberry. Then, as his grandfather had predicted, the beautiful Keepers of the Stars swarmed around him, playing alluring music on their flutes, tempting him to forsake his mission and remain with them.

Wek Wek, with the plight of his people heavy in his heart, called upon the strength of his mighty wings and resisted the persuasions of the Holukmeyumko. Flying back to his people, he dropped the precious seeds on the sea side of the mountains where they took root and flourished. The beautiful gift of music was restored to the people. Their spirits could soar once more.

NOTE: The authors adapted and paraphrased the preceding version of the legend of Wek Wek and the Holukmeyumko from a tale told by Dudley Carter and notes by Dudley's granddaughter, Anna Vaughan Hanson. Other resources that provided helpful information include *The Ohlone Way, Indian Life in the San Francisco-Monterey Bay Area* by Malcolm Margolin (Berkley, California: Heyday Books, 1978) and *Animal-Speak: The Spiritual & Magical Powers of Creatures Great & Small* by Ted Andrews (St. Paul, Minnesota: Llewellyn Publications, 2004).

Below Right: *Wek Wek and the Holukmeyumko*, 1935
Photographed in 1995 at the former Slough House Park in Redmond, Washington, where Dudley served as Artist-in-Residence in the final years of his life
Photograph 'Lyn Lambert

Dudley Carter envisioned further enhancement of *Wek Wek and the Holukmeyumko*. Sketch by Dudley Carter, courtesy Hedda Schafer Shepherd

Chapter 12

An Infusion of Geniuses

By 'Lyn Lambert

When most of the nation was in a downswing due to the Great Depression of the 1930s, things were looking up in San Francisco. The construction of two new bridges and business from their harbor and port gave San Franciscans reason to be optimistic. Scarcity of work in the Northwest timber industry moved Dudley Carter to think that he might be able to put his talents as an artist to work amidst the optimism in San Francisco, so in 1933 he and his family headed south.

The WPA Federal Art Project

The Works Progress Administration Federal Art Project (FAP), conceived by President Franklin D. Roosevelt's administration, was designed to employ out-of-work artists, to provide art for public buildings such as schools, libraries, and hospitals, and to infuse art and artists into the everyday life of communities throughout the United States. Dudley Carter was one of many artists engaged by the FAP in California. He worked half-time for the FAP and half-time for himself.

The first large redwood sculpture Dudley

Dudley and Teresa Carter in front of the Shasta-Cascade Building, 1940
Photo courtesy Dudley Carter

feet wide in top quality sugar pine, representing Northern California's indigenous people, its industry, and wild life.

Artists in Action

During the second season of the exposition, the Hall of Fine and Decorative Arts, also known as the Palace of Fine Arts, became a living, working, art exhibit, featuring artists in many media—an infusion of geniuses. Merriam Webster defines a genius as "a very smart or talented person who has a level of talent or intelligence that is very rare or remarkable."[1] Dudley Carter was one of those geniuses.

One reporter described the Art in Action exhibit as "a kind of twenty-ring circus of art".[2] The main attraction was famed Mexican muralist

carved while working for himself in California was *Condor*, which he submitted to an adjudication of artworks for the opening of the new San Francisco Art Museum. A prominent San Francisco architect, Timothy Pflueger, especially liked *Condor*.

As a member of the design committee for San Francisco's 1939 Golden Gate International Exposition (GGIE), Timothy Pflueger commissioned Dudley to design and execute the façade of the Shasta-Cascade Building. Dudley created a low relief carving, thirty-two feet high and twenty-six

Diego Rivera. Rivera's huge mural—almost 1,800 square feet—was known familiarly as *Pan American Unity* in keeping with the theme of the GGIE, which was peace and brotherhood among nations. More formally, Diego Rivera titled the work *The Marriage of the Artistic Expression of the North and South on this Continent*. The fresco covered most of one wall of the

---

[1] "Genius." Merriam-Webster.com. Accessed February 21, 2014. http://www.merriam-webster.com/dictionary/genius.

[2] Alfred Frankenstein, "Diverse Attractions at the Golden Gate Fair," *New York Times*, June 9, 1940.

Carving His Own Niche

Big Horn Ram, 1940
Redwood, 10' × 2.5' × 3.5'
Posing with *Big Horn Ram*, left to right, are Edward G. Robinson, film star and art collector whose portrait is in the war panel of Rivera's mural *Pan American Unity*; Dudley Carter; and Diego Rivera.
Photograph Arthur Niendorff, courtesy Emmanuel C. Montoya

> "Rivera saw the self-taught forest engineer from British Columbia, with his work echoing the work of coastal natives, to be a pivotal figure in the world of art."
>
> John Burnside, "A Most Remarkable Canadian," Coast News, British Columbia, May 13, 1991.

interior of the fine arts building. On the opposite wall, some 300 feet away, Swiss-born Herman Volz was creating a huge marble mosaic. In the center of the hall, Dudley Carter boldly swung his double-bitted axe while all around him numerous other notable artists demonstrated their talents.

Diego Rivera was so impressed with Dudley as he sculpted a huge redwood log into a ram using only the simplest techniques and tools, that the muralist featured the wood sculptor three times—as a sculptor, a woodsman, and a forest engineer—in the central panel of his magnificent work.

According to Sir Arthur Conan Doyle, "Mediocrity knows nothing higher than itself; but talent instantly recognizes genius." The talent and genius inherent in Rivera and Carter surely recognized each other, as the two artists became good friends.

Dudley recalled that in some ways he and Diego were much alike, in others very different. They both liked to work on a large scale, and both found that they could learn more from the primitive background of their own countries than they could from following modern trends here and abroad. Physically the two artists were very different. The paint-brush-wielding muralist weighed 315 pounds, the axe man, 122 pounds. Diego had many wives and concubines. Dudley found that one woman was enough.

There were usually about half a dozen artists at work in the fine arts building, starting around ten in the morning and winding up at ten at night. About every other night, several of the artists would take off for Chinatown after work. Dudley found Diego to be wonderful company, "He could consume great volumes of red wine and always enjoyed himself. He was as good as a show and helped everyone have a good time."[3]

There were also tense times while working with

[3]Carpenter, Patricia F. and Paul Totah, *The San Francisco Fair: Treasure Island, 1939–1940* (San Francisco: Scottwall Associates, 1989) 50–53.

An Infusion of Geniuses

60   *Carving His Own Niche*

Opposite page: *Goddess of the Forest*, 1940
Redwood, 32' × 7' × 7'
Restored portion remains in the collection of City College San Francisco
Photo courtesy Hedda Schafer Shepherd

Diego Rivera. Due to international politics and a lack of understanding, some people objected to Rivera and his art. Rivera had befriended the Russian Marxist revolutionary Leon Trotsky, who lived for a time with the artist and his wife Frida Kahlo in Mexico. While Diego was working at the fair, Trotsky was assassinated in Mexico, and many—including Rivera—were afraid that Rivera's life was in danger. Extra guards were assigned to the artists' building.

The Fusion of Genius

Rivera may have been the main attraction of the Art in Action feature of the exposition, but he was fascinated by the art of Dudley Carter. Speaking of the wood sculptor, Rivera said, "Here in the Fine Arts Building a man is making sculpture in wood. He was an engineer, an educated and sophisticated man who lived among the Indians. His art at first was like Indian art, an art form deeply rooted in the soil of the Americas without foreign influence. Now it is his own expression yet a great deal of Indian feeling has passed through him. That is the way art should be, first the assimilation, then the expression."[4]

Explaining his mural, *Marriage of the Artistic Expression of the North and South on This Continent*, Rivera wrote, "In this mural I projected the idea of the fusion of the genius of the South (Mexico), with its religious ardor and its gift for plastic expression, and the genius of the North (the United States), with its gift for creative mechanical expression. Symbolizing this union—and focal point of the whole composition—was a colossal Goddess of Life, half Indian, half machine." He goes on to explain, "This idea was elsewhere expressed in a portrait of Dudley Carter, an engineer who returned to a pure expression of plastics using only primitive materials and implements, such as a hand axe."[5]

Fairgoers and Diego Rivera were dazzled by Dudley Carter's first act, *Big Horn Ram*, but Dudley was determined to finish his performance with a truly grand finale. He planned to carve a sixty-ton redwood log into a work he would call *Goddess of the Forest*, with which he would demonstrate the totem principles of design. Misfortune struck, however, when the sixty-ton log Dudley obtained for his project was lost. The log and the two locomotives hauling it to San Francisco all fell into a canyon. The company supplying the timber could find only a thirty-ton replacement—still large enough for an artistic genius to make a big impression.

" . . . he who hopes to be universal in his art must plant in his own soil. Great art is like a tree which grows in a particular place and has a trunk, leaves, blossoms, boughs, fruit, and roots of its own. The more native art is, the more it belongs to the entire world, because taste is rooted in nature. When art is true, it is one with nature. This is the secret of primitive art and also of the art of the masters . . . "

Diego Rivera
My Art, My Life: An Autobiography

---

[4] Sand Point Naval Air Station handout, 1960, quoting Diego Rivera in 1940.

[5] Diego Rivera, *My Art, My Life: An Autobiography*, with Gladys March (New York: Dover Publications, Inc., 1991), 151–152.

Chapter 13

Craftsman or Artist?

From a conversation with Everett DuPen

I first came upon Dudley Carter in 1940 at San Francisco's Golden Gate International Exposition. There was Dudley, ascending in a rickety sort of elevator, ready to tackle a huge, and I mean huge, wood carving. As I remember, glass walls protected the public from the chips that flew everywhere as he swung his axe at a tremendous log.

Next to him, Diego Rivera was at work on his famous mural into which he painted Dudley three times. Initially, I thought Dudley was carving a totem pole, but *Goddess of the Forest* was not a totem pole. It was a splendid sculpture melding totemic standards with Dudley's own creative style.

Dudley Carter was smart to move to California when he did. The art community in San Francisco was excellent, very lively at that time, and it afforded him good exposure. My timing wasn't as good. I moved to San Francisco when World War II broke out. By that time, Carter had gone back to Seattle and the exposition site on Treasure Island was bulldozed to make way for a naval base.

In 1945 I heard about a job opening in the University of Washington's sculpture department. I applied, got the job, and began work in the fall of that year. It was at the University of Washington that I first got to know Dudley. I don't know how long Carter served as an instructor there, but he took over for Dudley Pratt after he left to work as an illustrator for the Boeing Aircraft Company

Carving His Own Niche

Dudley Carter and *Progress*, 1956
Red cedar, 9' × 8' × 2'
Carved originally for Rainier National Bank of Commerce, acquired by Security Pacific Bank, then Seafirst Bank. Eventually the work became part of the Seafirst Corporate Art Collection. Its current location is unknown.
Photograph courtesy Hedda Schafer Shepherd

during World War II.

I recall a rather dashing figure appearing in the UW sculpture studio one day, introducing himself as Dudley Carter and declaring, "That large piece over in the corner is mine. We'll get it out of here as soon as we can."

I don't remember what piece it was, but I do remember him working on an interesting panel he called *Progress*, which he did for the Rainier National Bank of Commerce at 6th and Olive in Seattle. I asked him how he managed to keep a huge piece of wood like that from warping, and he showed me how he put steel bars and angle irons on the back of the work. Additionally, he had learned from the Indians how to harden wood by firing it, lessening the chance of cracks and checks.

Rivalry of the Winds, the piece Dr. Richard Fuller and his mother bought for the Seattle Art Museum, also has steel rods and is plugged, making the rods

> "A man who works with his hands is a laborer; a man who works with his hands and heart is a craftsman; but a man who works with his hands and heart and head is an artist."
>
> Louis Nizer

invisible. That piece sat in an obscure location in Volunteer Park, sadly neglected and all but shrouded by holly bushes for many years. No doubt the steel rods helped retard nature's destructive process. Happily, the Seattle Art Museum rescued *Rivalry*. To their credit, they restored the piece and gave it a new home in the lobby of their Arcade Building just north of the museum in downtown Seattle. [Later the museum moved *Rivalry of the Winds* to the lobby of the Redmond Public Library, Redmond, Washington.]

Dudley worked on a large scale, but generally he first made models out of an oil-based clay. He tried to encourage me to do monumental work and would say, "Come over and get a log." I didn't care to do large-scale work, but that didn't keep us from enjoying a mutual professional friendship.

It was amazing what that man could do with an axe. He'd throw a double-bitted axe into a log and embed it every time, and he did that when he was far from young. Work, work, work, all the time! And he went everywhere—California, Oregon, British Columbia, all over the place. Dudley was quite a salesman. He received more commissions and was better paid than most sculptors. He did architectural sculpture, carved things for boats, and built Haida houses. The sales from his work were a steady incentive for Dudley. Bill McNae, one of my students, bought Dudley's Bellevue Haida house studio.

Despite his commercial success, many in the Northwest Institute of Sculpture did not like his work, did not value it. The institute, formed around 1955, included sculptors from Washington, Oregon, Idaho, and British Columbia. It doesn't exist anymore. At a Portland meeting when it was my turn to present the program, I showed slides of Dudley's work. It wasn't well received. They thought of him as a craftsman rather than an artist. They were sick and tired of totem poles. But I considered Dudley to be extremely creative. When working with public commissions as he did, an artist develops a commendable array of skills. I think folks in that group would change their minds now if they saw the whole body of art Dudley produced.

Although Dudley taught at the university, he did not have an academic background. He was one of those naturals. I consider Dudley to have been exceedingly talented—naturalistic, not realistic. His mastery of hollows—he worked those carving tools to make subtle changes to the shape of the wood and repeated the stylistic rhythm of his design. He knew how to distort so that the pieces would be very powerful when seen at a distance.

Dudley Carter was a salty character, salt of the earth. A craftsman? Yes. An artist? Obviously.

Everett DuPen (1912–2005), educated at the University of Southern California, the Chouinard Art Institute in Los Angeles, and Yale University. DuPen taught at the Carnegie Institute in New York City and Washington University in St. Louis, Missouri. He taught at the University of Washington Sculpture Department starting in 1945, eventually retiring as head of the university's division of sculpture. Known for his many works in Seattle—pieces of a thematic nature in churches and libraries, numerous works in private collections, and his large bronze fountain in front of the Washington State Library in Olympia. Photograph 'Lyn Lambert

Chapter 14

A Lumberjack in the Halls of Ivy

From an Interview with Duane Hanson by Liza Kirwin

As a youth growing up on a small dairy farm in Minnesota, I was always interested in carving, working with my hands, working in three dimensions with clay or wood, plaster, whatever. We had no art training in those days. My high school had maybe two or three art books. Our local college was no better. They had an instructor who had some art training, but they didn't offer any real art courses.

Then my parents moved out to Seattle about 1944. The University of Washington had a wonderful art program: art history, painting, and design. I studied there for two years.

At that time there was kind of a lumberjack guy who was teaching sculpture. He made us make little clay models. Then he took an axe—he had a big log there—and he started swinging at that log with that axe. I'll never forget it—and a figure would come out of that. Golly, that's amazing.

His name was Dudley Carter and I thought he was an old man then. He talked like he had dusters in his throat, "Think about form. You can have it a little more rounded here." I'll never forget that raspy voice, like he was going to drop dead any minute.

Then, three or four years ago—around 1985—my dad and I were watching TV and the reporter said, "Now, we have a very interesting sculptor to show you. This man carves with an axe. Dudley Carter."

Dudley Carter with a group of works he created during the time that he taught sculpture at the University of Washington
Photograph courtesy Hedda Schafer Shepherd

He was about ninety-five years old and still hacking away. "That's him!" I said to my dad. "That's him! Remember him?"

So I got introduced to what you might call an old-time tradition of carving and modeling through Dudley Carter. I gave a talk at the University of Washington in the spring of 1988 and I mentioned that one of my first teachers in sculpture was Dudley Carter—swinging an axe.

> "Sculptor Duane Hanson attributed his beginning in the arts world to Dudley Carter."
>
> "Duane Hanson," *Miami Talent Magazine*, June 1, 2012, http://www.miamitalentmag.com/emag/story/duane-hanson.

NOTE: This story was excerpted from an interview with artist Duane Hanson in Davie, Florida, August 1989. Liza Kirwin conducted the interview for the Archives of American Art/Smithsonian Institution, Washington, DC. Funding for the interview was provided by the Lannan Foundation.

Duane Hanson (1925–1996), sculptor and educator, born in Alexandria, Minnesota, received a master of fine arts degree from the Cranbrook Academy of Art in Bloomfield Hills, Michigan. Exhibited widely, nationally and internationally. Taught in public and private high schools in the US, American Army schools in Germany, Miami-Dade Junior College, and the University of Miami. Hanson is best known for his long series of super-realistic, life-size figures dressed in real clothes who are often overweight, expressing his long-running dialogue with consumerism, abundance, and America's penchant for overindulging itself. He died at the age of seventy-one of non-Hodgkin's lymphoma, likely caused by exposure to toxic resin and fixative fumes from sculpting.
Photograph courtesy Wesla Host Hanson

Bird Woman, 1947, red cedar, 12′ × 4′ × 10″
Carved around the time that Dudley was teaching sculpture at the University of Washington
Photograph courtesy Anna Vaughan Hanson

A Lumberjack in the Halls of Ivy   67

Chapter 15

An Original

From a conversation with Thomas Dunstan

I knew and worked with Dudley Carter for many years, dating back to 1948, but my first actual exposure to him and his work came in 1939 when I visited the world's fair in San Francisco. Dudley carved a marvelous colonnade of nine eagles that stood in the grand approach to one of the fair's museums. I don't think of them as totems for they had a classical theme to them. They were sugar pine, each three feet in diameter and about nine feet tall. Impressive!

Dudley had set up a studio at the fair where he carved with an axe, a feat I considered quite an art in itself. At that time, I was just twenty years old and studying architecture. Dudley received a good deal of publicity as a result of his work at the fair, and over the years I often read about him in various and sundry publications. When my practice was nicely established, I made it a point to look him up. Dudley Carter was a busy man. He did some freelance timber cruising and was operating a cedar products business. By then the market for large-scale wood sculptures was beginning to improve, so he was very busy.

In 1947 the Carter's house in Gibsons, BC, burnt to the ground, and Dudley moved his family to Bellevue where they rented an old farm. Around that time, he purchased a sizeable piece of property along the Pilchuk River near Granite Falls and about four acres on Bellevue-Redmond Road in Bellevue.

I built a house for myself in 1948 and commissioned Dudley to do a panel for it. The house featured a stone floor entry with an archway leading to the dining room. Dudley created a marvelous arch of lauan mahogany for the dining room entrance. It's a pretty big piece. The archway is five feet wide and seven to eight feet high. Dudley's carved panel, which outlines the opening, is eighteen inches wide.

Lauan mahogany, a blond mahogany, was not his usual medium, but I needed a material that could survive in a tight situation with people walking back and forth. Cedar would tend to split away and get broken off. Mahogany, being a denser material, would survive. So Dudley chose lauan mahogany for the arch. Working in mahogany must have been a piece of cake for him compared to working in cedar, which is so very unforgiving. Mahogany is much less demanding.

When my home was finished, I held an open house. A gentleman widely known in Seattle's clothing business attended. He liked the house and said to me, "I want you to build me a house just like yours."

I said, "You don't want a house just like mine. You want it different!"

"No," he said, "I don't want it different. I don't want a thing changed. I want you to build this exact house for me, including the carving around the doorway to the dining room!"

I duplicated the house and Dudley did a duplicate arch. I don't think the second arch ended up an actual duplicate. Dudley hated to copy anything, even his own designs. But it was the same configuration, it was lauan mahogany, and it stood in the same stone-floored entry with the same oak and cedar trim. You couldn't even obtain most of those materials now. My client could afford his house. I couldn't afford mine and had to give it up. But I'm sure that panel still exists in that house down on the shores of Lake Washington.

Dudley completed several pieces for my clients, for example, a door panel on a residence in the Blue Ridge neighborhood and another on the house next to a Congregational church in Magnolia. When my then-wife and I built a house on Yarrow Point, we incorporated the prow of a Dudley Carter Indian-style canoe into the end of a beam.

I also bought the marvelous *Female Head* that Dudley had carved in cedar. I either sold or gave it to a client when I remodeled a home for him. The same client also acquired one of Dudley's thunderbirds. Dudley did many thunderbirds. They were sort of a trademark of his and he did a beautiful job on them.

Female Head, 1943
Yellow cedar, 3′ high
Acquired by the Earl Amick family through Thomas Dunstan
Photograph courtesy JoAnne Amick

An Original

When my wife passed away, I rented an apartment across the street from Bellevue Square. Dudley had done a beautiful bowl that I admired and purchased, a feast bowl—the sort the Natives used to prepare food. It was four feet long, three feet wide, and about eight inches deep. I had a wet bar in my apartment, and I put plants in the bowl and hung it above the bar. It was very attractive.

At that time, I was doing about twenty houses for a developer in Sunset Hills and I moved out

Above: *Thunderbird*, ca. 1950s
Red cedar, 12′ × 6′
Acquired by the Earl Amick family through Thomas Dunstan, architect
Photograph courtesy JoAnne Amick

Right: *Bus Stop*, 1961
Red cedar, columns 18′ high
Commissioned for El Dorado Land Development through Thomas Dunstan, architect. Mercer Island, Washington
Photograph courtesy Hedda Schafer Shepherd

Below: *Feast Bowl*, 1956
Red cedar, 4′ long and 14″ wide
Typical of Dudley Carter's Native-style bowls; similar to those made by the Haida Indians of Alaska and Northern BC
Photograph courtesy Hedda Schafer Shepherd

An Original

of the apartment. I sold Dudley's feast bowl to the developer. He mounted it on the outside of his own house.

I designed the houses in a development called El Dorado Lane on Mercer Island that had a bus stop on site. I commissioned Dudley to do that bus stop. The design was interesting—the roof was a canopy of laminated two-by-fours shaped like a boomerang on a tilt. Three cedar posts ran through the canopy, anchoring it to the bench below. Dudley originally designed the posts as totem poles. But they would have cost a fortune and the developer wasn't open to that. We discussed it with Dudley and he came up with an inexpensive way of achieving the same feeling. He mounted carved figures of human and animal derivation on top of the cedar columns. The whole structure was nicely done and it sure beat building a bus stop out of glass and aluminum. Sadly, I think some eager beaver tore it down.

Whenever I asked Dudley to fulfill a specific architectural mission he always understood exactly what I wanted. I would visit his studio, and we would discuss materials and knock around the studio until we found a piece of wood that would work. He'd do a sketch and get the commission done.

He was capable of working with any material, but he really excelled with cedar. The beauty of his work was in his understanding of the grain of the wood. Cedar is one of the most difficult woods to work with. Success with cedar requires a sensitivity to the grain of each piece. You must study and understand each log and know how to work it as the Indians did—as Dudley did.

He did his best work when given a free rein. His work reflected the finesse and refinement of the carving that Indians did generations ago. How he could carve and create from wood with that axe of his—incredible skill! He was a real artisan. I was given much credit for my artistic awareness because I retained him and persuaded my clients to hire him.

I got to know Dudley socially and was invited to the Carters' rustic home on Bellevue-Redmond Road on various occasions. His charming wife would serve tea and we would chat. Dudley would share stories about his past—wonderful stories about his time among the Indians and timber cruising that revealed his great feeling for the Natives and the woods.

During Dudley's last years, I'd take my clients to his studio down by the Sammamish River just to admire his work. I also took my children and grandchildren. He always remembered me and took time to chat. We had a friendship that extended from 1948 until he passed away in 1992.

I was exceedingly privileged to have worked with Dudley Carter. He was an incredible person, tackling the most difficult tasks and performing them with flair, fine craftsmanship, and artistic skill. He was a genuine original.

Thomas Dunstan (1919–2013), native of the Northwest and longtime Seattle architect and developer. Working to support his young family while studying architecture at the University of Washington between 1939 and 1945, he never graduated, but he passed the state board exams in 1947 while employed by a licensed architect. He went on to a successful career designing over a thousand homes, some seventeen shopping centers, and numerous state buildings throughout the western United States. As an active octogenarian and resident of a retirement home, Dunstan continued to practice his profession long after most of his contemporaries had retired. Working from his retirement home office, one of his latest designs was an office building in central Washington.

Photograph 'Lyn Lambert

72   *Carving His Own Niche*

Chapter 16

Reviving History

From the writing of Albert H. Culverwell

As impressive as Dudley Carter's monumental works are, they were not foremost in my mind when I contacted him early in the 1950s. In my capacity as historian for the State of Washington, it was Dudley's knowledge of Indian culture and our forest resources that particularly interested me.

Part of my job with the Washington State Parks and Recreation Commission involved interpreting to the public the state's significant archeological and historical properties. In 1950 the commission acquired a notable piece of property, a portion of the site of Old Man House on Pacific Beach in Suquamish on Bainbridge Island. Old Man House, the largest Indian dwelling on Puget Sound, dated back to the early 1800s. It was the birthplace of Chief Sealth, the elected chief of six tribes, a man of unusual vision for whom the city of Seattle is named.

Historians disagreed about the original size of the dwelling, but it was thought to have covered an area of one and one quarter acres. In 1877 it was reported that the multi-family dwelling was 520 feet long and 60 feet wide. Another early authority maintained that the house had a length of 900 feet. Inside were some forty apartments separated by partitions of split logs. The structure faced the beach overlooking Agate Passage and was slightly curved to follow the outline of the shore. The great communal house was one of the most unusual Indian structures in the region.

Old Man House Interpretive Center, 1954
Red cedar, 12′ × 20′
Suquamish, Washington
Photograph Lisa Lambert

In 1951 archeologists from the University of Washington unearthed valuable information about the early housing project. Many of the house posts, split with elk horn wedges and stone hammers, were discovered. Replicating the dwelling was not feasible, so the parks commission settled on constructing an exhibit on the Suquamish site to interpret the archeological data for the public. I was aware of the work of Dudley Carter and believed that no one knew better than Dudley how to construct an Indian plank house, so I paid him a visit. He was decidedly enthusiastic about the prospect.

Using the archaeological findings and his own understanding of the methods and materials of the Northwest Natives, Dudley built an open construction of hefty cedar posts with a roof of overlapping planks secured in the style of ancient long houses. Within this shelter we placed the archeologists' interpretation of their discoveries.

Washington State Parks called upon Dudley again in 1961 to help with Fort Columbia at Chinook Point near the mouth of the Columbia River. The fort was established in 1896 to protect the river entrance. The US Army Coast Artillery Corps operated the fort prior to World War I and activated it again for a time during World War II. The area within view of Fort Columbia was home to the Chinook Indians and the site of many historically interesting events, so the old fort provided an ideal location for a museum and interpretive center.

When Fort Columbia became a state park somewhat unattractive signage marked its entrance. It didn't attract many visitors. We needed to enhance the entry and Dudley, now seventy years of age, was once again able to help us. We gave Dudley the plans for the project and he found the ideal tree, large enough to provide a timber of such dimensions as to extend over the roadway entrance. The sign had to be about forty feet long. He cut the tree down to size, hand axed and adzed the timber, and then chiseled, ever so precisely, the name of the park into it. Following the installation of the enormous sign and its supporting rock masonry pillars, attendance at the park picked up considerably—the power of art. And the sign was built to last.

I made a point of visiting the Carters on many occasions, sometimes to check on the progress of work being done for the parks, other times just to visit. Teresa always offered me a cup of tea and often an apple and some cheese. Dudley would

Fort Columbia Sign, 1961
Red cedar, 4′ × 41′ × 10″
Fort Columbia State Park, Washington
Photograph courtesy Albert Culverwell

remind me of the old adage about an apple a day keeping the doctor away—said I'd better believe it, and I did.

I enjoyed visiting the Carters. I never knew what I might experience. On one of my visits Dudley was busy trying his hand at making cedar bark clothing. Teresa showed me pictures of an attractive young lady sporting one of Dudley's cedar costumes. I don't think they ever caught on. In any event, Dudley never became known as the couturier of cedar.

There were always carvings in varying stages of completion around the place and I was drawn to

many of them. Over the years I purchased a number of pieces of Dudley's work. One of my favorites, called *Thunderbird*, is one that for some reason known only to Dudley was not up to snuff. I can't for the life of me see what its shortcoming is, but it didn't meet Dudley's standards. He sold it to me at a greatly reduced price.

My wife and I visited Dudley in the summer of 1991. He had recently celebrated his one-hundredth birthday and appeared to be in fine fettle, as busy as ever and still proclaiming the virtues of apples. It was encouraging for me to see a man, very much my senior, as active as he. I photographed the sculptures he had on display, intending to drum up a little

Albert Culverwell's collection of Dudley Carter sculptures
Above: *Thunderbird*
Right: *Last of the Sugarloaf Tribe*, 1961, red cedar, 3.5′ ×14″ × 10″
Following page: Detail of *Paddles*
Photographs courtesy Albert Culverwell

Reviving History

business for him in Southern California where I had retired.

    I enjoyed all my times with Dudley. Rubbing shoulders with Dudley Carter seemed to make me feel better. Was it Dudley? Or could it have been the apples?

Albert H. Culverwell (1913–2013), history and political science educator at Whitworth College and Western Washington College of Education (now Western Washington University). Employed by the US Forest Service as chief of interpretive services, Region Four, Ogden, Utah. Retired in 1982 after twenty-three years with the State of Washington as historian and supervisor of interpretation for the Washington State Parks Commission and as director of the Eastern Washington State Historical Society and the Cheney Cowles Memorial Museum in Spokane, Washington.

Photograph courtesy Albert Culverwell

Chapter 17

A Masterpiece

From a conversation with Kemper Freeman, Jr.

We met with officials of the City of Bellevue in 1980 to present our plans for a redevelopment of Bellevue Square. The city quite suitably expects art to be a part of such plans. We were content that Dudley Carter's *Forest Deity* would meet their artistic requirements. We couldn't believe our ears when someone who should have known better muttered, "That old stump? That isn't art!"

True enough, most fine art doesn't emerge from a tree trunk, but that degree of originality appealed to my grandfather, Miller Freeman, when he purchased *Forest Deity* from Dudley Carter in 1947.

Some might say that it's the nature of my family to do what others figure can't be done. For example, there were scoffers who were certain it was folly for my father to think of building a shopping center in a little community like Bellevue in the mid-1940s. In those days Bellevue was primarily a trading center for berry farmers and vineyardists, and the most excitement to be had was the annual Strawberry Festival. Bankers refused to grant my father a loan for the retail center project, so my grandfather and a few of his friends organized the First National Bank of Bellevue and set up the loan for my father to build his dream.

World War II brought about the departure of the Japanese farmers, contributing to the demise of the strawberry festivals. In September of 1947 someone had the bright idea to try an outdoor arts festival in Bellevue Square and almost a hundred artists showed up. They displayed four times that many paintings, but the main attraction of the whole affair was Dudley Carter. My grandfather was one among the many whose attention Dudley captivated. Later that year Grandfather purchased *Forest Deity*. He bought the sculpture not simply for the novelty of it. He perceived it to be a powerful work of art. He had it installed in front of the First National Bank of Bellevue, giving Bellevue its first piece of public art.

Bellevue's outdoor arts festival, officially organized as the Pacific Northwest Arts and Crafts Fair, became one of the nation's largest art shows, and the shopping center grew into a major regional center. Throughout that evolution, Dudley's *Forest Deity* has stood prominently in the Square. It has served as a symbol for the First National Bank of Bellevue and Bellevue Square itself. It was also one of the early logos of the City of Bellevue. Its image has appeared on the cover of telephone books and in and on many other publications. If *Forest Deity* isn't a work of art, I'd like to know what is!

Dudley Carter was quite a guy. I don't remember ever not knowing Dudley. I was a youngster of five when my grandfather bought *Forest Deity*. We used to call it the Indian. Dudley said that we could call it what we liked, but it depicted a forest spirit not a mortal creature of any ethnic origin.

When I was twelve or so, my family lived in half of the Clise Mansion in what was then called Willowmoor Farms and is now Marymoor Park in Redmond. I pedaled my bike all over the area, up and down the old Bellevue-Redmond Road. There were farms all along there and I worked on many of them. The Carters lived on that road. I remember riding by Dudley's carved sign and peering up the lane that led to his buildings on the hill. I made many visits to his place over many, many years. Dudley was such a friendly guy. He would take time to walk me around, showing me what he was up to. He had sculptures all over; they were stuck here and there among the trees and bushes. Dudley would part the branches and there would appear another beautiful carving.

Dudley exhibited his works and demonstrated his carving skills in the center court of Bellevue Square on a number of occasions over the years. He filled the whole court with his artwork. Apart from his ability to produce copious amounts of art, there was a quality about Dudley that I found particularly noteworthy, even enviable. When he was carving he

Forest Deity, 1947, red cedar, 14′ × 9′ × 4′
Photographed in 1991 at Bellevue Square, Bellevue, Washington, where it was installed in 1947 as a symbol for the new mall
Photograph 'Lyn Lambert

Forest Deity at its Bellevue Way location outside Bellevue Square with flag at half-staff to commemorate the sculptor at the time of his death in 1992. Photograph 'Lyn Lambert

would be totally absorbed, seemingly unaware of the crowds around him. Yet when people would come up and talk to him he would enter into conversation, then go right back to his work, having no trouble recapturing what he was doing. He would just pick up his axe and go right back at it. There were thousands of people a day observing him and many wanted to speak with him—that's a lot of distraction! But what he was doing was so clear to him it was almost like his work was preordained. I couldn't change focus like that and I was half his age.

The Bellevue Arts Commission awarded Dudley their Outstanding Artist Achievement Award in 1985. I was asked to emcee that event and I remember Dudley's reaction to be, "What's all the fuss about?" Sure, he attended the affair and no doubt he appreciated the award, but what was all the fuss about? He had a definite, discernable peace about him. You could put him in front of a microphone and he would speak so eloquently, so comfortably. By the time he had spoken just a few words, people at the ceremony who didn't even know him knew they were listening to *somebody*.

When Dudley last spoke to Bellevue's merchants' association he was way up in his nineties. He mentioned that he had, a few months earlier, gotten into his car and driven himself up to his place in Gibsons, British Columbia, to celebrate his birthday. That's quite a trip—Gibsons is on the other side of Vancouver, with a ferry ride involved. Not many folks in their nineties keep going like that. Thinking about Dudley reminds me of something my Arizona undertaker friend told me. He said he'd "never put away anyone who's still moving, so keep moving!" Dudley did his best to keep moving.

In all the years that *Forest Deity* has been displayed outdoors at the Square, it has never been subjected to any kind of vandalism. When Dudley died someone—I have no idea who—placed a flag at half-staff beside the sculpture. Dudley touched so many people and his work inspired that kind of respect.

My grandfather may not have been an art critic, but when he purchased *Forest Deity*, he recognized Dudley Carter as an artist. I'd say *Forest Deity*, the Indian, is Dudley Carter's masterpiece.

Forest Deity in its native surroundings, somewhere near Granite Falls, Washington
Photograph Horace Sykes, courtesy Paul Dorpat

"When art is true, it is one with nature. This is the secret of primitive art and also of the art of the masters."

Diego Rivera
My Art, My Life: An Autobiography

Full Circle by Anna Vaughan Hanson
Carved ducks, spooked by raptors, burst into flight around all sides of the huge stone fireplace in The Lodge at Bellevue Square.

Right: Kemper Freeman, Jr. and Anna Hanson at the dedication of *Full Circle* in July of 2008. Kemper Development Company honored artist Dudley Carter by commissioning his granddaughter Anna to carve the work from a historic Atlantic cedar that grew for years at Bellevue Square.

Photographs Red Fish Blue Fish Photography

Kemper Freeman, Jr., head of Kemper Development Company, developer of Bellevue Square and the Bellevue Collection. Past chairman of the International Council of Shopping Centers. Served in the Washington State Legislature in the 1970s. Often honored as one of Bellevue's best corporate citizens for his ongoing contributions to all aspects of community life. Determined to keep moving, Freeman enjoys snow skiing, boating, and trips in his RV, and like Dudley, he eschews retirement.
Photograph Mary Sikkema

Part III
Totemic Principles

"A lot of people repeat the Indian style, copy it. Carter abstracts the style and adds his own interpretation. It's really very eclectic and vigorous. Its hybrid health is the source of its power, and that's a positive judgment on his creativity."

— David Buerge

Northgate Totem as situated at Clearwater Casino, Suquamish, Washington, 2014
Photograph Lisa Lambert

Chapter 18

Totem of Lake Wilderness

By 'Lyn Lambert
Adapted from the writing of Dudley Carter

Totem poles are often called story poles for they serve as a substitute for the written word, something the first peoples did not employ. The poles are reminders.

They are to be understood more than read, as the symbols they carry are of little help if one does not already know their meaning. Some say that a totem pole is like a poem. It hints at more than it actually states.

In the late 1940s Dudley Carter was commissioned to create a large totem for the new lodge being built for Gaffney's Lake Wilderness Resort in Maple Valley, Washington. Designed to rise from the floor of the lodge and support a roof beam thirty-five feet above, the sculptured cedar column is western red cedar, logged from the slopes of Mt. Pilchuck. Dudley carved the pole in an upright position at the Western Washington Fair in September of 1949, attracting considerable attention from fairgoers.

In notes he submitted to the architects (Young & Richardson, Carlton & Detlie) of the lodge, Dudley revealed the meaning of his poetic imagery expressed in

Lake Wilderness Totem, 1949
Red cedar, 35′ × 5′ × 5′
Photograph Nancy Clendaniel Photography

Lake Wilderness had long been a popular hunting and fishing recreational area. In 1950 a new lodge opened at the resort, receiving the Grand Honor Award of the American Institute of Architects, Washington State Chapter. The totem pole, encompassed by a graceful spiral stairway, is the focal point of the building's main interior areas. In addition to its aesthetic and symbolic purposes, the carved post serves important physical functions: it is a roof column and it receives a pair of welded steel box beams that support a mezzanine.

King County acquired Lake Wilderness Park and its historic lodge and conference center in 1964. Later the county transferred the park and buildings to the City of Maple Valley. The building has been granted landmark status.

Dudley Carter, in his unique fashion of carving a pole upright, can be seen to the left of the column, thirty feet up on his scaffolding. The carving of the *Lake Wilderness Totem* became a popular attraction at the Western Washington Fair in September 1949. Photograph courtesy Dudley Carter

the pole's carvings. A photograph of the *Lake Wilderness Totem* in situ appears on page 269.

The flora and fauna characters are all native to the Northwest. The top figure, symbolizing Kain Gaffney, the host and founder of the resort, bears the burden and responsibility of it all. He seems to be gazing out across Lake Wilderness toward Mt. Rainier, wishing for someone else to hold up the roof while he goes fishing in the lake.

Mountain Hawk next, below and in front, is the guardian spirit who keeps away evil, such as high-pressure salesmen. Mountain Goat Kids follow, a friendly and playful pair, representing the atmosphere of the lodge. Then appears Mourning Dove, a symbol of peace also known as Wild Pigeon, who is able to exercise good influence upon the weather. Fire Bird, a mythical avian creature, keeps fire under control and is shown subduing the flame rising between the horns of Ram. A bighorn mountain sheep, Ram, embodies the rugged

Details of *Gaffney's Lake Wilderness Totem* in progress at the Western Washington Fair, September 1949
Photographs courtesy King County Parks

Cascade and Olympic Mountains. In front of Ram, a symbol of strength who takes seriously his part in supporting the building and the column above, is Great Horned Owl, holding a dogwood blossom. The blossom, called Eye of Coyote by local Indians, enhances Owl's confidence, awareness, and craftiness. Perched on the horn of Mountain Ram is Chipmunk, who is wondering, as the viewer likely wonders, why he was not given a tail. At the top and rear of the column appears a young trillium with a nest of loons' eggs in its leaves. The eggs will be safe there, for legend has it that disturbing a trillium, the first wild flower of spring, will bring on continued rain and stormy weather. If you should hear the maniacal laugh of the great loon flying high at night, there will be rain the following day; if it gives the call on the waters of Lake Wilderness, the sun will shine tomorrow.

Lower down the column, Frog is supporting a steel beam. After devouring Dragonfly, Frog has grown in stature and feels equal to Mountain Lion below, who is poised for attack. Mountain Lion is angry with Frog, who not only defies the force of gravity while supporting the beam, but is also undaunted by Mountain Lion, who desires to have that position. Two Mythical Birds appear on the west side of the column. They make the contact between the medium and the characters.

Chapter 19

The Northgate Connection

From conversations with Marvin Boys

Northgate Totem is enormously significant to me. Not only is it the tallest of Dudley Carter's monumental works, it is the one through which I came to know Dudley.

Most of my professional life was spent with Allied Stores, a national retailing chain. In 1952 Allied expanded their shopping mall in Seattle called Northgate. When I joined them as their director of store and shopping mall development for the western states, Dudley Carter had already been commissioned to do the totem, an artistic feature the company expected would become a landmark.

Allied broke from retailing tradition with Northgate Mall, becoming the first major retailer in the country to own a center and invite their major competitors to join them as tenants. Dudley Carter, an artist known to respect and yet depart from tradition, was a natural choice to produce the Native-style art envisioned by John Graham, the Seattle architect hired by Allied to plan the new center.

Dudley designed a fifty-nine-foot pole, and in his typically unorthodox way, planted it in the center of a thirty-two-foot war canoe. He agreed to do the work on site, side by side with the construction crew. He thought that would attract attention and bring out the press—good publicity for himself and for Northgate Mall.

I met Dudley for the first time when Weyerhaeuser delivered the huge cedar log. Dudley had cruised the forest and personally selected the tree that was to become the Northgate Totem. Not only that, he felled the seven-foot-diameter tree himself. The man fascinated me and I soon discovered we had much in common. We were both products of families formed in hard times and had learned to make do or do without. Each of us had an appreciation of wood—as if the same sap coursed through our veins. I had studied forestry, working summers

Dudley Carter with *Northgate Totem*, 1952, red cedar, 59′ × 7′ × 7′ with canoe, 32′ long. Photograph courtesy Dudley Carter

Dudley Carter with *Prince of the Grizzlies*, photographed at his outdoor studio in 1955, red cedar, 12′ × 28″ × 28″
Commissioned for the restaurant of the downtown Seattle Bon Marché. Photograph courtesy Mavis Carter Vaughan

as a timber cruiser, and then went on to get my civil engineering degree at the University of Washington. Dudley picked up his knowledge of forestry and engineering on the job.

I became so intrigued with the man and his abilities that I would check on his progress practically every day. Dudley worked well within deadlines and adjusted readily to the demands of construction. All the engineers on the project were impressed with the way Dudley made his massive totem earthquake resistant. No doubt he made use of knowledge he gained doing civil engineering work on hydroelectric projects in Canada. Working with him was personally enjoyable and immeasurably beneficial to the company, and I vowed to use his work in future developments whenever feasible.

Northgate Totem, as expected, became a popular landmark, but Dudley was never content with it. He and the architect disagreed on the size of the eagle's wings. Dudley gave in and carved the oversized wings the eagle wears. As the totem aged, management of the shopping center arranged to have the pole repainted, and when Dudley saw the results he remarked disgustedly that "they let house painters loose on it." Others commented that "it looked like a chocolate eagle on a stick." It was a far cry from the subtle coloring originally applied by Bill Holm.

Dudley Carter with *Bird of the Air*, photographed at his outdoor studio in 1955, red cedar, 10′ × 7′ × 22″
Commissioned for the restaurant of the downtown Seattle Bon Marché. Photograph courtesy Hedda Schafer Shepherd

The Northgate Connection

With Northgate finished, Allied began an addition to the Bon Marché, their major store in downtown Seattle, and we contracted with Dudley to do the décor for the store's new restaurant area. He designed and carved two totems, *Prince of the Grizzlies* and *Bird of the Air*, one for the entrance, the other for a corner. He also included a mural depicting the Indian legend that inspired the totems. He split cedar boards sixteen to eighteen inches wide and twenty feet long to provide a surface for the painting. Having seen murals done by the award-winning Seattle artist Jean Beall, wife of Boeing executive Wellwood Beall, Dudley requested that she be commissioned to paint the mural. Beall painted the totems also, doing them in traditional Native fashion.

Dudley's art was so well received that we decided to commission him to do carvings for a tearoom addition to the Bon Marché in Spokane. He completed the works well in advance of the opening. I shipped them to our warehouse in Spokane so they'd be available when needed. Well, lo and behold, about two weeks before we were due to open, the warehouse burned down. All the carvings were destroyed. I was devastated. Amazingly, Dudley came up with replacement works, managing to meet the deadline for the opening of the new addition.

My appreciation of Dudley led me to begin a personal collection of his sculptures. Most of the works in our garden gallery are carved from driftwood salvaged at Dudley's place at Gibsons, on the Sunshine Coast in British Columbia. People are often surprised at the fine condition of our outdoor sculptures, but with good care they should last forever. Each is raised up from a concrete base by a steel support, allowing air to circulate beneath the wood. I give them a good dose of wood preservative every year and wrap them with plastic for the winter. *Ram Head*, a treasured gift from Dudley, and *Mountain Majesty*, a wall-mounted relief carving, are displayed indoors.

Lady of the Sea, ca. 1970, red cedar, 6′ high
Collection of Marvin and June Boys,
Bellevue, Washington
Photograph Mary Sikkema

In the 1970s, Allied Stores planned a major shopping center on the east side of Lake Washington. It was to be as large as, or larger than, Allied's Southcenter Mall, and I began to acquire property to accommodate the project. I accumulated one hundred and twenty acres for Allied that, coincidentally, were in close proximity to Dudley's home and studio on Bel-Red Road. I had fallen in love with the property and envisioned keeping the land as near to its natural state as possible with buildings primarily of wood. We named the project Evergreen East and again hired John Graham to be the architect. John often made use of Dudley's talent. He drew up his plans for Evergreen East with specific accommodations for a number of Dudley's carvings. Allied purchased a total of sixteen Dudley Carter sculptures and we transported the group to a Seattle storage facility. The collection of eight major and eight minor pieces—some old, some new—were representative of about forty years of Dudley's carving career and dated back to 1935.

We began to clear the property to make way

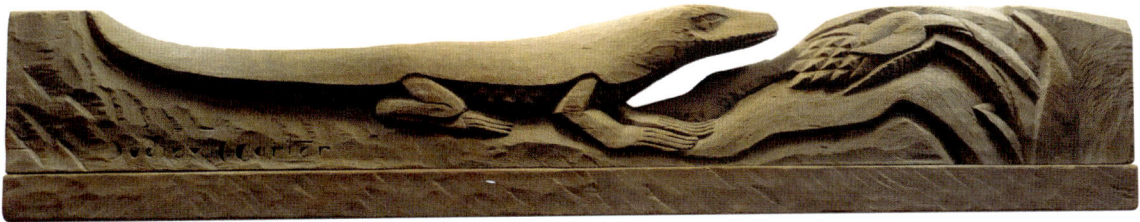

Desert Scout, 1960, 18″ × 7′ × 6″. Part of Allied Stores' purchase in 1975. Photograph King County Library System

for Evergreen East. All manner of unimaginable political problems began to erupt. The cities of Bellevue and Redmond bickered over pieces of the pie, and other area shopping center developers feared competition from a new kid on the block. Allied, uncomfortable in the midst of conflict, withdrew from the fray and sold the land to another nationally known developer with the understanding that he would build Evergreen East. That developer capitulated, abandoned the shopping center plans, and sold the land. I was so disappointed I resigned from Allied just six months before I was due to retire.

As time passed, I began to worry about the status of the sculptures purchased for the Evergreen East project. Some seemed to have disappeared. The collection called out for public display, and it was a shame to let the works vanish into oblivion, perhaps winding up in private collections. I talked to Dudley about the situation and offered to help him recover them. He was hopeful, but I was unsuccessful. Dudley took the disappointment in stride, telling me the sale had done a lot to set his sculpting business on firm financial ground, and the whole affair gave him considerable exposure. Meanwhile, he had other dreams in mind and in the works.

His active imagination was busy dreaming up the six-ton *Legend of the Moon*. It pleased me considerably that I could play a part in the realization of that dream when I arranged for a contractor

Sculptures from the Allied Stores' collection acquired by Marvin Boys in 1995, intended for public display. Photographs 'Lyn Lambert

Left: *Wek Wek and the Holukmeyumko*, 1935, red cedar, 12′ × 5.5′ × 5.5′
Above: *Two Thunderbirds*, 1976, red cedar, 2′ × 3′ × 12′ long

The Northgate Connection

Marvin Boys, Dudley Carter, and Mike Hoonan, one of Dudley's many apprentices, in Dudley's Slough House Park garage/studio discussing architect's plans for a new studio, 1991
Photograph 'Lyn Lambert

friend to help Dudley move it from his outdoor studio to its Marymoor Park location.

Dudley was a proud man in the finest sense of the word, a man of firm convictions. I always respected him and marveled at his talent. Not only that, I cherished the man. Over the years we became very good friends. We both grew extremely hard of hearing, but we communicated by shouting until we thought we understood each other. This often became a source of amusement to others who happened to be present.

Dudley was over ninety when circumstances made it necessary for him to move from his Bel-Red Road property. It troubled me terribly when I learned that the developer who took over the proposed Evergreen East property wanted to acquire a larger package than I had purchased. Dudley, as he told me later, reluctantly agreed to sell his property to the developer "to keep peace in the family." Dudley had understood that the terms of the sale would allow him to remain there as long as he desired, but that was not to be. His land was destined to become part of the headquarters of Microsoft. Dudley had to leave on short notice.

He considered moving to Gibsons or to California, but some members of King County's Arts Commission realized that he was an asset to the community, a treasure, and they wanted to keep him in the area. Dudley understood that the county intended to have him live and work in Marymoor Park where his *Legend of the Moon* was a welcome addition. But, instead of being an artist-in-residence, he ended up carving in the trash collection area and renting a room where he could live off-site. A patron later provided better living accommodations for him, but it was still an appalling situation.

Without telling Dudley, I went to the county and put up a fuss about the way he was being treated, but it took the urging of many Carter friends before the county finally arranged to set him up as artist-in-residence at Slough House Park in Redmond.

Dudley was living in the Slough House when I received a call from his family relaying the sad news that his son-in-law, David, had been killed in a freak accident while travelling in Nova Scotia. They asked that I visit Dudley and let him know. That was one of the hardest tasks I ever undertook. I talked to him a bit about general things—then I told him of the tragedy. He didn't say a word. He just turned away, walked over to his axe, picked it up, and started working. Tears still well up when I recall that incident.

I visited Dudley frequently after he settled into Slough House Park. His circumstances were considerably better there than they'd been at Marymoor, but they were far from ideal. It troubled me to see this man in his nineties working outside in the cold and the wet for lack of suitable studio space. I hired an architect who drew up superb plans for a studio and a sculpture garden on the grounds of the Slough House. I presented the plans to King County and told them I'd raise the funds to see the project through. The county wasn't interested. I got absolutely nowhere—another of life's great

Menace de Modernisme, 1984, red cedar, 8.5' × 5'2" × 32"
Purchased by Marvin Boys, along with *Hatching Bird* on right, from the Dudley Carter Estate, intended for public display
Photograph 'Lyn Lambert

Haida-style studio was situated on the site.

The foundation hoped to raise funds to acquire some of Dudley's carvings to form the beginning of the sculpture garden. Then, out of the blue one morning in January of 1995, I received a call from a senior vice-president of the Bon Marché. He knew the whereabouts of six of the Carter sculptures that were to have been the heart and soul of the aborted Evergreen East. He also knew how anxious I was to see those sculptures displayed publicly and asked where I would like to have them delivered! I was stunned. I had to think fast. Some of the pieces were monumental in size. Mini storage was out of the question. I contacted King County Parks and convinced them to let me store them at Slough

disappointments.

Following Dudley's death in 1992, I joined with a group of his friends and fans to form a nonprofit organization known formally as the Dudley C. Carter Northwest Arts and Cultural Foundation. We planned to work with King County to establish a sculpture garden and an arts program at the Slough House Park, hoping to encourage the county to renovate the park and commemorate Dudley by naming it after him. That seemed only right, considering the nature of the property, Dudley's stature as an artist, and the fact that his last

Hatching Bird, 1989, red cedar, 7' × 22" × 14"
Photograph Lisa Lambert

The Northgate Connection

House Park. The Bon Marché very generously delivered the works to the park—a major effort requiring two trips with a large flat bed truck and a huge crane.

Unfortunately, as enthusiastic as its participants were, just a year or so after its incorporation the Dudley Carter Foundation ran into difficulties and disbanded, so there was no organization in place to oversee the sculptures and pursue the plans for the park. I held out hope, however, that the county would come through with a Dudley Carter Park and I purchased four additional sculptures from Dudley's estate. I met with county and city officials countless times, but to date nothing definitive has developed. The sculptures still sit rather forlornly, some tucked away in storage, others in the deserted park in Redmond.

In a sense, I'm like a foster parent, looking after Dudley's orphaned offspring until a prescient public entity will permanently adopt them. All we need is the right connection.

Marvin Boys *(*1913–1997) with *Ram Head*, 1976, yellow cedar, 2.5′ × 22″ × 20″, a gift from Dudley. In his youth, Boys drove a logging truck, cruised timber, and played semi-professional baseball. He served five and a half years in the military during and following World War II. Boys was a general contractor prior to spending twenty-eight years with Allied Stores as director of store and shopping mall development. As an active octogenarian, he delivered tons of produce to food banks in the Puget Sound area. Boys died suddenly in November 1997, still hopeful that a Dudley Carter Park and Sculpture Garden would become a reality.
Photograph 'Lyn Lambert

NOTE: Marvin Boys passed away suddenly and unexpectedly in 1997. At the time of Marvin's death, disposition of the sculptures he acquired and the plans for a Dudley Carter Arts and Cultural Center were in limbo. In 2012, the City of Redmond designated the property where Dudley served as artist-in-residence as Dudley Carter Park. They hired landscape architects who designed an art center, gathering place, and sculpture garden. As of the writing of this book, the project has not been fully funded.

Chapter 20

Mink and Wolf Totem

By 'Lyn Lambert

When Shell Oil Company planned their Anacortes, Washington, refinery in 1954 they aimed to make the refinery and its personnel an integral part of the surrounding community. Erecting a traditional symbol of the Pacific Northwest seemed appropriate, so they commissioned Dudley Carter to create a totem pole depicting a story that was part of the mythology of the early populace of the area.

Dudley drew inspiration for the pole, called *Mink and Wolf Totem*, from a legend told to him by an Indian woman. He recorded the story verbatim and anthropologists at the University of Washington later authenticated it. The legend is one of rivalry between Mink—a legendary hero common to the area's Snohomish, Swinomish, and Upper and Lower Skagit people—and Wolf. It encompasses elements of achievement, theft, death, imprisonment, and eventually, escape.

Wolf, jealous of Mink's success as a salmon fisher, sends his eldest son to rob Mink's trap. Mink takes the form of a human and kills the son of Wolf. He hangs the wolf's pelt from his ceiling for all to see, holds a powwow at his house, and sings his power—letting all know why Wolf's son was killed.

Wolf orders his other sons to revenge their brother's death. Mink, prepared for that eventuality, escapes through a secret exit under his house. Later, old woman Devilfish, who was either an octopus or

Mink and Wolf Totem, 1955, red cedar, 46′ × 5.5′ × 5.5′
Photograph 'Lyn Lambert

because his heart is pure, and he returns home, presumably to live happily ever after.

In their 1995 book, *Northwest Coast Native and Native-Style Art*, authors Lloyd Averill and Daphne Morris characterize the Shell Refinery Pole as "… Dudley Carter at his idiosyncratic best—or worst, depending on your point of view." They describe the manner in which Dudley, "uncharacteristically (for a totem)" carved designs into the back of the pole "that resemble line drawings more than anything in the coastal tradition." The carvings

The reverse side of *Mink and Wolf Totem*
Photograph courtesy of the Anacortes Museum

squid, tricks Mink and holds him captive in her underwater lair. Mink, growing thin and haggard, must convince Devilfish to let him go. Mink remembers that devilfish are afraid of sunshine and convinces Devilfish that his uncle, the Sun, will dry up all devilfish if she doesn't release him. She takes Mink to the shore and sets him free.

In this legendary tale, as in all great myths and legends, justice and right triumph. Mink not only gives an enemy, Wolf, his just desserts, he also talks his way out of the clutches of a designing woman. Mink's strength becomes as the strength of ten

94   *Totemic Principles*

clearly portray the main characters of the Mink and Wolf legend.

Uncle Sun appears at the top of the pole. Below is Devilfish, grasping Mink by his hind legs. Near the bottom, above Dudley's oft-used pineapple cross-hatching, is Mink in human form, wearing the skin of Wolf's son. On either side of the incised designs are a series of painted formline patterns added by Bill Holm, who assisted Carter in painting the pole. The colors used were mixed from ground pigments as Native carvers once prepared them.

"This pole by Dudley Carter is a puzzle," comment authors Averill and Morris, who are baffled by the artist's treatment of the front of the pole. The boldly carved front side, where one would expect to see the legend portrayed, is carved in the totemic manner, but it does not appear to declare the primary statement of the myth. The figures seem largely unrelated to the story of Mink and Wolf.

At the top is a series of rings—a clan status symbol—on the head of a quadruped, which might be Mink, with a small fish in its mouth. Below that an eagle, or perhaps a hawk, appears above a figure resembling a land otter with what may be a serpent in its mouth. The bottom figure is a mysterious humanoid that inspired refinery employees to affectionately name the pole Cedar Sam. With the exception of the top character, Averill and Morris found it hard to tie the figures to Mink and Wolf mythology. Only the artist knows their true significance.

Dudley carved the pole in his outdoor studio on Bel-Red Road in Bellevue. Since 1955, it has stood in its idyllic setting in front of the refinery's administration building. With Padilla Bay and Mount Baker as its backdrop and a reflecting pond at its foot, it is hard to imagine a more fitting setting for such a work of art. The pole is accessible to the public in the refinery's unrestricted area on March's Point Road off Highway 20, east of Anacortes.

Posterior detail of *Mink and Wolf Totem*
Surprisingly, Dudley carved a copyright symbol on the pole.
Photograph 'Lyn Lambert

NOTE: Material that aided greatly in the compilation of the above story was provided to the authors by Fran Bulawa of the Shell Oil Products Company. Valuable also was *Northwest Coast Native and Native-Style Art* by Lloyd J. Averill and Daphne K. Morris (Seattle: University of Washington Press, 1995, 137–138).

Chapter 21

Spiritual Perceptions

From a conversation with James Washington, Jr.

Art is not a product of the intellect, art has to be perceived. You can't simply see it, you must feel it. It is born of intuition and relies upon the same for interpretation. Being a man of faith, Dudley understood that Native totem poles, just like the Bible, carry messages intended to remind readers that they can become better people, but they must be written and read with the understanding of the heart. Dudley Carter's work has that spiritual quality.

My first meeting with Dudley Carter occurred at a Chi Omega alumnae art show at the University of Washington in 1957 held at the sorority's chapterhouse. Some 150 artists participated. Dudley and I were among twenty sculptors included in the show and I immediately connected with his work. It was vibrantly alive. I sensed that we shared the same ideals for our artistic creations, and after talking with him awhile, I was convinced that he too viewed art as a means of revealing the spirituality of matter. There is life and expressive energy, the nature of the Absolute that some call God and some call Love, in everything. Dudley Carter was a true artist—a student of the Absolute. George Washington Carver proposed that if you love a thing, be it a peanut or a potato, it will give up its secrets to you. Dudley could certainly romance wood. He wooed the secrets right out of it.

In 1960 I was asked to oversee an artists-in-action affair to be held in downtown Seattle's Westlake Mall. My first order of business was to invite significant local artists to participate in the event. Serendipitously, Dudley had been commissioned to do a large totem pole for the naval air station in Seattle's Sand Point neighborhood. I managed to score a coup by persuading him to carve the pole in the downtown mall. Dudley, a performing artist at heart, took no time to agree to join in.

He knew that he could make a spectacular presentation by carving the pole upright. Without a doubt, he became the main attraction, generating a lot of publicity for the event. If you erect an immense wooden pole, which looked to me as if it towered eighty feet up, in the middle of a major city street and work from 10:00 a.m. to 10:00 p.m. daily—rain or shine—mightily cleaving the pole with lumberjack's axes, you are bound to attract attention. Newspapers regularly reported his progress. One paper claimed that Dudley put on one of the longest and most interesting shows ever seen downtown. He was nearly seventy years of age at the time.

Dudley Carter carving the *Naval Air Station Totem* in the heart of downtown Seattle
The artist always drew a crowd at this artists-in-action event during the summer of 1960. Photograph courtesy Anna Vaughan Hanson

Spiritual Perceptions

The Westlake show, which was held in the middle of August in 1960, featured a variety of painters, sculptors, and musicians. We had a wonderful time. As I remember, the show was scheduled to run for a few weeks, but Dudley's act carried over until he completed his work around the beginning of

A crane raised the nearly half-ton thunderbird's head to top off the forty-six-foot totem as it stood in Westlake Mall. Photograph courtesy Anna Vaughan Hanson

Top right: The *Naval Air Station Totem* awaiting Dudley's finishing touches prior to its installation. Photograph courtesy Anna Vaughan Hanson. Bottom left: Dudley Carter, having felled the fifty-four-inch-diameter tree intended to become the Sand Point totem, prepares the log for removal from the forest near Oso, Washington. Photograph courtesy Anna Vaughan Hanson
Bottom right: Dudley applying the final touches to the Sand Point totem. Photograph courtesy Dudley Carter

Dudley Carter and the *Naval Air Station Totem* at Sand Point, 1960, red cedar, 46' × 4.5' × 4.5' with a wingspan of 14'
Photograph courtesy Anna Vaughan Hanson

October. The huge pole, which Dudley's records indicate was only forty-six feet tall not the eighty I perceived it to be, was a product of community action—a fine example of synergism. Dudley hewed the tree himself; a logging company hauled it to Seattle; a local contracting firm used a crane to set it up and later remove it; a telephone company guyed the pole; and a scaffolding outfit furnished the scaffold. These and many others donated their time and services to the Thunderbird Club so the pole could be carved in the mall.

The Thunderbirds, a group of naval air reservists and veterans of active duty, commissioned the totem for the Sand Point Naval Air Station. Their name stems from the original Naval Air Station emblem, which was a totem pole topped with a mythical Indian thunderbird.

Dudley did a masterly job on the Sand Point totem. He kept an eye out for five months before he found the tree he would use in the forest lands of a large lumber concern near Oso, Washington. He reckoned the solid, tight-ring, western red cedar had been growing for 800 years. The totem is eight-and-a-half tons of ancient and modern symbolism. The topmost figure, carved separately and weighing around a half a ton itself, is a thunderbird representing the power of the Naval Air Service. A human countenance is carved on the thunderbird's breast, implying the creature's human attributes. On its wings it wears the insignia of the Naval Air Service. The thunderbird, displaying its supremacy, is perched upon its prey, a whale that is representative of the submarine menace the naval air organization combats. The whale's dorsal fin suggests a periscope cutting through the water, which flows toward a frogman interlocked with the whale's tail. The fin is incised with a human face indicative of the human mind controlling it. Positioned below the whale, as if imperiled by it, is a man-bear holding a shield and anchor and embracing a deep-sea diver. The part-

In appreciation of his work on the *Naval Air Station Totem*, the Thunderbirds presented Dudley with the first of two golden axes he would receive.

Dudley checks his model of *Legend of the Moon*. The model was stolen while on loan to Marymoor Museum—a major loss. Dudley claimed the model's value is half that of the sculpture itself. *Suntower* is in the background.
Photograph courtesy Charlene Skoors Root

man, part-bear figure symbolizes human intelligence endowed with the strength of a grizzly. It represents the civilian and military personnel who support the Naval Air Reserve.

The great totem stood in front of the Sand Point Naval Air Station Recreational Building until the station was closed in 1995. The pole later became the centerpiece of the new Naval Support Complex at Smokey Point, north of Everett, Washington.

Dudley and I became true lifelong friends. My wife Janie and I visited him and Mrs. Carter frequently, often being invited to join them for meals. They did eat differently. It wasn't unusual for them to have frozen, cooked chicken for dinner—still frozen. They liked it that way. Maybe that was his secret to longevity—frozen chicken!

In 1977 I served on a jury for King County's Arts Commission to select a work of art to be placed at Marymoor Park in Redmond. Valued at $20,000, a one-percent for art commission, it was substantial. Numerous proposals, including one from Dudley Carter, were submitted. For no good reason that I could see, the majority of the jury favored a steel sculpture, which didn't seem to me to speak at all to the heart, nor did it suit the intended location. It was no match for Dudley's *Legend of the Moon*, a towering piece inspired by a myth of great significance to the Salish people who formerly occupied the land where the artwork was to be placed. I held out, feeling that the other jurors had a material bias. They were not sensing the spiritual aspect at all, and I told them they were trying to sell me on a piece of material. Maybe it was divine grace, but I managed to sway the jury. I still remember the pleasure it gave me to telephone my eighty-six-year-old friend and give him the news that he had won the Marymoor Park commission.

Mark Tobey, a renowned painter who had a profound influence on Northwest art for almost half a century—to whom I was apprenticed for a time—said, "In this life you either have it or you don't." I'm convinced that Dudley Carter had it.

James W. Washington, Jr. (1911–2000), painter and stone sculptor in the Northwest tradition, known widely for his sensitively carved figures of small mammals and forest creatures. Born in Mississippi to the Reverend and Mrs. James W. Washington, he moved to Washington State in 1944 and worked as a civilian electrician at the Bremerton Navy Yard. Invited in 1946 to exhibit his paintings at the Little Gallery of Seattle's Frederick and Nelson department store, he soon became apprenticed to Mark Tobey. His first major exhibition was in 1948 at the Seattle Art Museum. Although widely accepted as a painter, he was drawn to stone sculpture, experimenting in that medium in 1952. By 1960 his flourishing art career allowed him to end his thirty-year career with the US Government. Washington, an artist exhibited widely and honored extensively, was a popular guest speaker and published poet. His works, known to emphasize the unity of nature that bespeaks the unity of God, are in numerous museums and private collections. Photograph Mary Sikkema

> "A North American Indian totem pole, like much of the symbolism of what used to be called 'primitive' religions, expresses a vision of man and his relation to the universe that is extremely subtle and sophisticated. For one to grasp the meaning of these symbols it is necessary not only to have accurate information about the particular tradition in question, it is even more important to be able to see and hear with the intelligence of the heart."
>
> James Mitchell, 1977, *The Random House Encyclopedia*. New York: Random House.

Chapter 22

Transitions and Transformations

Reminiscences of Geordie Tocher

Dudley Carter gave me a chance to get myself sorted out during a rather rocky time in my life in the late 1970s. I had encountered him years earlier, sometime in the 1960s, on the beach in front of my house at Cypress Park in West Vancouver, British Columbia.

I was making paddles, or some other small thing, just for that endorphin-stoked state that often comes upon me through the act of carving. I looked up and saw a man standing about thirty feet away, just standing there and smiling. I don't usually stop working when spectators gather, but something about his demeanor caused me to pause. He approached me and said straight out, "Hello, I'm Dudley Carter."

Talk about a thrill! He had no need to further identify himself—his reputation had preceded him. He told me he was working in Seattle and had driven up to Vancouver that day to look for wood. After a while, he invited me to his daughter's home about half a mile down the beach where I was invited in for tea.

We visited each other often over the years and I came to know his family. Teresa struck me as a happy person, full of joy. I remember wondering about the effect of artists on people close to them—carving is an obsessive, selfish thing in some respects. But it seemed to me that Teresa and Dudley had a pretty good life together.

Dudley spent much of the summer of 1975 carving for the West Vancouver Parks and Recreation Commission on Dundarave Beach. That's a special spot for me. I like to visit the beach

Legend of the Moon, 1978, red cedar, 35′ × 11′ × 6′
Photograph 'Lyn Lambert

performance in the park.

Sometime in 1976 or 1977 Dudley asked me if I'd bring one of his works, *Suntower*, to Bellevue from Burnaby where it had been displayed at a gallery. *Suntower* is a thirteen-foot sculpture assembled from red and yellow cedar that Dudley did at the United Nations Habitat Forum in Vancouver in 1976. I disassembled it, securing the pieces on top and inside my van, and headed for the States wondering if I'd have a problem getting across the border. At the customs inspection point, I told the officials my van held a piece of sculpting. They simply told me to go ahead—that surprised me. In those days I was a longhaired, heavily bearded character driving a decrepit van—just the combination that border officials generally look at askance.

Arriving at Dudley's, I found he had another assignment in mind for me. Would I be interested in helping him find a log for his project at Marymoor Park in Redmond, Washington? Of course I would be interested.

I can't recall if we drove my vehicle or his Oldsmobile station wagon, but we set off on a beautiful drive over the Cascade Mountains and up a winding road to a timber company's mill yard. We chatted with the superintendent, a nice chap who let us browse around the yard. Dudley found a log that

and pier there. At the end of the pier, the longest in West Vancouver, is a plaque commemorating my voyage in the *Orenda*, the canoe I built and sailed to Hawaii.

Dudley gave daily demonstrations at Dundarave from 10 a.m. to 5 p.m. I tried to get down to the beach every evening to help him store his work. If I wasn't available, some other good Samaritan helped out. A restaurant nearby afforded overnight storage space for Dudley's gear and sculptings for the duration of his

Dudley Carter strides by *Legend of the Moon* in progress.
Photograph courtesy Charlene Skoors Root

Transitions and Transformations

Top left: (Left to right) Geordie Tocher, Chuck Skoors (Dudley's friend, neighbor, and frequent helper) and Dudley confer while working on *Legend of the Moon*. Top center: Geordie Tocher (left) and Chuck Skoors (right) with unfinished elements of *Legend of the Moon*. Top right: Renting a crane truck greatly facilitated assembly of the massive sculpture. Bottom left: Dudley and Chuck Skoors dealing with *Legend of the Moon*'s internal structure. Bottom right: The work of art continues. Dudley Carter and volunteers or apprentices with *Legend of the Moon*. Photographs courtesy Charlene Skoors Root

he pronounced a "fine big stick." We measured and marked it, reserved it for Dudley, and returned to Bellevue. Dudley, ever the perfectionist, went back to the mill yard several times to check out the log. He wanted to be absolutely certain it was the best cedar available for the project.

When the log arrived at Dudley's studio, he called me again, wondering if I'd like to have a hand in the production of the Marymoor work. In no time I found myself back in Bellevue.

That was a difficult, unsettled time in my life. I had been involved in what might best be described as a complicated relationship. It seemed like a good time for me to take off. Taking off was not a problem. My van was a home on wheels and Dudley's yard would be an ideal campsite.

Dudley's design for the Marymoor sculpture, a work that would depict the Snoqualmie legend of Moon the Transformer, called for the huge tree to be split artfully into two shells—a major undertaking that Dudley tried to accomplish with the aid of large jacks and any available manpower. There always seemed to be willing individuals around to help with the burdensome aspects of Dudley's creative endeavors. His nearest neighbor, a big, very pleasant fellow named Chuck, often came over to assist. Using only jacks and manpower to move the log made the process slow going, so I suggested Dudley consider using a crane. I had experience running crane equipment and found an outfit willing to rent a crane truck to me by the hour, saving the prohibitive cost of hiring an operator. This delighted

Dudley, and we were able to gently lift and turn the log so he could operate on it as deftly as a surgeon would deal with his patient. It felt good to be able to help Dudley like that.

The fact that he was nearly deaf made it hard for us to readily exchange spoken thoughts. Our working conversations were often carried out through winks, nods, and smiles. If we could catch each other's eye, we generally managed to get our point across. But we did chat together during quiet times. I was interested in Dudley's philosophy—what made him tick.

The depth of Dudley's devotion to his faith and to the wisdom of the Bible became apparent. He spent time every day with the scriptures, and if circumstances seemed to warrant it, he could easily come forth with an appropriate passage. But I believe Dudley gleaned his sense of the Almighty as much from nature as he did from scripture.

Sir Francis Bacon, the English statesman and philosopher born in the sixteenth century, suggested that there are two books set out for us to study. Taken together, the two will prevent us from going astray. The first, according to Bacon, is the book of the Scriptures, which reveals God's will. The second is the volume of the Creatures, which reveals God's power.

Dudley certainly had plenty of opportunity to study the book of the Creatures, witnessing firsthand the awesome power of God. He faced much of the worst that nature could dish out, but he also discovered an indescribable peace in the wilderness. Having been a timber worker too, I knew what Dudley meant when he spoke of the forest cathedral.

Imagine yourself dueling with the elements, making your way through the most inhospitable territory—not knowing what lay ahead and questioning the wisdom of being there at all. Then imagine finding yourself, all of a sudden, in a place of breathtaking beauty—nothing but green. Your high-top boots sink into moss easily a foot deep. It is a place so dark that not a piece of brush exists, only moss—moss-covered boulders and moss-covered trees—huge trees, towering hundreds of feet up, their trunks wrapped all around in moss—a dark, quiescent, green place. Then you glimpse a beam of sunlight ahead, penetrating the darkness and pushing its rays down through the trees. You are drawn to that light. It is quiet—not even a whisper of wind. You can't speak. You have no need to speak. Walking becomes effortless. You move through the gentle quiet to the center of the sunlight and stand transfixed. The hair on the back of your neck bristles. Only the silence speaks. You are in a magnificent cathedral and you sit. Who knows for how long? You are a part of eternity. That is worship Dudley Carter style. Experiences like that added to Dudley's Indian-ness and gave him a physical connection to spirituality that enabled him to envision works the likes of *Legend of the Moon*.

Getting close to Dudley, sharing our common understandings through the creation of that work for Marymoor, was a truly transforming experience. By the time we completed the sculpture, I had a new handle on life. I returned to Vancouver determined to build a canoe and sail it to Hawaii. And I did just that. Quite likely, neither Dudley nor I had any idea spending time with him was what I needed, but in any event, a good dose of Dudley turned out to be a godsend.

Geordie Tocher (See "Zen of the Axe" on page 39 for Tocher's bio.)

Chapter 23

Legend of Moon the Transformer

Adapted by David M. Buerge

Long ago, in the land of the Snoqualmie people, two sisters camped out to dig fern roots on the beautiful prairie above Snoqualmie Falls. As they lay on their blankets among the lacy fronds, watching the stars wheel overhead, Younger Sister asked of the elder, "How would you like it if we got those stars up there as husbands?"

"Don't say that," cautioned Older Sister, knowing how dangerous idle wishes could be. But Younger Sister wished a winking white star to be her husband and a bright red star as a husband for her sister.

When they awoke the next morning, the sisters discovered themselves in a strange house. Younger Sister found next to her an old white-haired man, while beside Older Sister was a handsome red man in the prime of life. The sisters had no idea where they were. Eventually, they became used to their new surroundings and lived very much as they had lived before, but in their hearts they longed to find a way back home. In time, Older Sister became pregnant and bore a child, a boy who became the moon.

> Students of Northwest Coast Indian mythology believe Dudley Carter interpreted this important Salish myth quite freely when he created *Legend of the Moon*. Harmonizing the mythic story with Carter's dramatic sculpture, David Buerge prepared this adaptation of the Snoqualmie story primarily from two versions of the myth recorded early in the 1900s.

While gathering roots one day, one of the sisters' digging sticks poked through the ground and a great wind rushed up from the hole. Peering down through the opening, the sisters rejoiced to see their old familiar world. They then realized that they had been taken up into Sky Country and were living with the Star People whose hearth fires spangled the heavens. Aching to see their parents, they secretly wove a long rope of cedar branches. When it was long enough, they lowered it through the hole and began to climb down, carrying the moon child with them.

Meanwhile on Earth, the sisters' grieving parents had called upon powerful shamans to sing their songs, dance their dances, and fly far and wide to search for their missing children, but with no luck. Only Blue Jay and Squirrel were still singing when at last a rope magically appeared from the heavens, and the sisters lowered themselves to the prairie with the moon child. The shamans' lament became a song of joy when the parents ran from their house to embrace their daughters and marvel at the beautiful baby.

Word spread quickly that everyone was invited to come celebrate the sisters' miraculous return. At the gathering, the sisters taught the people to swing on the rope in a long, joyous arc from one mountain-

Legend of the Moon, 1978, red cedar, 35′ × 11′ × 6′
Marymoor Park, Redmond, Washington. Photograph courtesy Anna Vaughan Hanson

Legend of the Moon Transformer 107

top to another. In the meantime, blind old Grandmother Toad took care of the moon child. However, while rocking him to sleep she dozed off, and one of the invited guests, Chum Salmon, crept into the house, kidnapped the child, and carried him away to his longhouse under the western ocean.

Heartbroken at their new loss, the family again hired shamans to make a search. The weeping sisters washed the child's clothes, left behind by Chum Salmon. As they wrung them out they heard a cry. The wringings had become another child, a boy who became Sun, younger brother of Moon.

For a long time, the shamans searched for Moon. It was Blue Jay who, after making a dangerous journey to the far edge of the world, finally found him in Chum Salmon's house. Moon had grown to manhood, married the daughter of Chum Salmon, and was now the father of sons. Blue Jay revealed to Moon the story of his miraculous parentage and his kidnapping. Blue Jay pleaded with Moon to return to his grieving family. Moon agreed, but first he prevailed upon Chum Salmon's people to visit their human in-laws yearly and offer them their robes of flesh to repay them for their sorrow.

Waxing with power, Moon returned to his human family, driving the salmon upriver before him. On the way he fought monsters and titans that dominated the earth, transforming them into useful animals and benign landmarks, thereby changing the world into a happier home for humankind.

Moon made the people fully human and told them they could climb the rope to get whatever they needed in Sky Country. At the prairie, Moon and his brother, Sun, climbed the rope into Sky Country and competed to see who would light this new world. As Sun walked the trail leading across the sky from one edge of the world to the other he made a hot bright light. When Moon followed he gave a cool, pale light. While this was going on Rat, in Sky Country, gnawed the rope until it broke. It fell in a great coiled heap onto the prairie below, severing the connection between Sky Country and Earth.

Moon and his younger brother remained in the sky. Sun gives light and heat during the day while the changing Moon watches over Earth at night, carrying old Grandmother Toad, who holds on tight so she won't lose him this time. We see her as the frog in the moon when Moon makes his silent journey. The rope no longer joins the Heaven and the Earth, but the labors of Moon bind the two worlds together, a continuing force enabling the powers of each to enrich the lives of all who come after.

NOTE: David Buerge's rendering of North Wind and Storm Wind appears on page 33. His primary resource for this adaptation of Moon the Transformer was Arthur Ballard's detailed version of the legend, published in "Mythology of Puget Sound," *University of Washington Publications in Anthropology*, Seattle, Vol. 3, No. 2, pp 69–80. Snuqualmie Charlie, a Snoqualmie elder from the village at Tolt born around 1850, related the tale to Ballard. A shorter version told to ethnographer Hermann Haeberlin by Skookum George, a Snoqualmie, was also helpful ("Mythology of Puget Sound," *Journal of American Folklore*, Vol. 37 (145–146), 1924, 373–374).

Chapter 24

A Tribute for Two

By 'Lyn Lambert

Tucked away in the memorial garden of a Seattle parish church stands a commemorative totem. Proudly, silently, it celebrates the lives of two men with little in common save their devotion to God and their desire to evince God's will through service to others.

When Frank Calvert, a founding member of the Episcopal church of Saint Dunstan's of the Highlands, died in 1959 his family wished to honor him and his exemplary Christian life. They chose to do so through the image of a historical church figure of regional significance.

Chief Spokan Garry—a Washington State hero of the faith largely ignored by history—was suggested as a likely candidate by the vicar of the Highlands' parish, Canon Thomas E. Jessett. Canon Jessett, a historiographer as well as an Episcopal priest of considerable attainment, wrote extensively of Pacific Northwest history, and among his published works is a biography of Chief Spokan Garry.

Spokan Garry was chief of the Spokanes, a Salishan tribe or group of tribes whose territory lay along the Spokane River in the area of the present city of Spokane. His Salish language name was Slough-Keetcha. One of the earliest Natives baptized in the land that later became the State of Washington, Chief Garry was the area's first Indian Christian missionary and an educator and statesman. For over half a century, under the most forbidding of circumstances and armed only with a weapon of peace, Garry fought for land rights and the preservation of his people.

Signage marking the sculpture of *Chief Spokan Garry* at Saint Dunstan's of the Highlands Parish Church, Seattle
Photograph 'Lyn Lambert

Chief Spokan Garry detail, 1961
Red cedar, 12′ × 4.5′ × 22″
Located at Saint Dunstan's of the Highlands Parish Church, Seattle, Washington. The chief's left hand, holding open his treasured Bible, bears initials, evidence of a latter-day vandal.
Photograph 'Lyn Lambert

He was born in 1811, just a few months after the arrival of the first white traders to the area of the Salmon Trout people, near the present town of Cheney, Washington. Garry's father was Chief Illim-Spokanee, a man already old when Garry was born.

The father, in the custom of Native elders, enjoyed regaling his son with stories, tales that would create in the boy a desire to become a good speaker and a wise leader—brave, upright, and strong. The chief taught his son to honor old people and strangers as well and to do all in his power to help them. One story made a particularly deep impression on young Slough-Keetcha.

Illim-Spokanee spoke of a terrible night, a night he would never forget. Great thunder rumbled through the skies and a fierce trembling shook the earth. By daylight, everything—trees, rocks, lodges, even the hills—wore a thick blanket of ash. The people were terrified, certain the end of the world was upon them. Fear was about to turn to panic when a man of many years with an air of serenity about him appeared. Raising his hand in the sign of peace, he told the people he came with a message. He assured them this was not the end of the world and much more would come to pass before that time. He told them that mysterious people with skin of a different color, speaking strange words and wearing peculiar clothes, would come before the world's end. Wise ones would be with them who would teach the people from marks made on leaves bound together in a bundle. The world would continue until the arrival of those people. His commanding way brought order out of confusion, and the people set about clearing away the ashes. No one thought to ask the old stranger from whence he received his authority and a few days later he died. Historians set this story at the time of the eruption of Mount Saint Helens in 1790.

The message of the serene old man prepared Chief Illim-Spokanee for a friendly association with the earliest white traders. When mysterious palefaces in peculiar clothing arrived speaking strange words and bringing with them their books—marks made on leaves bound together in a bundle—the aged

Totemic Principles

chief was ready to accept them and their teachings without apprehension or consternation.

So accepting was Illim-Spokanee that he turned his young son, fourteen years of age, over to Hudson's Bay fur traders to be taken across the mountains, a seventy-five-day journey of some eighteen hundred miles. Clergymen in charge of the Church of England Missionary Society near Fort Garry, now Winnipeg, Canada, had requisitioned traders to keep their eyes open for bright young Indian lads and bring them to the Anglican Red River Mission School. It was the aim of the clergy to educate the Indian boys and return them to their tribes to act as assistants to missionaries who were yet to come, aiding in the conversion of the tribes. Before he left for the school, Slough-Keetcha was renamed Spokan Garry in honor of his tribe and an official of the Hudson's Bay Company, Nicholas Garry.

Spokan Garry returned to his tribe after an absence of four years, a year after the death of his father. Grateful for the knowledge he gained at the Red River Mission, he took other young Indian boys to the mission school to be educated.

In his early years as leader of the Spokanes, Garry proved to be an influential teacher, attracting Indians from many tribes to hear him. He taught English and simple agriculture and established a straightforward form of Christianity emphasizing brotherly love, peaceful behavior, and humility—a doctrine well received by the Salishan people. Garry's statesmanship and knowledge of the white man's ways established him as a revered leader of his people. Always a friend to the white man and opposed to war, he spoke for the Spokanes in their dealings with representatives of the United States.

Unfortunately, the Native leader's influence lessened with the coming of the white missionaries. Being of differing denominations, the missionaries, rather than building on the simple form of Christianity Garry preached, criticized his teachings. The religious deputies managed to create discord, fragmenting tribal unity at the very time concerted action was essential in the struggle for their survival. This clash of cultures caused Chief Garry to suffer enormously. Eventually, rejected by his people and forcibly deprived of his farm by white men, he died a vagabond in the land of his birth. Had he died at a time when his influence was strong, Chief Spokan Garry would have been acclaimed as a great leader of his people.

The family of Frank Calvert held this tragic and heroic figure in esteem when they asked Dudley Carter to create their memorial. The *Chief Spokan Garry* statue acknowledges early Episcopal history, its sunshine and its shadows, and more recent church history in its tribute to Frank Calvert.

Dudley Carter must have felt an affinity, a spiritual kinship, to Chief Garry as he carved the cedar likeness of the early missionary. Dudley was a member of the Christadelphians, a group of believers who practice their faith in a manner they hold is true to the church of the first century. Lacking the trappings of high church worship and avoiding denominationalism or politicizing, Christadelphians emphasize brotherly love, peaceful behavior, and humility. And that is what Spokan Garry's life was all about, a testimony that the true tenets of Christianity and those of indigenous spirituality need not be out of tune.

Dudley carved his representation of Chief Spokan Garry from a portrait of the chief made at the Walla Walla Treaty Council in 1855. The chief's right hand is held up in the sign of peace, and he holds in his left hand his Bible—marks made on leaves bound in a bundle.

NOTE: A valuable source of information for this story was the historical biography *Chief Spokan Garry 1811–1892* by Thomas E. Jessett, published in 1960 by T.S. Denison & Company, Inc., Minneapolis.

Chapter 25

Little Orphan Alder

By Don Clark

Totem poles are always carved of cedar. I should know. My forester daddy was in the cedar business for years. In the late 1950s he retired from the University of Washington and the Washington State Forest Products Institute to pursue his new love for—what he called—Little Orphan Alder, the tree foresters loved to hate.

As secretary-manager of the Northwest Hardwood Association, my father became the champion of alder—the perfect wood for just about anything. You can stain it; you can paint it; you can make it look like any wood you wish—great for furniture, why not for totems? So he, or maybe the hardwood association, commissioned Dudley Carter to carve a totem of alder, but funds ran out before the pole was completed.

My father dreamed of having Dudley demonstrate the carving of the alder totem pole before the members of the Northwest Hardwood Association in Olympia. Arrangements were made for Dudley and the totem-in-progress to appear in Olympia for

> Foresters long considered the alder a weed because of its rapid growth and the way in which it invaded clear cuts, competing for space and light and killing planted conifers. When the virtues of Western Washington and Oregon alder were recognized, the timber industry switched from poisoning alder to planting it. Scientists, manufacturers, and artists have come to revere the tree.

the demonstration, but on that day the totem didn't show up on time. Ergo, my father had an unrealized dream, and Dudley Carter had an unfinished alder totem in his back yard.

As secretary of the Northgate Rotary Club, I was involved at that time in cementing a relationship between four local Rotary Clubs and our adopted sister Rotary Club in New Lynn, New Zealand. We needed a meaningful and perpetual memorial to this bonding, one that the New Zealanders could put on display and one that reflected our Pacific Northwest culture. A totem pole, how logical!

Working with several Seattle sister clubs, the Northgate Rotary Club was able to put up the bucks for Dudley to finish his alder totem. We picked it up on a Saturday and set it up in the Northgate meeting room, ready for Monday's luncheon meeting. I shall never forget that Monday. The work of art had developed two major splits, one running from head to toe. We were not aware that wet alder, abruptly introduced to a warm, dry environment, is noted for this tendency to disjoint itself. Red faced, I removed the disgraced totem to my patio at home where—with bolts, screws, dowels, wood putty, and a coat of paint—I restored the work of art to near normal and off it went to New Zealand.

I have searched high and low for a picture of Dudley Carter's one and only alder totem pole.

Little Orphan Alder Kidnapped!
The July 18, 2007, edition of the *New Zealand Herald* reported that an owl and ram totem was abducted from West Lynn Gardens early on July 13. Donated to the New Lynn Rotary Club in 1964, the pole must have been the Dudley Carter sculpture donated by the Seattle-area Rotary Clubs. Bolted to steel flanges set in concrete, it was believed it would have taken up to four people to remove the massive work and hoist it over the garden's locked gates.

The *Seattle Times*, August 1, 1964, reported news of Dudley Carter's *Owl and Ram Totem*, which four Seattle area Rotary Clubs were sending off to the New Lynn Rotary Club in New Zealand. The seven-foot-tall totem went on a farewell tour, attending luncheon meetings of the clubs prior to being shipped to New Zealand where it was destined for display in a suburban Auckland park.

Nada. Nien. Non. But newspaper articles at the time featured pictures showing delighted New Zealanders gathered around the pole—no hint of any splits in the pole or our new New Zealand relationship.

Don Clark (1925–2006), native of the Pacific NW, served with the US Navy in WWII, received a degree in journalism from the University of Washington, and went on to enjoy a long and successful career in advertising and journalism in Alaska and Washington State. To satisfy his lighter side, Clark entertained the people of Seattle as Captain Kidd of the city's Seafair Pirates. Continuing to love things of a naval nature, he helped found a nonprofit archaeological diving organization established to assist major North American museums. Clark authored and published two historical books, retired, and settled in Ocean Shores, Washington, where he continued to enjoy life as a freelance writer. Photograph courtesy Don Clark

Chapter 26

A Grand Totem for a Prairie School

From the writing of Ann McLeod

I t's unclear to me now how we decided that our school needed a totem pole. After all, we are located in the land of the Plains Indians, a people not known to display such symbols. But a totem pole we have. And it is not just any totem pole—it is a Dudley Carter original.

I was a counselor at Grande Prairie Composite High School in Alberta, Canada, when the class of 1976, along with students of past graduating classes of the six-year-old school, decided they would leave a meaningful legacy to the school. The students, respectful of our area's first peoples and appreciative of their endowment, had named our intramural sports teams after Plains Indian tribes. The student council was known as the tribal council, the interschool sports teams were the Totems and the Tomahawks, and our winter carnival was dubbed Pow Wow Daze. A totem pole, albeit an art form more typical of coastal Indians, was deemed an appropriate legacy.

In determining who might carve the pole, we checked with Jasper Place Composite High School in Edmonton, as they have a totem. Someone there

Grande Prairie Composite High School Totem, 1976
Grande Prairie, Alberta, Canada
Photograph D.R. Wilson

gave us Dudley Carter's name. We tracked him down, and it went on from there.

Once we made contact with Mr. Carter, the whole process became quite simple. He was excited about the project, and together we tossed around a few ideas about what characters would befit a totem destined for a school in Northern Alberta. We settled on a great horned owl as representative of the province, a beaver as symbolic of Canada, and a buffalo to represent our Plains Indians. A small swan would be etched on the owl's wing, signifying Grande Prairie, and names of Albertan Indian tribes would appear at the base of the pole. Mr. Carter went to work on the pole at Dundarave in West Vancouver, British Columbia.

As the totem neared completion, our concern became transportation of the pole to Northern Alberta. Luck was with us. The father of one of the players on the basketball team I coached happened to own a trucking company and had a truck scheduled to make a delivery to the West Coast. Timing was right and the truck would be returning empty—so the pole was conveyed courtesy Borstad Cartage. Mr. Carter looked after all the arrangements, including the packaging, from his end.

The eagerly awaited $3,000 pole arrived at the school to be duly installed according to Mr. Carter's explicit instructions. Faculty and students were elated to learn that the artist himself would fly up

Above: Dudley Carter and the *Grande Prairie Composite High School Totem*, 1976, red cedar, 17' × 30" × 30"
Photograph *Grande Prairie Herald Tribune* / QMI Agency
Left: Letter from Dudley to Ann McLeod, who has always regretted not having him carve an owl for her
Photocopy courtesy Ann McLeod

A Grand Totem for a Prairie School

to Grande Prairie to officially unveil the totem at the Pow Wow Daze celebration. My husband and I had the honor of showing him around town, and it was a delight to spend time with him. We drove out to the Wapiti River area. I recall Mr. Carter being particularly interested in the trees, the local logging industry, and the pulp mill. He was alert—interested in everything around him—humble, amusing, kind, and much younger than his years, which were over eighty at the time.

Michelle King Gray, the young lady chosen to be the Pow Wow Daze Princess that year, retains fond memories of Dudley Carter to this day, as well as a special memento to remember him by. Told the day before the unveiling that he was to present flowers to the princess, Dudley worked through the night carving a miniature totem pole to give to her.

Michelle, years later, recalled being instantly captivated by Mr. Carter for he held "a kind of attraction that made you feel comfortable and at ease. He was not outgoing in a talkative way. He was outgoing from the inside in what seemed a genuine love of people." Michelle, now living in Arizona, studied sculpture and describes herself as an "art freak."

When the totem was first erected there was some criticism that there were no arms and no bright colors, just natural cedar. I've often had nightmares that someday someone might decide to paint it. Interestingly, the totem has never suffered a single bit of vandalism, not even the often irresistible carving of initials.

Ann McLeod, following her years as a high school faculty member, became self-employed in the community in a variety of small businesses. In addition to McLeod's reminiscences, which she related in a letter to the authors, information for this story was gleaned from an article about Grande Prairie's totem in the June 20, 1995, *Grande Prairie Daily Herald-Tribune*, contributed by writer and public relations consultant Sue Farrell Holler.

A local newspaper pictured Dudley in a splendid tribal headdress with Michelle King, princess of the Grande Prairie Composite High School's winter carnival. They hold the miniature totem pole Dudley had carved for Michelle the night before the celebration.
Photograph *Grande Prairie Herald Tribune*/QMI Agency

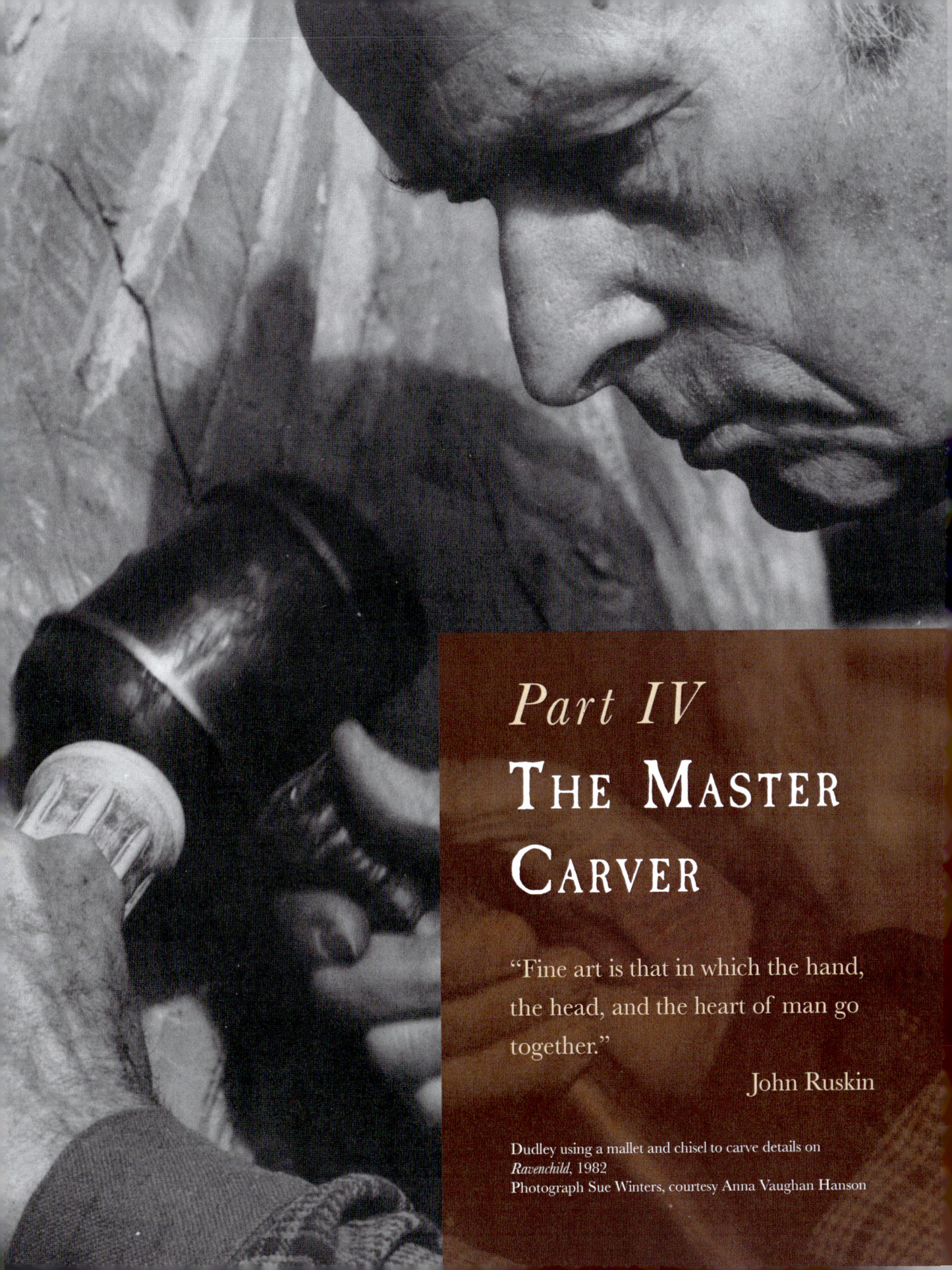

Part IV
THE MASTER CARVER

"Fine art is that in which the hand, the head, and the heart of man go together."

John Ruskin

Dudley using a mallet and chisel to carve details on *Ravenchild*, 1982
Photograph Sue Winters, courtesy Anna Vaughan Hanson

Chapter 27

At Home in the House of the Master

From a conversation with Bill McNae

In the noisy midway of the 1949 Puyallup fair, I caught sight of a man on a scaffolding, swinging an axe with all his might, shaping a giant totem pole. He appeared to be forty or fifty feet up—no guardrail protecting him—looking as comfortable and confident as if he were working on terra firma. I was awestruck.

My brother and I were at the fair celebrating my recent release from the armed service. As a youngster, I'd been enchanted by the totem poles I'd seen in the Royal BC Museum in Victoria, British Columbia, but I'd never seen one in the making. My brother told me the totem had been commissioned for Gaffney's Lake Wilderness Resort and the axe carver with the unusual technique was Dudley Carter.

But it wasn't until 1963, when I began teaching art at Chinook Junior High School in Bellevue, that I actually met Dudley. The school had just opened and the front yard was as the building contractors had left it—bulldozer tracks, rotting tree stumps, and blackberry vines everywhere. The school's principal challenged me to put my art training to use and see what could be done to beautify the entrance to the building—a stimulating challenge for a new art instructor.

I laid out flowerbeds with rhododendrons and azaleas, favorites of mine that require little maintenance and offer beautiful reward, but the landscaping called for more than flowering bushes. I envisioned a twelve- or thirteen-foot wood carving of the school's mascot, the Kodiak bear, as a focal point. The PTA board liked the idea and asked me to get some bids on a carving. One of the board members put forth the name of a friend known to be a good wood-carver and offered to contact him, but to my mind he was no Dudley Carter. Carter was number one, and there was no two or three as far as I was concerned.

A telephone call to Dudley Carter's home connected me with Mrs. Carter, who set up a time for me to visit. I could hardly wait for that meeting. Dudley and Teresa Carter received me graciously, as if they'd known me for years. I told Dudley about the project and he said he happened to have a beautiful piece of western red cedar that would quite likely fill the bill. When it came to the matter of price, he said, "The going rate for a totem these days is a hundred dollars a foot, so a twelve-footer would come to twelve hundred dollars."

I swallowed hard—back then such a figure would floor the members of the PTA. Then Dudley went on to say, "I always cut my price in half for anything that's being done for kids."

In no time Dudley came up with a design for a bear totem. He deftly sketched out a bear wearing a tall ceremonial hat indicating superior power. Its great paws held its favorite food, a Chinook salmon, source of the Kodiak's strength and symbolic of the school's name.

After seeing the design, the shop teacher and the school's other art teacher agreed with me that, regardless of cost, no one but Dudley should do the Chinook totem. I couldn't wait to present Dudley's proposal to the PTA. The carver friend of the board member came in with a bid of twelve hundred dollars—it didn't stand a chance.

When Dudley began to work on the totem, I asked him if I could come around on weekends and take pictures of his progress. He agreed, so I got to poke around and watch him in action. As time went on, I found myself hard at work.

One day Dudley said, "If you want to get some experience and a little exercise to boot, here's a four-inch lip adze."

I considered myself to be in pretty fair shape, but Dudley, some seventy years old, worked without a drop of perspiration on his forehead. On the other hand, I was wringing wet. Dudley piled up more chips in half an hour than I could produce in a week. My adzing technique left much to be desired, and Dudley wryly suggested I wear a couple of stovepipes to protect my legs.

To further my formal art training, I enrolled in the master of arts program at the University of Washington and spent as much time as I could in the

Chinook Bear Totem, 1964, red cedar, 14′ × 30″ × 28″
Chinook Middle School, Bellevue, Washington
Photograph Mary Sikkema

At Home in the House of the Master

Dudley Carter and *Replica of a Haida House #2*, 1956, red cedar, 17′ × 30′
This work of art served as Dudley Carter's studio on Bellevue-Redmond Road in Bellevue, Washington. Purchased in September 1968 by Bill McNae, dismantled in 1980, and later reconstructed on Whidbey Island, Washington. Photograph courtesy Dudley Carter

sculpture studio there. I enjoyed working with wood, but most of the sculptors at the university molded their designs with wax or clay and cast them in bronze. My instructors encouraged me to work in my medium of choice, but they didn't demonstrate wood carving techniques. On the other hand, Dudley, truly a master carver, would willingly demonstrate his skills and offer his advice. He also provided me with many fine pieces of cedar.

When I wasn't teaching at Chinook or studying at the university, I could often be found at Dudley's place. I loved the idyllic forest setting and the split cedar home where Dudley and his wife lived. In a small clearing, Dudley's splendid Haida house studio stood with its marvelous carved door. That door was nonfunctional for it had no hinges. In any event, should occupants manage to open the door to step outside, they would be met with a sheer drop—straight down a fifteen-foot embankment.

The Haida house sat on a concrete slab with a hole—maybe four feet square and three or four feet deep—in the middle of the slab. Dudley had rigged a turntable in the hole and secured an eyebolt on the beam directly above it. He could drop the end of a log in the hole, hoist it upright, and rotate it to assist the carving process. The studio's ridgepole was thirteen feet high, so a fifteen- or sixteen-foot log could stand upright. Two holes in the roof let in natural light, and by climbing a tree adjacent to the studio and peering through the openings, Dudley could get a bird's-eye view of his work. He laid boards across the holes when they were not in use.

Dudley really preferred to work outside whenever he could, whatever the weather—rain, snow, or sleet. To keep himself from freezing in the winter, he

Dudley using a mallet and chisel to carve details on *Ravenchild*, 1982
Photograph Sue Winters, courtesy Anna Vaughan Hanson

reconfigured a fifty-gallon steel drum and mounted it horizontally on two steel-rimmed wheels. He'd pull the contraption close to the sculpture he wanted to work on, start a fire in the drum, and "keep on keepin' on," as he'd put it.

He had dozens of axes with which he did the bulk of his work, and then he'd finish up with chisels. He didn't use knives as many Native carvers would. He used chisels with a mallet or hand

At Home in the House of the Master

pressure to do finer carving. And he was very, very particular about his tools. Even when new, he often ground the edge of the tool to his own preference. Practically all his chisels were Marples—he was partial to English steel. And could he split cedar boards! Thirty-foot-long boards, thirty inches wide, were no problem for Dudley. He'd take a wedge and a froe and peel those boards off, one after the other.

Teresa was a beautiful lady, very gracious, the epitome of everyone's grandmother. Dudley called her Toots and she called him Ducko. Only one neighbor lived near the Carter's place; Teresa, isolated like that, must have craved companionship. She didn't drive a car and depended on Dudley to take her wherever she had to go. When my wife accompanied me on my visits, the two ladies would talk and talk like old friends.

Teresa was known to be a matter-of-fact individual. A relic of an electric stove sat outside the back door of the Carters' home. I thought it must have been junk, but Teresa set me straight. "Oh, no!" she said, "I cook out there in the summer. It's much cooler in the house if you don't cook inside."

Teresa Carter made it possible for me to acquire Dudley's Bel-Red Road Haida house studio. She approached me one day and asked, "Would you be interested in buying Ducko's studio?"

I didn't even ask her how much, I just said, "Yes! Yes, if you will accept monthly payments."

By that time Dudley had become very hard of hearing and I gathered that Teresa was acting as his business agent. She and I formalized the agreement in 1968, and Dudley continued to live and work in the studio for some twelve years after I bought it.

When I was ready to move the building to property I had purchased on Whidbey Island, Dudley wanted to buy it back. He said, "I'll pay for all the new material and you can build a new house right next to this one so you can get all the dimensions you need."

I spent a week or two making phone calls to timber companies to locate similar material. They just laughed at me and said, "You gotta be kidding. That stuff went out of existence years ago!" There was no way I could replicate Dudley's Haida house, so I just couldn't sell it back to him.

Dismantling, transporting, and reconstructing the house on our property on Whidbey proved to be quite a project. I numbered and measured every piece and made detailed drawings before I began the dismantling process.

The Haida house didn't encompass enough space for my wife, my son, and me, so we had a contractor dig out a full basement. Dudley came out to see the place after we had it pretty well set up. Obviously very upset, to put it mildly, he said I had ruined the Haida house because such dwellings don't have basements. Though

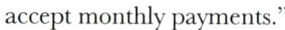

Reconstruction of Dudley's studio, *Replica of a Haida House #2*, on Whidbey Island. Photographs courtesy Bill McNae

disappointed, he offered some suggestions for improving our setup. He proposed that I build a forty-foot-wide deck onto which the carved door would open. The deck would provide an expansive outlook over the water and allow for closer viewing of the carved corner posts, the door, and the eight-foot bear that towers above the roofline. He also recommended that we plant shrubbery in front of the basement to conceal the excavation. We followed his instructions.

In many ways Dudley Carter seemed a real-life superhero. I believed that young people might find him inspirational. I asked the school district to buy the video *Dudley Carter* produced by Abby Sher, so I could show it to my classes each semester. I'd impress upon the students, "This guy is unbelievable. Ninety years old and look what he's doing. What are you capable of?"

Dudley knew real hard work and tough times, yet he was always content. Were he to have a financial worth of twenty billion dollars, I'm sure he'd still have gone to the thrift store for his clothing. If he had carte blanche at the local grocery store, he'd content himself with a head of lettuce, a chunk of cheese, perhaps a package of nuts, and most definitely, a bag of apples. He'd pass up the T-bone steaks. Forget those. And no ice cream! He'd be living and working exactly as he always had. You can't put a price on accomplishment and contentment.

I have a number of fine pieces of Native-style art hanging on my walls. Any one of a hundred carvers may have carved them because they all follow traditional standards. That's not bad, but I don't know who did them. Dudley Carter's style is distinctive. If you see one of his sculptures, you say, "Ah-ha! Dudley must have done that!"

Certainly only Dudley Carter could have fashioned this wonderful dwelling, the former Haida studio that is now our home. I feel Dudley's spiritual presence each time I walk through the front door. His spirit, his sense of design, and his place in history permeate the dwelling like the fragrance of freshly split old-growth cedar.

Bill McNae (1925–2014) photographed with *Semone*, 1965, red cedar, 7′ × 24″ × 2″, a panel by Dudley Carter. McNae served in the US Navy, farmed in Alberta for four years, was a draftsman with the Boeing Company, and taught art at Chinook Middle School in Bellevue, Washington, for twenty-five years and wood carving at Bellevue Community College before retiring to enjoy his carving interests at his home, the former Dudley Carter studio. Photograph Mary Sikkema

At Home in the House of the Master

At Play in the House of the Master
By Anna Vaughan Hanson

My earliest memories of my grandfather seem to always go back to the days when his studio was in Bellevue. To cross the border into the US by train or car was always an adventure. And to spend half your summer—one whole month—as a wild, reckless child, free to explore the seemingly endless acres of forest, was paradise. To the rhythmical beat of the axe my brothers and I would head out the back door, through the outdoor kitchen, slip by the Haida house studio, and wade through a sea of wood chips to our adventure playground beyond. For a few brief moments we were immersed in cedar. All our senses knew of nothing but cedar. As I waded through, knee deep in chips, I always had the urge to linger, to stay a while, but too many adventures lay ahead. With several giant leaps, chips flying, we broke free and were away.

Massive cedars would come and go. The immense logs, tamed by the axe, would be transformed into bold, fantastic creatures of the sea or forest. An absolute miracle.

My grandfather always imagined that one day he and I—each with our double-bitted axes, side by side—would be transforming a giant burly cedar into a masterpiece. Although I did apprentice with him occasionally, we never did actually tackle the same sculpture together. When I was a child he once brought me a block of wood. Upon it he drew a bold, stylized bear in the Northwest Coast tradition. I watched him carve one side, he left me to carve the other.

Over the years I've delved into marble and bronze sculpture, but my fascination with cedar has never left. Carving by hand with the axe and chisels, carving bold stylized shapes—the essence of the form, I will always be drawn to it. I strive to be true to the medium, to preserve the natural character of the wood. I have studied fine arts and graphic design, but watching the magician at work, letting the shape and grain of the wood speak to him, is where I really received my education—among a sea of cedar chips.

Ducko passed away on the evening of April 7, 1992, on my fortieth birthday. In his fortieth year he was carving his first major sculpture, *Rivalry of the Winds*. On that April evening, he passed on the baton, his double-bitted axe.

He has been gone for years, but as I carve using his axe and chisels in a Haida house studio, he is never far away. So now in a sense we are carving sculptures together.

NOTE: Anna wrote this piece recalling her early memories of her grandfather and his studio in February 2015. Sadly, in 2018 she contracted and succumbed to pancreatic cancer. Like her grandfather, Anna continued carving right up until her final weeks. We like to think that she and her grandfather are very much at home—at work and at play—in the house of their Master. Another story by Anna, "River of Life," appears on page 254.

Chapter 28

Secrets Revealed

From a conversation with Donald McAusland

Collecting Dudley Carter sculptures and trying my own hand at wood carving have been predilections of mine since I first came across Dudley demonstrating his carving technique in Bellevue Square. That wiry little man, all muscle and sinew, turning out powerful sculptures—I was charmed.

Right away, I bought two of Dudley's small pieces, small by Dudley's standards, for the rooftop patio of a building I own across from Bellevue Square. I acquired another Carter sculpture from my friend Wellwood Beall. Wellwood, a Boeing executive, had purchased an interesting work from Dudley—a sculptured seagull high atop an upended driftwood log. He had a Boeing truck come out with a big lift and install it in the swimming pool area of the Beall's beautiful estate. When his wife, Jeanne, the artist who worked with Dudley on his Bon Marché mural commission, came home and saw it, she took one look and declared it was "out of scale" and had to go. So Wellwood sold it to me. It was an ideal addition to the landscaping of my downtown Bellevue building, and no longer would Bellevue Square be the only establishment in town with a Dudley Carter work of art out front. For years the seagull soared there, but when vandals applied some paint to it, I decided to move the work to my home. Now it's out of scale there.

Ten years or so after I moved the seagull to my home, Dudley was visiting us and I said, "Dudley, that bird up there is looking pretty old and tired."

Woman with Gift. My favorite piece is *Riding the Comb*, a Native paddler at the crest of a driftwood wave. It's the one most admired by others. The third is a piece I don't think Dudley considered particularly important for he didn't give it a title, as far as I know. It is a beautiful bird carrying a branch in its beak. It doesn't take a stretch of my imagination to see the creature as a bird of peace.

I enjoy my own artistic endeavors, particularly painting, but out of admiration for Dudley Carter I felt an urge to learn to carve. I told Dudley I wanted to carve, explaining that I didn't mean whittle like I did in Boy Scouts. I wanted to learn to sculpt wood.

"Well, Don, let me show you something," he said as he led me over to *Woman with Gift*. "Wood carving is very simple. It is just a series of Vs." He

Seagull on a Post, 1960, red cedar, 10′ × 5′ × 12″
After Don McAusland's death, his family donated *Seagull on a Post* to the City of Redmond for installation in Dudley Carter Park.
Photograph Lisa Lambert

He got on a ladder, inspected the bird, and agreed that the creature needed help. About three days later Dudley put a new bird up there while I was away. He said he wanted it to be right.

There are three other Dudley Carter carvings in our courtyard. One is a woman, one of Dudley's early works. She holds a bowl of sorts, as if it is an offering. She strikes me as Egyptian so I call the piece My Egyptian Queen. Dudley titled it

Woman with Gift, 1963, red cedar, 5′ × 2′ × 16″
Photograph 'Lyn Lambert

Secrets Revealed

pointed to the carving saying, "There's a big V in her eyelid here, a small V on her ear, a V here and another over here. And if you look under here, there's another V. Everything is Vs. All you have to do is take a chisel and make Vs. Or, if you want to make large Vs, you take an axe. That's how simple it is."

And I could see he was right. When you look at it the way he did, there's nothing to it. Dudley's lessons were one of the beguiling things about him. I received another lesson when I pointed out to him that there were pencil lines visible on his carvings. He gave me a look that inasmuch said, "Don't you know anything about art?" He asked me if I had ever been to the Louvre and went on to explain, "Great artists do a pencil sketch first, and they don't go around with an eraser afterwards. The pencil lines indicate it's an original. Now you know you have an original!"

The pencil marks have worn off my Dudley Carter carvings now. I'm sorry about that because I learned something from them. I now sketch before I paint.

I complimented Dudley on a carving one time, and he replied, "It's not the carving that is beautiful, it's the piece of driftwood that produced it." He often insisted, "It isn't the carving. It's the wood."

One summer while on a cruise up the coast of British Columbia, I saw a piece of driftwood that set me to thinking about that comment. I'd often seen salmon migrating up the rivers of Alaska and I could see a salmon in that piece of wood. "It's just perfect," I thought. I understand it's now illegal to remove driftwood from the shore, but I couldn't resist. I put it in the boat and took it home.

I tried so hard to carve that migrating salmon, but it just didn't look right. I didn't know what I'd done wrong. So I consulted with the master. Dudley studied it a bit and then said, "Well, I'll tell you what. Take a mirror and place it behind the piece on

Seated Ram, 1959, red cedar, 16″ × 12″ × 8″
Photograph 'Lyn Lambert

your workbench. Then stand back and look at the mirror image. Next time you see me, tell me what you saw." Then he added, "And another thing, don't try to finish it next weekend. Study the carving in the mirror. If you decide the tail is too long, take a little bit off. Then leave it for a while. Go do some gardening. Come back and see it tomorrow. Don't try to do it too fast."

Dudley worked like that. He had works in progress all around his studio, indoors and out. He'd sculpt a little on this piece for a while, then work on another, and so forth. He'd let a carving sit unfinished and think about it until inspiration came to him.

The mirror trick gave me an entirely new perspective. I followed Dudley's advice and got the salmon to suit me. I got my gardening done too.

Most of my Dudley Carter carvings are displayed outside, but I keep my smallest Dudley Carter treasure, *Seated Ram*, in the house. Dudley carved it when he was in San Francisco. It's remarkably heavy for its size, weighing over forty pounds. It is supposedly red cedar, but it seems more like some type of hardwood. Dudley won an award for that piece.

He was quite a storyteller, known for entertaining anyone within earshot with stories of his experiences with the Indians. But he also enjoyed hearing of others' involvement with the Natives. I told him of my grandfather's near demise during the Modoc Indian Wars of 1872–1873. General Canby was in charge of the military, and my grandfather, A.B. Meacham, was Superintendent of Indian Affairs for the Oregon Territory under Abraham Lincoln. He went with Canby to have truce talks with the Modoc leaders. They killed Canby and shot my grandfather three or four times. A young brave then sat on his chest trying to scalp my bald grandfather. Grandfather received several chinks in his head before an Indian woman he had befriended appeared and told the warriors to flee as the Federal Troops were coming. Canby, Oregon, got its name from the slain general, and a town on the west fringe of the Blue Mountains near Pendleton is named Meacham after my grandfather. My grandfather wrote a book documenting his experiences titled *Wigwam and War-Path: Or, The Royal Chief in Chains*.

Dudley was in his eighties when he decided to compete for a commission from the State of Oregon for a collection of sculptures depicting the history of Oregon. He remembered the stories I'd told him about my grandfather and asked if he could borrow his book to bone up on Oregon history in preparation for his proposal. He went to Weyerhaeuser for trees for the project. They told him he could have anything he wanted from their forests and they would put their cruisers at his disposal. I asked him later if he got some trees and he replied, "I got a couple of spurs."

What he finally found were three huge trees. When I asked him how in the world he planned to carve all that himself, he said, "Oh, I have my students and my friends." And that's how he operated.

Before Dudley could carry out his plans for the Oregon project, he had to leave his Bel-Red Road studio. He made an arrangement with King County to move all his belongings to Marymoor Park and to do his carving there. He thought he was going to be able to live in the park, but he couldn't pull that off. Nor could any of us who tried to sway the county, no matter what strings we pulled. County rules wouldn't permit people to live in parks. I have no reason to suspect that Dudley spent a night or two at Marymoor, but I sure hope he did. He wouldn't need much in the way of accommodation—just a hollow log or a wood bench and a jacket for a blanket. Dudley Carter lived very much the way he practiced his art—he kept things simple.

Don McAusland and Dudley Carter with *Riding the Comb*, 1977, red cedar, 4′ × 5′ × 22″
Photograph courtesy Don McAusland

Donald M. McAusland (1917–2009), born in Yarrow Point, Washington. Graduate of Stanford University, 1938. Served five years as a naval aviator in the Pacific. Owned and operated Lake Washington Farm and Garden Store prior to establishing McAusland Realty in Bellevue, Washington. Retired at age seventy, trading the rainy winter months of the Pacific Northwest for the sunnier climes of Rancho Mirage, California.

Chapter 29

Forest Reflections

From a conversation with Robert Chervenak

In 1963 when I was designing a building that would house the University of Washington Forest Sciences Laboratory, I knew I wanted a Dudley Carter work as part of that building. I had seen his art on several occasions and knew he used wood to its best advantage, applying his sculpting tools so his design seemed to grow out of the tree itself. He didn't simply work with wood. Dudley delighted in it and in the forests that produced it. On this building for the school of forestry, Carter was the natural choice and I knew he would understand what I was after.

The university system required that a competition be announced for commissioned art, subjecting proposals to a panel of judges. So to guarantee that Dudley would do the work, I made his art an integral part of the building. Buildings need doors. Carved wood entrance doors would be ideal for a school of forestry building, and Dudley could be hired directly as the best contractor for the job.

I wondered how Dudley would respond to a commission restricting him to precise architectural

Winkenwerder Forest Sciences Laboratory main entrance, University of Washington. Photograph Sara Lachman, Pacific Coast Architecture Database

restraints. He did a variety of work, not just totem poles. But he did huge pieces, like his carving for Bellevue Square, and he carved with an axe! Perhaps entrance doors would seem too insignificant to a man who called himself a monumental wood sculptor, or the detail of the carvings might be too small for an axe carver.

We got together and I told him the building would house the forest products institute. I explained that I wanted the subject of the carving to tie in with the building's purpose. As an added incentive, I told him that Winkenwerder, for whom the building was to be named, was a forester from Canada. I thought that might mean something to Carter. Foresters lived in a close-knit community in those days, and Carter knew almost everyone in that profession. He accepted the commission.

Dudley's studio was a fascinating place and I often looked for excuses to visit him there. Initially, I wondered if I'd have to remind him of the confines of the doors or explain more fully the message that I hoped the carvings would convey. I discovered he knew exactly what I was after, and in no way did architectural restrictions stifle his creativity. He could work within restrictions as well as do mammoth carvings that defied restrictions. I was amazed to see him make what my mind's eye envisioned appear in those cedar panels. He wasn't much for chitchatting, a pretty straightforward guy just working his own brand of magic.

In some respects, I wish we had chosen to go with a more significant piece of Dudley's art, yet everyone who walks through those doors encounters the forests that they represent. Many may pause a moment to reflect on the forests.

Door Panels, Winkenwerder Forest Sciences Laboratory, 1963
Red cedar, three panels, each 9′ × 22″
Designed for the University of Washington, Seattle, Washington. Photograph 'Lyn Lambert

Robert A. Chervenak (1924–2010), FAIA, served with the US Air Force during WWII as an aerial and ground photographer. He entered the University of Washington on the GI Bill, graduating at the top of his class in 1951. Chervenak taught design at the University of Washington as an associate professor of architecture. In addition to the Hugo Winkenwerder Forestry Laboratory, which received a national design award, Chervenak designed Bloedel Hall, also on the campus of the University of Washington, and numerous other public buildings and private residences. His firm designed hundreds of churches and church-related projects throughout the West Coast region. Photograph 'Lyn Lambert

Forest Reflections

Chapter 30

Desert Studio

From a conversation with Earl J. Neel

I met Dudley Carter in 1959 or 1960 when I was managing the family business, Neel's Nursery, in Palm Springs, California. Dudley came by wanting to rent some of our crane equipment to unload a truck full of huge timbers. He looked like a rather frail old man, and I couldn't imagine what he planned to do with the logs. I had to ask and his reply surprised me.

"Carve them," he said. He went on to describe the sizeable sculptures and relief carvings he had done for the San Francisco fair and mentioned some of his totems in the Seattle area. The man and his plans intrigued me. I offered to unload the timber right there at the nursery and to store it for him if he would agree to do his carving on the premises.

The fourteen-acre nursery, founded by my father in the 1920s, had three hundred feet of frontage along Highway 111 near Araby Drive. That was our display window, where we presented a selection of our landscape designs—reflection pools, lily ponds, waterfalls, and fountains—along with the trees of the desert. Cycads, a form of prehistoric tree from the dinosaur era that we brought from the Virgin Islands, particularly impressed Dudley. Ancient fig trees and a thick-trunked hundred-year-old pomegranate also interested him. And then there were the blue spruces and green pine trees, miniature cousins of the conifers Dudley grew up among.

Left: A segment of *High Mountain Companions*, 1962
Redwood, approximately 6′ × 2.5′ × 2′
Photographed at Neel's Nursery, Palm Springs,
California. *Easter Parade*, 1960, in the lower right of the
photograph is in the collection of Dudley Carter's family.
Photograph courtesy Dudley Carter

Below: *High Mountain Companions* at Slough House Park,
Redmond, Washington. Purchased in 1975 for the Allied
Stores' collection, later acquired by Marvin Boys and
loaned to Redmond Town Center, Redmond, Washington.
Photograph 'Lyn Lambert

He seemed very much at home as we walked along the rows of trees and cans of shrubs. I pointed out places where he might set up a work area, and we settled on a spot in the frontage strip where people driving by could see him at work. Dudley would be an animated display. We made our agreement and unloaded the timber then and there.

Dudley had no trouble becoming acclimated. It's much the same with a man as it is with a plant—properly planted in the right spot and given the attention they need, just about anything or anyone will thrive, even in the desert.

Watching Dudley and listening to his stories became a popular pastime for many Palm Springs residents and visitors. They were fascinated by his tales of becoming ill when he lived with the Indians, and how, as a timber cruiser eating only canned food for months, he was hit with a nearly deadly dose of scurvy. The illnesses took their toll and made Dudley look frail, yet when he plied his axe to those timbers his frailty vanished. He carved with the vigor of a man much younger than his seventy-plus years. Palm Springs' people were impressed.

The rich and famous were among the Dudley-watchers. Walter Annenberg became a great

admirer and one of Dudley's California friends. Mr. Annenberg was the noted philanthropist who commanded a huge communications operation—radio, television, and publishing. He also occupied

Desert Studio

what was considered the most prestigious post in the United States Diplomatic service—ambassador to the United Kingdom. Comedian Bob Hope often came down to catch the wood-carver's act. He loved Dudley's work and intended to purchase some of his creations. Dudley said Hope's wife, Dolores, put the kibosh on that. He presumed her taste ran more along the lines of lackluster plaster cast figures.

Dudley made good use of redwood and sugar pine when he worked in Palm Springs. He did a lot of work on speculation, but also brought in commissions, most of which went out of town. Among his Palm Springs creations were *Desert Scout, Springtime, High Mountain Companions*, and *Wildlife*, which all became part of the Allied Stores' purchase. Dudley carved *Segment of Creation* and *Easter Parade* at our nursery.

In 1962 my wife and I purchased a magnificent home close to downtown Palm Springs, and I commissioned Dudley to do a divider for it. It is a fine piece, natural redwood about six feet tall and twelve feet long. A carved head, representative of an Indian, tops each upright board. Reluctantly, I sold that home—an 8,000-square-foot home is a bit much for an elderly man living on his own. I wanted to take Dudley's divider with me, but the purchasers insisted that it remain with the house.

There is scarcely any place, especially in the old sections of Palm Springs, where the surroundings have not been enhanced by the efforts of Neel's nursery. The citizens of Palm Springs dedicated the mile of lighted palms, a thousand trees along Palm Canyon Drive, to the memory of my father, claiming that he "made the desert blossom like the rose."

Dudley migrated to Palm Springs to do his carving at Neel's Nursery every winter for about twenty years. He loved the oasis in the sun-drenched desert. My foremost notion of Dudley Carter is that he was one of the finest men I've met.

Earl J. Neel (1917–2001) grew up working weekends and summer vacations planting, cultivating, and landscaping with his father, who operated one of Palm Springs' longest-operating businesses. Apart from WWII, when he served in the US Navy, Neel never strayed far from the desert. Nursery work was his great interest and fondest hobby. He also served as an officer of the Desert Museum. As an enthusiastic golfer, he played every day well into his eighties.
Photograph courtesy Earl J. Neel

Desert Scout, 1960
Redwood, 18" × 7' × 6"
Carved and pictured at Neel's Nursery, Palm Springs. Purchased for Allied Stores, Seattle Washington in 1975. Donated to King County Library System for display in the Redmond Public Library.
Photograph courtesy Anna Vaughan Hanson

Chapter 31

Great Expectations,
Diminished Actualities—
Fine Art Forthcoming Nonetheless

In 1977 Dudley Carter was presented with an opportunity that would excite any artist—a request for a major public artwork carrying with it a six-figure commission. However, things didn't quite pan out, and to express his concerns about the situation, Dudley wrote the following memo. To whom? We're not sure, but most likely it was directed to Seattle's John Graham & Associates, designers of the Clackamas Town Center. The memo indicates some of the challenges creating public art can present and speaks of the degree of determination, flexibility, and ability to compromise possessed by Dudley, an artist well into his eighties. It also shows that, like many of us, Dudley (or his typist) had difficulty spelling some of Washington State's names.

CLACKAMAS TREE SCULPTURE PROJECT
DUDLEY C. CARTER
SCULPTOR

3075 Bellevue-Redmond Road
Bellevue, WA 98008
Phone: 206/885-1947
August 15, 1979

The Clackamas sculpture project (representing the background of Oregon) was first presented to me in the fall and winter of 1977 as six units. I realized it was not practical for one man to execute such a huge project—within the time limit of two years—without thoroughly organizing help, finding suitable timber and suitable locations to work at three or four different points along the Pacific coast. This would enable the taking advantage of weather conditions (important since most of the work must be done outdoors), material and help. Hence, I took a trip to Santa Cruz, California in March for one month in 1978. By that time photographs of my work had been used to illustrate the type of sculpture proposed by the architects. From then on I was committed to this project. I could not afford to lose any time so I immediately started experimenting, making models and doing research work on the background of Oregon to prepare such subject matter as "The Move West", "The Covered Wagon" (two people and four to six oxen), "The Pioneers' Waterwheel" (a mobile sculpture with movable figures and 20' to 30' in height), "The Primitive Indian Dance", "The Pioneers" (the life so familiar to me as I had been one of them), and the proposal for the Meier and Frank Court (all these sculptures and more each to be probably more than 30% over life size). It appeared to be an attractive commission with a contract price which would probably exceed $150,000.

I found the help, the timber and places to work in California for probably three months each winter. I continued experimenting with models and scouting for timber in Washington, Oregon and British Columbia. Hopes faded with the more ground I covered, for it seemed there was no such timber available. Traveling expenses mounted with motels, phone calls and thousands of miles of travel with the car. It finally boiled down that four of the major timber companies may possibly have been able to supply the size and quality of timber we required, Miller of Granite Falls, Washington; Rayonier of Hoquim [sic], North Bend and Longview, Washington. Prices quoted ran, generally, $1,200 per thousand for the #1 cedar. We required somewhere in the neighborhood of 15,000 board feet, which would be approximately $18,000 delivered. This was raised later by the #1 tree having about 4,000 board feet more than first estimated.

I had friends, some of the top-level executives in the industry, trying to negotiate the purchase of timber for me since early spring, 1979. It turned out that Weyerhauser [sic] was our most likely source of cedar. However, negotiations finally broke down with no prospect of a deal. It seemed my only hope was to negotiate with some of the top-level men in the industry myself. Perhaps my reputation with "Sculpture from the Great Trees of the West" had aroused the interest of some of them and this would help in the acquisition of timber.

My friend, the manager of Weyerhauser [sic] at North Bend, volunteered to introduce me to the company manager at Longview, Ted Nelson. He has charge of a huge forest area producing some of the best timber on the market. Meeting him on May 18, 1979, opened the door for the deal we made. Ted Nelson had known of my work and showed great interest in it and the project at Clackamas. He had seen me at work carving the 30-ton "Goddess of the Forest" at the Golden Gate Exposition in 1940 and was very willing to cooperate in supplying us with the finest cedar for our purpose. This would be specially selected and handled with slings to protect the bark as well as the wood.

The last of these three large trees was delivered August 9. Larger than we had originally planned, it raised the scale about 4,000 feet more than the first estimate—consequently raising the market price to well over $20,000 as compared with Rayonier and Miller. Ted Nelson negotiated a price cut in our favor with a savings of well over $10,000 delivered to Clackamas. This savings was made possibly only by my effort an expense in locating and negotiating on material over the period of 1977, 1978 and 1979. It is understood we place a bronze plaque on the project indicating the timber is supplied by Weyerhauser [sic].

To go back to what this means to the present sculptor's contract: In the early spring of 1979, five of the six units were dropped; and somewhere about that time it was decided that the sculptor would not stand the cost of the sculpture project (which was now the designing and carving of the three trees in the Meier and Frank court). He would be engaged with a fee of $58,000, and the developers would stand the costs. There would be a time limit of two years. This time limit was later cut back to one year and the fee to $30,000. Now, however, it looks like two summers will be used up, which is equivalent to two years since it is not practical to do much during the winter.

I agree with the suggestions of the new designs—subject matter from the forest and nature as being appropriate (as presented at the July 5 meeting). However, it represents a fresh start and more delay. In addition to the preliminary work of making models and scouting for timber in 1977, 1978 and 1979, I have been working almost continuously on this project since the first of May, 1979. I'm not sure where the year of work is intended to start, nor have I been informed on the terms of the contract we are making shortly except that I have been advised my expenses should be paid.

I thought you should have this statement directly from me since it no doubt will have some bearing on the contract.

Chapter 32

Beyond Expectations

By Abby Sher

In the spring of 1977 my brother Ron and I learned we would soon be receiving the proceeds of an investment our father had made in our names when we were children. It was going to be more than we required for our immediate needs, so we decided to invest in a property together. Ron, who lives in the Seattle area, found a beachfront property he wanted to show me in the San Juan Islands.

I flew up to Seattle from Los Angeles to see it. With his wife, Eva-Maria, we drove to Anacortes, took the one-hour ferry ride to Orcas Island, and from the ferry landing made our way to the property we were considering. It met our criteria as an investment, but gazing out to sea, we noticed a small forest-covered island less than a mile off the coast. It turned out that this seventeen-acre island was also for sale and for roughly the same price as the beachfront property. In little more than an hour we were speeding toward Reef Island on the motorboat of our realtor, Wally Gudgell.

As we approached the island, we saw the outlines of a small wooden house unlike any we'd seen before. It sat on a rise, just above the high-tide level. Once inside, we could see that all of its parts were fitted together using no nails at all. The floor was dirt and the doors were missing. But it was otherwise in good condition. According to Wally, the front door was in storage for safekeeping because

Reef Island's *Replica of a Haida House #3*, 1958, red cedar, 14' × 22'. Photograph courtesy Anna Vaughan Hanson

it featured a large carving of an eagle. We sensed a mystery unfolding and were excited as we explored the island's forests, beaches, and moss-covered slopes dotted with wildflowers.

Barely a week later, Ron and I were in the seller's office in Seattle. In addition to the many technical questions we asked regarding the island and our possible purchase of it, we also had questions about the house. When was it built? Who built it, and for whom? Might the builder be able to help us complete it for our use?

We were told that a previous owner, a Mrs. Hart, had commissioned an artist, Dudley Carter, to build the house for her. It was first constructed in Bellevue, Washington, then disassembled, the parts labeled, and reconstructed on Reef Island. There was even a short film of its assembly on Reef. Although the house was a replica of the kind of houses the Haida Indians had built in western Canada, its builder, Dudley Carter, was not himself an Indian. We were advised that he was very old, very hard of hearing, pretty much out of it, and we would be wasting our time looking him up.

In spite of the warning and not expecting much, we decided to look him up anyway. Maybe he could conjure up some recollection of what was intended for the house or show us drawings of the original design.

When we arrived at Dudley's, we found him—in a stocking cap, well-worn checkered pants, and plaid shirt of a different pattern—outdoors, busy at work in the yard of another, larger Haida Indian-style house. Peering inside, we saw that he had been sleeping in a sleeping bag. Outside, scattered everywhere, were large and small cedar sculptures: some in progress and some finished, large pieces of driftwood ready for carving, and stacks of hand-split cedar.

Beyond Expectations

Dudley greeted us warmly, and when he heard we were looking into buying Reef Island, he was delighted. When we asked him if he could recommend someone to help us make the house habitable, he pulled a small calendar from his pocket. After studying it for a moment, he said he could make the time—though this was not what we had asked. He explained that he'd been commissioned to depict the westward movement of the pioneers in larger-than-life-size relief carvings on the façade of a new regional shopping center to be built in Clackamas, Oregon, and the project was on hold. He showed us drawings of covered wagons, mule trains, and pioneers. Students would transfer the drawings onto wood for Dudley to carve and install on the shopping center's façade.

Next, Dudley showed us his scrapbooks. One of them had a double-page spread from a 1941 *Life* magazine of the mural Diego Rivera had painted at the Golden Gate International Exposition on Treasure Island in San Francisco Bay in 1939. I was a great admirer of Diego Rivera and was amazed to see that Dudley was represented at the very center of the mural carving a monumental wooden sculpture with an axe. This was only one of three representations of Dudley. In another, Dudley was standing with a small notebook protruding from his pocket, and it was on this notebook that Rivera signed the mural!

Dudley explained to us that the notebook was his timber cruiser's notebook and that timber cruising had been his occupation for many years. The job of a timber cruiser, he told us, was to survey the forests on foot and by canoe, charting and estimating the value of the timber stands so logging companies could bid on the timber in a particular tract. The job entailed traveling and camping in the woods for weeks or even months at a time. He also briefly mentioned his teenage years in an Indian village in Canada, where he'd first taken an interest in carving.

Ron and I soon realized that, rather than being "out of it," Dudley, who was eighty-seven at the time, was as sharp as anyone I've ever known of any age. The breadth of his experience was far-reaching and his vivid memories dated back to the late nineteenth century. We were enthralled.

Filmmaker Abby Sher and Dudley took to the forest in 1979 to reenact his days as a timber cruiser for Abby's film, *Dudley Carter*. Photograph courtesy Abby Sher

Whereas we were initially worried at the thought of Dudley working on the island, which had no dock, no drinking water except what we carried by boat, no electricity, no phone service, no cooking facilities, and no bathroom, it soon became clear that on the island Dudley would be in his element. If he were to die there, he would have died living the life he loved. We also knew he had much to teach us.

Once Ron and I had completed our purchase of the island, we returned there, this time with Dudley, to plan our next steps. When we arrived, straightaway Dudley set up a timber cruiser's campfire so we'd have a way to cook before the house was ready for a fireplace. It was around this campfire that we got to know Dudley, spending many happy evenings listening to the well-told stories of his fascinating life.

Next, Dudley set to work making a back door

for the Haida house. Once the door was in, he created a lock for it that didn't require a key—only a piece of wood, a string, and knowing the trick to open it. He also made wooden shutters to prevent storms from battering the big sea-facing glass windows. He advised us on the floor and a fireplace for indoor cooking, and we brought in others to do this work.

The "Portland Project," as Dudley called the Clackamas shopping center commission he'd told us about when we first met, was still on hold, so there was time for more projects on the island. Dudley built an outhouse for us with a beautifully designed—and signed—hand-split cedar door featuring a carving of a half moon. He also built a bunkhouse with a corner post incorporating a carving of a ram's head. He used the same nail-free construction he had learned from the Indians for both structures.

In the fall of 1978, after working on and off the island for several months, Dudley heard the Portland project was a go, and although scaled back from the original proposal, it would still be an exciting and challenging commission. Instead of creating relief carvings for the shopping center's façade, Dudley would now be carving three old-growth cedars for the center's interior. They would be placed between the food court and the skating rink and rise up beside the escalator to the floors above.

Not long before I met Dudley, I had helped a friend make a short film and, in doing so, had learned the basic steps of filmmaking. As I watched Dudley working and listened to his vivid descriptions of the various chapters of his remarkable life, I began to want to share my experience of him with others. When he told me he was about to begin work on the shopping center project, I decided to make a film. The carving by axe of the trees would constitute the present action of the film, intercut with the story of the Northwest over nearly a century as experienced by Dudley: homesteading in British Columbia; living as a teenager in a Kwakiutl Indian village, Alert Bay, where his father was a teacher; working on the construction of the Stave Lake Dam; life in the woods as a timber cruiser; the Depression; entering a soap-carving contest where he won an art scholarship and a commission from the Seattle Art Museum; witnessing the building of the Golden Gate Bridge in San Francisco; carving at the Golden Gate International Exposition while Diego Rivera was painting him into his mural; and the many other dramatic and colorful chapters of Dudley's life. Although I was a novice, Dudley's enormous enthusiasm for the film project and his absolute confidence that I would do his life justice made up for any lack of courage I might have felt.

Dudley finished his Reef Island projects and set about finding three trees of a size suitable for the Clackamas commission. He eventually located them on Mount Saint Helens and supervised their removal and transport, making sure to preserve the bark, as he said, "so they look like they're timbers straight from the forest." Remarkably, the trees were removed just eight months before Mount Saint Helens erupted, leaving a trail of lava where the forest had been.

I wasn't organized to begin filming when the trees were cut down and transported from Mount Saint Helens to Clackamas, though Ron was present for this first stage. Instead, I used photographs combined with sound effects to represent these events. I was, however, on the site for the trees' arrival in Clackamas and filmed as a crane hoisted them from the truck beds and, under Dudley's expert supervision, placed them where they would be carved.

As a practical matter, Dudley decided to live in a small trailer on what would become the shopping center's parking lot. The carving of the trees and the building of the shopping center would take about the same amount of time. So when the center and the sculptures were finished, Dudley could move

Santa Monica's Mayfair Theater marquee announcing the showing of Abby Sher's film, *Dudley Carter*
Photograph courtesy Abby Sher

his trailer in time for the parking lot to be paved.

In addition to filming Dudley on the site as he worked with his axe from dawn until sometimes late into the night, I found existing film footage of Dudley's earlier life. This included a 1940s *Eyes and Ears of the World* newsreel entitled "Sculptor Uses Forest for Studio!" featuring Dudley carving a massive living cedar tree, film footage from the 1939 Golden Gate International Exposition, and the footage of Dudley assembling the Haida house on Reef Island. I also found historical photographs that illustrated events exactly as Dudley remembered them, such as his description of a Kwakiutl Indian potlatch. This was thrilling for both of us.

There were some chapters of Dudley's life for which we didn't have film footage or photographs, and for these Dudley made drawings or reenacted his experiences. We filmed him during a snowstorm snowshoeing along the banks of a raging river, acting as if he was surveying the forests. On another day we filmed him building a timber cruiser's campfire over which he hung a pot he'd just filled with snow for boiling water; then he set up his tent and pretended to be making his cruiser's notes at the end of the day. What fun we had!

When the film was finished, Dudley, then ninety-one, flew to Los Angeles to be guest of honor at a screening I held for friends and family in the Mayfair Theater, an old movie house in Santa Monica. He attended other screenings too, such as the one at the Forest History Society in Seattle and at Gibsons where his daughter and son-in-law lived. But for the most part, Dudley was on to other projects. I would visit him from time to time, and he always had something new to show me. In his early nineties, he was still making proposals that would have taken him years to complete.

It was a great privilege to know Dudley and to spend as much time with him as I did.

Abby Sher lives in Los Angeles. After filming Dudley and his sculptures at Clackamas, she loved the idea of art in a shopping center so much that she developed Edgemar, a mixed-use center in Santa Monica where she founded the Santa Monica Museum of Art. Sher currently serves on the board of the Southern California Institute of Architecture and wild Up, a modern music collective.
Photograph courtesy Abby Sher

Attitude is Everything
By Ron Sher

Dudley was a good friend. It was a very rich experience for me that our lives overlapped and intersected for a period of twelve or thirteen years. I first met Dudley when he was eighty-seven, and I had the pleasure of celebrating his one-hundredth birthday with him. So much of my Dudley connection is best described by anecdotes—or call them vignettes.

I mention the rich experience, for the connection to Dudley was also a connection to the past. I remember Dudley telling me about a man he had worked with in the woods when Dudley was probably in his early twenties. The man was about eighty and had come to California for the 1849 Gold Rush. I was about fifty years younger than Dudley, old enough to treasure the connection through time.

Dudley talked about how the old Indian ways were changed by three factors: the chain saw, the outboard engine, and liquor. Dudley was fortunate to have lived as a teenager and young man in the remote tribal parts of the Northwest where the effects of these changes were still in their naissance. The thought that the man I knew had witnessed potlatches and tree burials, carved sea canoes, and learned cedar construction with primitive hand tools was remarkable.

The changes in lifestyle that Dudley experienced were also remarkable: from the early years, when he spent months at a time in the forest as a timber cruiser—where most of his provisions were the same as those on shipboard, and he was afflicted by what he called "a scurvy condition"—to the visit my wife and I took him on to Disneyland with our two young daughters when he was ninety-two. He took the Jungle Cruise ride, but he especially enjoyed careening down the Matterhorn on a bobsled. I hadn't thought it was such a wise move, taking him on the bobsled, but Dudley insisted, reminiscing how as a child he and his brothers had done somersaults in a canoe while running rapids. Dudley had tremendous energy and joie de vivre.

Dudley's life and experiences spanned an era of enormous change, yet he was able to adapt very well; he had one foot solidly planted in the past, evident in the cadence of his speech, his colorful expressions, and his quaint, slightly British accent. He had a twinkle in his eye and a wonderful sense of humor.

Dudley was always very frugal and for many years scraped by, cobbling together a livelihood mainly through his art, his timber cruising, and his cedar products business. He was always concerned about having sufficient reserves and spent money only on necessities. One time I remember he found two pairs of soccer shoes for ten dollars and wore them for years, cleats and all.

Just to function on his own, with his poor hearing and eyesight, would have been a problem to a lesser man. A phone conversation was very difficult because of his hearing. It was amazing that he could even drive, but he did, navigating by landmarks instead of street signs. He couldn't get a driver's license in Bellevue, but every two years he would make a pilgrimage to a rural licensing bureau in Sedro Woolley where he was somehow able to extend his license. Driving with or near Dudley was terrifying, so I did the driving except when I was exhausted. We drove down to Mount Saint Helens and then way up the mountain to an amazing stand of old-growth western red cedars. We climbed around in the woods with the Weyerhaeuser employees while Dudley selected the three trees he wished to use for the Clackamas project. He was very specific about how he wanted them felled and that the bark had to be protected; much of the discussion was conducted in gestures due to Dudley's hearing issue.

Dudley had about ten acres in Redmond, which is now part of the Microsoft campus. That is where we originally met him and where he built the second of his four Haida houses. It had beautiful carvings on the two front corners and on and above the central front door. With the door closed the combined carvings resembled a thirteen-foot-high totem pole. Dudley sold this Haida house to an art teacher he knew with the understanding that the teacher would take delivery upon retirement, which he did. But Dudley, already in his early nineties at the time, was too busy at work on the Clackamas project to build himself another house, so he hired Kim Hoelting, who had been his apprentice and was a builder and craftsman, to help with the structural parts of a fourth Haida house on the Redmond property.

About fifty yards behind the Redmond house was an opening in the trees where Dudley had piles and piles of cedar scattered, it seemed, but actually in a large oval. To me, the piles looked mostly like construction debris that should be cleaned up and burned. I certainly learned otherwise. One afternoon Dudley gave me a tour of the scattered cedar. Each pile represented a project that he had planned—and some were major projects.

He was excited about each pile—he knew where the wood came from and how he would construct and carve it. He was eager to get started when he had the time. In spite of having immense hearing problems and failing eyesight, and weighing only about 120 pounds, Dudley was indomitable. At ninety, he could camp out on Reef Island or hop on an airplane to Disneyland. He could and would adapt, but he didn't change. One of my favorite expressions is "attitude is everything," and Dudley had one of the most consistently positive attitudes I've ever encountered.

Ron Sher is an investor and developer who specializes in projects that will enhance communities. He is also the founder and owner of Third Place Books. Sher is active in environmental issues focusing mainly around cycling, livable cities, and land use issues—principally open space and farm land. He shares his time between his farm on Whidbey Island and a residence in Bellevue, Washington.
Photograph courtesy Ron Sher

Chapter 33

A Timely Request

From a conversation with Ted Nelson

It was springtime 1979 when I received a telephone call at my office at the Weyerhaeuser Company in Longview, Washington. A lady with a youthful voice described logs her wood-carver friend, Dudley Carter, wanted for a project. The name Dudley Carter didn't register with me at the time, but as a raw materials manager for the company at Longview, it was not unusual for me to get requests from the public. I told the caller I'd be glad to talk about it, and we booked an appointment May 18th.

The day of the appointment came and the two arrived at my office. In walked an elderly man—I later learned that he was eighty-eight years old at the time—a diminutive old gentleman. The woman was a little smaller even than he, dark haired, maybe about thirty years old, and pretty! The old gentleman could hardly hear and the young lady was his interpreter. I was just bowled over—I couldn't help but like that pair. Soon, I was calling him Dudley. The young lady was Abby Sher, who was producing a film about Dudley.

Dudley explained that he needed three large cedar logs. He'd been commissioned to create a major sculpture for a shopping center to be built in

Clackamas, a suburb southeast of Portland, Oregon. He produced a portfolio filled with pictures of his work and lists of honors and awards he'd received. I was impressed and immediately realized I'd seen his work before. The portfolio included a photograph of Dudley with Edward G. Robinson and Diego Rivera beside a sculpture Dudley had done at the San Francisco fair in 1940. I remembered being at the fair as a kid of about ten and seeing his sculpture there—it made an impression on me. And here was Dudley, in my office nearly forty years later, looking for more wood to swing his axes at.

Dudley spoke a bit about his early days, highlighting the time he spent as a timber cruiser evaluating stands of great trees. I told him I'd also cruised timber while working as a forester for the Diamond Match Company. We had a good chat about archaic procedures employed in the early days and talked about logging camps, sharing colorful stories that came from those experiences. We laughed about having two sets of long john's, a wet pair and a dry pair. We slept in the dry pair. The wet pair never dried and we'd have to don them again the next morning. By the time we finished talking I really wanted to help Dudley with his project.

I called George Kilen, a forester on my staff, and asked him to go with Dudley to locate trees to meet his specifications. George was about six-foot-six, such a contrast to Dudley.

George took Dudley and Abby to the forests at the headwaters of the Toutle River near Mount Saint Helens, where suitable trees were likely to be found. They were gone for several days before they settled on three cedars that met Dudley's criteria.

We agreed that Weyerhaeuser would fall the trees and deliver them to Clackamas. Dudley would pay for the trees, and Weyerhaeuser would absorb the cost of harvesting and delivery. Dudley was more than satisfied with the price we negotiated. The last of the three large trees was delivered to the shopping center site on August 9, 1979.

Thinking back on the timing of things, I realized that Dudley first came to my office with his request for the trees exactly one year prior to the day that the volcano erupted. If Dudley hadn't needed those trees for his project, they'd be somewhere up in Saskatchewan now, turned to ash by the eruption's devastating blast. Instead, they are preserved as works of art. Dudley titled the three-part work *Reflections of the Primitive Background of the West Coast*. To me, they are reflections of a friendship formed as a result of a timely request.

Ted Nelson (1931–2010) with his wife, Sharlene, and *Owl*, a gift from Dudley. After Nelson arranged to obtain cedars for Dudley's Clackamas project, the Nelsons maintained a close friendship with the artist. Sharlene Nelson authored two fine articles about Dudley Carter. One ran in the fall 1980 edition of Mountain West Airlines' magazine. The other appeared in *Highlights for Children*, November 1992. After Ted Nelson's retirement from the Weyerhaeuser Company, he and Sharlene enjoyed life as freelance writers. They published guidebooks about West Coast lighthouses and the Columbia-Snake River Inland Waterway and wrote books for children about logging in the Old West, national parks and monuments, and famous people.

Photograph Mary Sikkema

Chapter 34

Delivering Three Big Cedars

By Jesse Wilt

This story first appeared in *Loggers World*, December 1979, and is reprinted here with the permission of Kevin Core, owner, *Loggers World* magazine. The definitions have been added.

Getting out an old growth red cedar, and delivering it unbroken, is a large order, and when it's hollow in the center with core rot, the job looks pretty near impossible. But let a couple loggers hash it over for a day or two and they'll come up with a solution. Then add a World's Champion climber, two expert cutters, a top-notch cat skinner, a shovel operator who knows his stuff, and a loading crew with lots of savvy, and the job is practically done. All it takes from there on is a truck driver that can snake an oversize load through Portland's rush hour traffic and two 30-ton cranes to pick the load off and lay it down very gently at the end of the trip.

> **Cat Skinner**
> *The person who operates a Caterpillar tractor*

At least, that's what spelled success when Weyerhaeuser Company undertook to deliver three old growth cedar logs to a new shopping center site in Portland where they become raw material for wood sculptor Dudley Carter.

Locating three trees to supply the logs took

Larry Downing and Duane Hardy looking the situation over. They put the strap on the tree to see just how Larry could manage it when he got up in the tree.

quite a bit of looking. While there's some big cedar still standing to choose from, these had to be of exact size and conformation and each one was hand picked by Mr. Carter. George Kilen, a Forester in Weyerhaeuser's Longview Raw Materials division, spent several days cruising the Coldwater and Castle Creek areas of Camp Baker with Mr. Carter looking for exactly the right trees.

The first two were smaller (one six foot and one eight foot in diameter) and were cut and delivered without too much special care. The third one, however, had complications. Located in a canyon below the 3713 road up Castle Creek, it was eleven feet at the base, and had about a ten-degree lean downhill. The answer to the lean was to use jacks and drop it uphill, but a couple of whacks with the back of an axe and it sounded like a ripe watermelon, so the big problem was how to keep it from breaking up as it fell.

They've been using metal straps to keep loads of logs together for quite a while, especially on bundles of sinkers, so somebody suggested using these bands on the tree, with a climber putting them in place. Larry Downing from Castle Rock, Camp Baker Head Cutter and holder of more than one world's championship in tree topping and speed climbing, got the job. He spent half of an extra hot July day getting the straps all in place and clamped tight. Put a strap every five feet up to the first limbs, about fifty feet. Bullbuck Duane Hardy and George Kilen were groundmen, toting supplies and bullcooking.

It looked like a storybook job out there in the big timber on a nice day, but the no-see-'ums were so thick under the

Bullbuck
Foreman of a cutting crew

Bullcooking
Assisting with camp chores – in this case helping the crew loading logs

Larry Downing at work! There weren't many limbs in the way but there was one big burl at the upper end that the artist wanted left intact, as he would incorporate it into the total carving. When putting on the metal straps Larry would pin one end of the strap to the tree then carry the strap around the tree to hook it up.

The Master Carver

Duane Hardy working in with the tail holt cat to clear the stumps and rocks out of the way, making a soft bed to drop the tree on.

trees they wiped them off their faces and arms by the handful. They'd get under a guy's hard hat and set up a show line along the edge of his hairline, and between them and the sweat rolling down his face it was just plain misery. By the time the sun got down into the canyon far enough to drive the gnats off, it was eleven o'clock and since the whole area was on 'hoot-owl' it was time to quit. The day the cutters came in it was cold and foggy in the canyon, and the gnats were waiting for them, hungrier than ever.

Duane Hardy cleared out a bed for the tree using an old tail holt cat. Some windfalls and the stumps left when the right of way timber was felled had to be moved out of the way, and some good-sized rocks rolled down the sidehill. If there was any way to make certain this tree had an easy landing, these fellows were looking for it.

Cutters were Dick Music and Jerry Davis, both with a lot of years at Camp Baker. They spent quite a while checking out the best lay for least breakage, and that ten-degree downhill lean didn't help matters, either.

Hoot-owl
A logging operation limited to the early morning hours when fire danger later in the day will require a cessation of operations

When they put in the face cut it showed up the extensive core rot, and the chances of getting the old boy down in one piece began to look pretty poor. There were only about sixteen inches of solid wood on the outside and the center was honeycomb.

George Kilen and Dick Music decided a few more straps just above the cut would be a good idea. At this point the chances for success looked pretty poor.

Cutter Dick Music, taking a good look at the downhill lean.

Delivering Three Big Cedars   149

THREE BIG CEDARS:

It was good, holding wood and the jacks had a solid base. Dick Music works on the final cut while Jerry Davis and George Kilen wait by the jack pump.

It's starting to talk as the jacks go to work.

By cutting into what appeared to be a more solid "foot" on the back side of the tree, Dick said he thought they'd find a bigger area of holding wood for the jacks, and he was sure right about that. Then with the jacks in place and everything ready to go, they added several more straps just above the cut for extra insurance. Everybody on the place had their fingers crossed when they finally dropped the tree, but it came down nice and soft and easy, right into the slot cleared for it, and only one of the holding straps broke. But yarding it out to the road busted several more, and they had to be replaced. It was a heck of a lot easier, though, with it laying on the ground.

Yarding
The act or process of conveying logs to a landing

It was a week later, on another hot August day, when the shovel moved in to load the log out. The truck was contracted from Al Price Log Trucking of Kelso. It was truck number 7, a KW with a

Cummins 380, and driven by Dean Buck. Dean has been driving for Al for two and a half years, mostly out of Randle and Astoria. He'd hauled one of the smaller logs, and wanted this one loaded with the big end to the front but there just wasn't any way to get it between the eight-foot stakes. Five feet from the butt it still measured ten feet. Loaded small end to the front, it had a pretty good sway going down the logging road to Camp Baker, but some added binders took care of that problem.

KW
Kenworth truck. Kenworth is an American manufacturer of medium and heavy-duty trucks based in Kirkland, Washington.

The first stop on the way out was at Camp Baker scale ramp where scalers Dale King and Jack Farrand scaled it out as #1 Sawmill, 46 feet long, 11 feet 3 inches on the butt and 60 inches on the small end. Gross scale was 8,040 feet and it weighed 58,300 pounds. Hauling required two overwidth permits, one for Washington and one for Oregon.

Moving down Interstate 5 was a smooth, easy trip shepherded by Al Price driving pilot car. The only near casualties were some out-of-state tourists who'd obviously never seen a big log before. They'd get so interested in looking they forgot about driving, until they'd suddenly realize just how big that load was they were getting so close to. Then they'd get scared and take off like a rabbit heading for the briar patch. Cross chatter on CB had a lot to say, too, and some of it not too complimentary, wondering what in heck we planned to do with an old, rotten log. One CB'er even had us hauling this one down to set up on the Capital steps at Salem. Sounded like a novel idea, but old schoolmate Vic Atiyeh might not approve.

Destination was a new multi-million dollar shopping center under construction between I-205 and 82nd Street in SE Portland. The two logs already delivered were waiting inside an eight-foot

Tree was fell by Dick Music and Jerry Davis. Tail Holt Cat brought the big Cedar up to the road. Choker setters were two cutters and a forester. Bullbuck ran Cat and bossed the job. In the picture above the yarding job is all but done. Log is out and ready to be loaded.

Log couldn't be loaded out big end forward, too big to fit between the stakes. Tom Reynolds operated the loading machine. Working on the job were George Kilen, Jerry Berrier the logging foreman, John Pluard second loading, Tom Reynolds the load machine operator and truck driver Dean Buck. Log is about loaded and ready for the trip to Portland.

Dick Music putting in the face cut and hoping for some solid wood.

Delivering Three Big Cedars

Left: Straps in place. Purpose to keep the tree from splitting. Right: Al Price trucking doing the hauling, Larry Price is the Vice-President of the trucking firm. In the picture above George Kilen and Dean Buck are checking binders and other details before pulling onto I-5 for the last leg of the journey to Portland.

cyclone fence for this third member to arrive. Also waiting were two thirty-ton cranes all set up and ready, and they eased the old boy off the truck, over the fence and onto the blocks between the other two logs. It was a neat, precise very careful job of unloading.

You know, there was sure a lot of extra special care taken with this old, hollow log.

Now, it's ready for Dudley Carter to turn it into one of his unique wood sculptures. Mr. Carter, a very unusual gentleman himself, was born in New Westminster, BC. He's no stranger to logging, either, as his first job was greasing skids for his father's logging company out of Tipperary, BC. He worked as a faller, was also a timber cruiser, and then a Forestry Engineer. Started carving in 1932 and was the featured artist at the San Francisco World's Fair in 1939. He's also been a professor of Sculpture at the University of Washington. Two of his many awards in the world of art were the Music and Art Foundation Award in 1950, and the HUD International Sculpture Award in 1973.

Working in wood, his tools a double-bitted falling axe and an adze, he has become internationally famous. His sculptures nearly all based on Pacific-Northwest Indian legends, can be found all over the world from Seattle to New Zealand to New York. Most are on a grand scale, ranging in size up to fifty-six feet tall, and from four to twelve feet in diameter.

This group at the shopping center will, according to Mr. Carter, be completed about the time of his next birthday, on May 6, 1980, when he will be 89 years old.

End of the journey! Truck is spotted between the cranes that will unload the log and set it inside the shopping center, behind the fence. The first two big cedar logs are inside the fence and this 'big brother' soon shall be. These three logs will become three wood sculpture figures in the entry of the Sunnyside shopping center now under construction.

Chapter 35

Spirit of the Northwest

From the writing of James C. Michaelsen

My first meeting with Dudley Carter was with a design team around a conference room table in 1977. I was project director with the architectural firm of John Graham & Company, working on the Clackamas Town Center in Oregon. To emphasize the spirit of the Northwest, the designers wanted to commission major sculptures for the interior courts of the shopping mall. The subjects were selected early on, and Dudley Carter was the first artist considered for the job.

Talk at the meeting revolved around such things as themes, scheduling, and fees. In a matter of minutes, I realized that Mr. Carter was deaf. He was much older than I had expected, and although he wore a hearing aid, he could be as deaf as he chose to be at any moment. Part of the meeting concerned hearing aid batteries and our offer to send out for new ones. This offer was declined—firmly.

The Clackamas sculpture concept was a large order, but as I came to know and appreciate Dudley's work, I thought him to be perfect for the job—with one exception. Well into his eighties and deaf as a stone, a number of us wondered if he could go the course and complete the monumental

Spirit of the Northwest   153

Primitive Woman in progress, 1979–1980, at Clackamas Town Center construction site prior to the move to her permanent location. Photograph Al Russell

Primitive Woman during the move to her permanent location inside Clackamas Town Center, Portland, Oregon. Photograph Al Russell

studio on Bel-Red Road to deliver some sketches of architectural details. Dark and off the road a bit, I got the impression his place was swarming with dogs, big ones. To gain entrance we needed to pull a rope that rang bells or turned on a light to announce visitors. Dudley appeared and led us to his studio. While showing us models of works in progress, he suddenly—from a standing start—jumped atop his worktable like a monkey. At no time in my life could I have done the same.

Once Dudley got the go ahead, he was off and running, eager to get the show on the road. In the midst of all the activity involving document preparation, owner approval, and agency approval, I kept imagining Dudley out there somewhere contacting tree growers, cruising the forests selecting trees, and overseeing the arrival of the giant logs at the job site. This took a great deal of manpower and horsepower, but Dudley kept after the crew until he had the logs just as he wanted them. Damage to the trees and their bark had to be held to a minimum.

work on time. Opening dates are of vital importance to mall developers. However, Dudley seemed to be so eager to begin work, so full of energy, that we began to feel we were holding up the job if we didn't turn him loose. The owners felt the same in spite of the age factor.

My wife and I had reason to visit Dudley's

From the day the logs arrived on site, Dudley was atop them rain or shine, swinging his axe or his adze or wielding his chain saw with no let up. It wasn't long before he moved a small house trailer on site next to his logs. Local authorities had some problems with a live-in trailer on site, but it was next

Mythical Beast is permanently placed.

The *Forest Garland* cedar moves into position with *Mythical Beast*.

Primitive Woman on the move, the cedar's hollowness exposed. Photographs Al Russell

Spirit of the Northwest

Primitive Woman being installed in the center's interior
Photograph Al Russell

to impossible to argue with Dudley. His batteries could go dead on a moment's notice. The trailer stayed.

As construction progressed it reached a point where the logs had to be brought inside and set in place. It took heavy machinery to move them—machinery that would not fit through the center's doors—so the building would have to be completed around the sculptures. Dudley resisted this strongly, but it had to be done. He disappeared from the job for a few days. When he returned he found his precious logs in their own court. Lighting had been installed and the logs were not damaged. He just took off his jacket, donned his hard hat, grabbed his tools, and scrambled up the scaffolding to send the chips flying once more.

Dudley Carter never came across as the artist stereotype the workmen had expected. He seemed to be one of them—a worker, a lumberjack who dressed like them and could work wonders with his tools. Fascinated by what he was creating and in awe of his skills, they had the best introduction to sculpture anyone could ever have.

When *Primitive Woman*—or the Madonna, as she was known on site—was upright and the sculptor had brought his work down to a respectable point on her bosom, the owners' representative, impressed with Dudley's work, suggested he continue his carving down a bit more. People who had been following the work with interest were aghast—the Madonna with a low-cut décolletage? Shocking! After a while, the fervor subsided and the work went on.

Massive cedar trees aren't always as hearty as they appear. Al Russell, project architect for Clackamas and an avid photographer, provided us with a generous assortment of photographs taken during

Forest Garland, 1980, red cedar, 36' × 7'
Part of *Reflections of the Primitive Background of the West Coast*, Clackamas Town Center, Portland, Oregon
Photograph 'Lyn Lambert

Primitive Woman, 1980
Red cedar, 30' × 8'
Part of *Reflections of the Primitive Background of the West Coast,* Clackamas Town Center, Portland, Oregon
Photograph 'Lyn Lambert

looked scruffy, to say the least. Foreseeing this problem, Mr. Carter had carefully peeled and saved the bark he had removed to reach the carving surfaces. Now he brought out the meticulously cut pieces to fit the damaged areas and attached them with copper nails. A little color touch-up and the trees looked pristine once again.

Dudley titled his artistic triad—composed of *Mythical Beast, Primitive Woman,* and *Forest Garland*—*Reflections of the Primitive Background of the West Coast.* An enormous amount of intelligence, hard work, and cooperative effort went into the threesome, and in them Dudley Carter created a true expression of the spirit of the Northwest.

construction. As the photos show, some trees are solid and some are far from it. Some seem to be made of separate trunks rising from the same root system, growing together toward the top. One can see how fragile they were and appreciate the care that was taken to avoid damage.

The treatment the logs had endured since their harvesting—transport on a logging truck and the move to the mall interior—had left their marks. Once they were in a standing position, the cedars

Spirit of the Northwest 157

Mythical Beast, 1980, red cedar, 39′ × 6′
Part of *Reflections of the Primitive Background of the West Coast*,
Clackamas Town Center, Portland, Oregon
Photograph 'Lyn Lambert

James Michaelsen (1920–2015) graduated from Illinois Institute of Technology. After WWII, he returned to Chicago, worked in his father's architectural firm, and then joined the Harper Richards design group before leaving Chicago to take a position with the John Graham firm in Seattle. He was made an associate in 1970. He retired in 1983 to travel, settling in Florida in 1988.
Photograph Gary Jentoft, Seattle

Mythical Beast at Columbia Gorge Interpretive Center Museum, Stevenson, Washington
Photograph Lisa Lambert

> To make way for a $100 million makeover and expansion of the Clackamas Town Center in the summer of 2004, three heavy-duty cranes and an eight-man crew lifted the giant artworks from their foundation, loaded them onto trucks, and sent them off to a new home at the Columbia Gorge Interpretive Center Museum in Stevenson, Washington. Too large to fit inside the museum, the three huge sculpted cedars now stand outside the entrance.
>
> The memory of *Reflections of the Primitive Background of the Northwest* will be kept alive at the Clackamas shopping mall in the form of an eighteen-inch-high scale model created by Portland artist and sculptor Robert Watts.

Chapter 36

A Most Decent Proposal

From the writing of Nancy Crozier

In September of 1979, as a third-year student at the Museum Art School in Portland, now the Pacific Northwest College of Art and Design, I ran across an ad requesting a sculptor's assistant. Short of funds, curious, and eager to find art-related work during the school year, I rang the number.

I explained that the hours would have to be after school and wondered how much daylight that would allow for sculpting. The artist-advertiser said that what he really needed was a contact in town to drive him places, purchase supplies, and help him arrange living quarters on his work site. He explained that the contractors at the construction site where he would be working didn't want him to camp on site, but he had a plan in mind.

My potential employer invited me to meet him and see the site—Clackamas Town Center. I wasn't prepared for what awaited me. Three enormous tree trunks lay in a flat bulldozed area flanked by portable buildings and not much else.

Even more surprising was the wizened, wiry character whose energy and sparkle rivaled that of my youngest friends. I resolved immediately to take the post and do what I could to help this aged man achieve his Herculean task. Dudley told me he was eighty-nine, but I never really knew how old he was for sure. His age didn't seem to bother him or anyone else for that matter.

Dudley's first concern was getting some sort of lodging on the site. Since he would be there

Dudley holds a clay and wood maquette of *Primitive Woman*, one of his triad of cedars at Clackamas Town Center, Portland, Oregon.
Photograph Sharlene Nelson

several months, I suggested that a trailer might do. After some investigation, it appeared that buying one secondhand would be the most practical solution. Dudley didn't want to purchase a trailer, but said he would rent one from me if I would buy it. My student budget had no room in it for a trailer. So Dudley worked out a loan and I became the owner of a little trailer I had spotted. I arranged for it to be brought to the site and assumed the role of landlady.

I performed a variety of odd jobs for Dudley, none of which involved carving. I brought groceries and propane to his trailer home, where he quickly settled in under what I considered Spartan circumstances. He said they were luxurious, maintaining that he could sleep just as well in the hollow of a tree. He even set up an outdoor shower, and it bothered him not at all to make use of it!

Once a week we would go to dinner together, and Dudley entertained me with stories of his youth and his art career. Interspersed with tales of adventure were accounts of illnesses and injuries he had endured. He had a decided hobble that he attributed to a foot injury. It plagued him particularly in wet weather. It was true testimony to his grit that he carried on carving in the most inclement weather and under such primitive conditions.

He came to my home a few times to see how I was getting on with my work. Even though he had his own pressing deadlines, he found time to encourage and support me and to share suggestions regarding carving techniques. He was a well of wisdom.

I marveled at the progress Dudley made with his Clackamas carvings. The energy he put into the work was incredible. Even so, the process took longer than he expected. A technical hitch—difficulty in retaining bark on some of the uncarved portions of the tree trunks—although anticipated by Dudley, slowed things down considerably. On top of the carving complications, Dudley lived and worked amid the shopping center confusion, often having to move the trailer to accommodate the building process. Additionally, he had to make himself available to a film crew. He had agreed to be the subject of a documentary produced by Abby Sher, a filmmaker from Los Angeles. A good portion of the film featured the making of the Clackamas carvings. Through everything Dudley remained his usual gracious and almost maddeningly unruffled self, giving everyone his time.

His composure was really put to the test as a result of a stupid accident I had. While running errands and getting groceries for Dudley, I had an accident that virtually wrote off his car. I felt

At work on *Primitive Woman*. The oil drum on the left of the platform contained scraps from carving that Dudley burned to keep warm. He worked day and night, rain or shine. Plastic covering shielded him a bit from the elements, floodlights allowed him to work at night. Photograph Sharlene Nelson

Above and right: *Primitive Woman* and Dudley pose together as work progresses, 1980. Construction workers dubbed the lady Madonna. Photographs Sharlene Nelson

but had to decline.[1]

We corresponded often over the next ten years and I always felt I would see him again. I hoped to see his whole sculptural collection. It was not to be. I married and settled in England where I sculpted, taught, studied, and bore two children.

This amazing man touched my life profoundly, and my determination to sculpt and live in a creative vein was indelibly reinforced by his example.

Nancy Crozier was reared in Canada and attended art school in Portland, Oregon. In November 1996, when she wrote her recollections of Dudley, she resided in Middlesex, England, the busy young mother of two children, managing to sculpt and teach as well.

[1] *Dudley's wife Teresa passed away in 1975.*

dreadful, but it didn't even seem to upset him. He said it was a good thing—that he planned to trade the car in anyway. I never knew if this was true, but I was grateful to him for his equanimity.

With the imminent completion of the Clackamas project I grew increasingly despondent. But sadness changed to astonishment when Dudley surprised me with a marriage proposal! We had become good friends and our common interest in carving and art meant we never lacked for conversation. Dudley suggested a purely platonic relationship, one in which companionship was the bond between us. He said he would be able to help me in my career. I was truly flattered and deeply moved by his sincerity,

Chapter 37

Garland of Earthly Delights

Perceptions of Jon Kraft

When I study *Forest Garland* I envision Dudley Carter contemplating his own impending mortality and coming to grips with it through lessons learned in his relationship with the natural world.

The garland follows the grain of the wood. Dudley makes no attempt to manipulate or control what is given, rather he accentuates it and, simply and gracefully, fills the space with rich detail. This work speaks to me of Dudley's will to die the way he lived, in concert with nature.

Earth and sky merge about midpoint in the sculpture. Dudley has placed a small circular form here. Is it a blossom? Or is it a ripe seed about to fall to earth? I think it is a seed and it represents Dudley's own return to the earth.

Three ravens plunge headlong earthward and three butterflies flutter toward the sky. Three flowers nestle together, rising from undulating furrows of the earth. Forest Garland is one of three pieces of sculpture that comprise one work of art. Dudley makes lavish use of the threesome, a symbol for the cycle of life.

One raven's beak reaches toward a butterfly, which in fact ravens eat. They represent, to me, Dudley's acceptance of death—his awareness that life lives on life and that death is nearing. As the ravens head toward earth, butterflies and plants reach for the sky. That speaks to me of death and rebirth; what falls to earth is transformed into new life.

Dudley has placed coyote—creator and trickster in Native lore—in sky territory. There is always hidden wisdom where coyote appears. Coyote suggests a balance of sense and senselessness, wisdom and folly, and reminds us that playtime is necessary for health.

Forest Garland, 1980, red cedar, 36' × 7'
Clackamas Town Center, Portland, Oregon
Photograph Mary Sikkema

I like to think that Dudley explored his own mortality in this massive tree harvested from the flanks of Mount Saint Helens less than a year before it erupted. This great cedar escaped annihilation, and in this lively carving, Dudley Carter reminds us that death is not annihilation but transformation.

Jon Kraft with a mask of his own creation, a commissioned work inspired by Kwakwaka'wakw mythology and Asian tradition. Pursuing his interest in art, Kraft found himself at Dudley Carter's studio in Slough House Park in Redmond, Washington, shortly after Dudley's death. Apprenticed to Haida carver Ralph Bennett, artist-in-residence at the park, Kraft had an opportunity to define and refine his talent. Spending time with Dudley's sculptures displayed in the park, studying and restoring other Carter works in the Puget Sound area, and carving in Dudley's studio, he absorbed a sense of the spirit of the old master while learning much from Bennett. His work reflects his love of nature and his regard for Native ways, but is very much of his own design. At the time of this photo, Kraft was a busy husband, father, and sculptor, visiting area schools and other public venues to demonstrate his skills.
Photograph Mary Sikkema

Chapter 38

Meeting the Man in the Mural

Reminiscences of Masha Zakheim

When I began teaching at City College of San Francisco in the mid-1960s, I very quickly discovered in the college's Little Theater the amazing fresco, *Pan American Unity*, by Mexican artist Diego Rivera, who had been a friend of my father's. It is a very large work, twenty-two feet high and seventy-four feet long, created in ten sections at the Golden Gate International Exposition on Treasure Island in 1940.

Rivera worked on it daily during the Art in Action program conceived by architect Timothy Pflueger to replace a hastily departed European masterpieces exhibit, a feature of the first year of the fair. European owners had recalled the works, concerned over their safety with the outbreak of World War II.

Realizing what a fantastic teaching device the mural was, I began introducing it to my English classes as a subject for essays and to my humanities classes for art analyses. By the early 1980s I had learned on the job about the mural's fresco genre, the ground-earth palette, and its fascinating vignettes calling forth political, cultural, and historical subjects, both Mexican and local San Franciscan. Above all, the people portrayed by Rivera intrigued me.

When I heard that a figure so important that Rivera portrays him three times in the central section of the mural would be coming to San Francisco, I was elated. Indeed, that central figure wielding his timber cruising-cum-sculpting axe was Dudley

Dudley Carter portrayed three times in Diego Rivera's 1940 mural *Pan American Unity* at City College of San Francisco
Photograph Roberto Marquez, courtesy Masha Zakheim

Carter. By this time I had known Dudley for fifteen years, but only through Rivera's painted image. I timidly approached Mireille Piazzoni Wood, a friend of Dudley's and daughter of the well-known San Fransisco oil muralist Gottardo Piazzoni, about meeting Dudley, and she responded that—not only would it be all right—she would be delighted to introduce us.

We met when Dudley and his granddaughter, Anna, came to visit on their way back from a trip to the Yucatan in 1981. I have a photograph of Dudley and Anna taken at that time in front of Dudley's large redwood carving *Big Horn Ram*, a mountain ram that Rivera also depicted in his mural. *Ram* and Dudley are centrally located in the mural. Years later, Dudley would tell me that Rivera wanted him in the central frames of his fresco because Dudley was a totally North American artist, having never studied abroad. He had learned his sculpturing craft from the Native Americans of the Northwest, a fact that impressed Rivera. Students of the mural suspect that Rivera may have been further impressed by Dudley's art because it is highly evocative of the work of Mexican artist Mardonio Magana, another sculptor favored with inclusion in the huge mural.

At the time of Dudley's visit, *Ram* stood out of doors, freestanding in a bed of long grasses, and I was very embarrassed to show the sculpture to him. It had served as a football team mascot for the City College of San Francisco Rams, and fans of rival football teams had badly vandalized its natural wood finish with a coat of orange paint, now peeling. Not only had it been gratuitously painted, there were also random burn marks and even a few nails left over from ephemeral posted notices.

Yet Dudley took everything in stride. Although he was ninety years old, he told me that he could come down from Seattle the following year to restore the sculpture. I was dubious that a man that age could make such a commitment. But sure enough, a year or so later he arrived with the actual axe that I had come to recognize from its portrayal in the Rivera fresco.

Since I live not far from the CCSF campus and had to go there to teach every day, I invited Dudley to stay with me and go along in the car when I went to school. At first he said that he would walk the four miles to the campus every day; however, when he realized that the four miles wound up and down some very steep San Francisco hills, he accepted my transportation offer during the three weeks he stayed at my house.

Because of rheumatic fever contracted when he was four years old, Dudley was nearly deaf. One had to stand quite close to his good ear and speak very boldly for him to hear. Yet he was friendly and infinitely patient. His concentration on the work at hand was intense. It was a pleasure to watch him work carefully and methodically on his sculpture projects.

The lobby of Conlan Hall, the administration building that would serve as the new indoor location for *Ram*, became the studio where Dudley worked every day, using the same axe he had originally

> According to Brooks Key, writing for the City College of San Francisco newspaper the *Guardsman*, the *Ram* stood as a focal point for outdoor student events. "Everyone from politicians to folk singers . . . rallied 'round the Ram. It remains a symbol of strength."
>
> Brooks Key, "Sculptor visits college to see campus mascot," *Guardsman*, March 11, 1981.

Ninety-one-year-old Dudley Carter posing with his portrait in Diego Rivera's *Pan American Unity* mural. Depicted on Dudley's right is Timothy Pflueger, an architect of the GGIE. The lobby of the Diego Rivera Theatre of San Francisco City College is the present home of the 1,800-square-foot fresco.
Photograph Emmanuel C. Montoya

Meeting the Man in the Mural

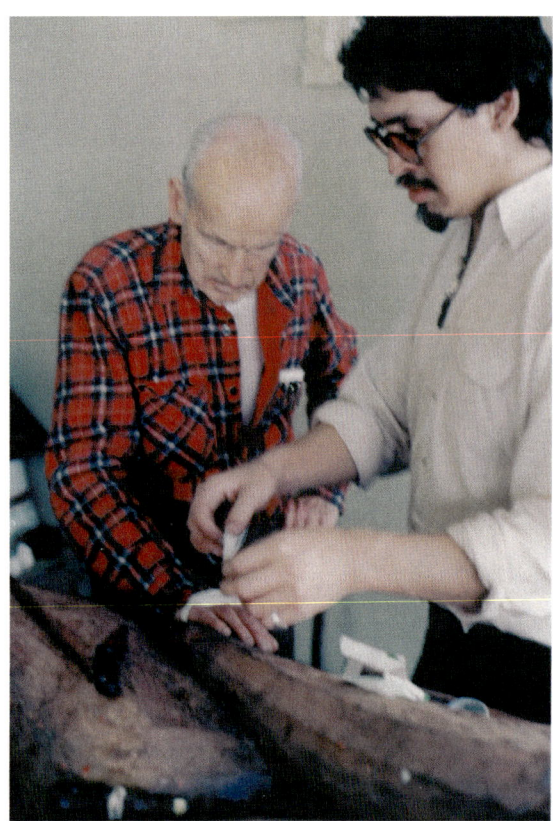

CCSF Student Emmanuel Montoya bandaging Dudley's knuckles during restoration of the *Ram*
Photograph courtesy Emmanuel Montoya

finished the project, Dudley gave the college a sculpture he titled *The Beast*.

While in San Francisco working on *Ram*, Dudley went to Golden Gate Park to view his monumental

> "With chisel the artist unveils the beautiful calligraphy nature has embedded like grain in the wood... The Sculptor's blood from wounds gives life to the wood."
>
> Bernard Zakheim
> Masha Zakheim, *Coit Tower San Francisco: Its History and Art*, San Francisco, Volcano Press, 1983, 131.

employed to carve the sculpture forty-two years earlier. Art department faculty quickly became attached to Dudley and many found themselves scraping paint side by side with the sculptor.

Some of my students signed on as apprentice scrapers too. Emmanuel Montoya, a student from one of my English classes, helped with both the restoration and with entertaining Dudley when they weren't chipping off paint. Montoya became a good friend of Dudley's and an accomplished muralist, printmaker, and administrator at the San Francisco Art Institute.

The faculty made some plaster casts of Dudley's hand holding the famous axe, as well as miniature casts in metal of the refurbished *Ram*. When he had

The Beast, 1986
Redwood, 6′ × 3.5′
Photograph Emmanuel Montoya

sculpture *Goddess of the Forest*, also fashioned at the Golden Gate International Exhibition. It depicts a Native American goddess figure holding an eagle and a bear cub. But what a shock to find that his gift to the park had rotted out at the core. Capillary action had drawn rainwater up through its center from the poorly drained base on which it stood. Once again a work of Dudley's required restoration, though the damage this time came from nature and neglect rather than from vandalism.

While Dudley was still working here in 1983, the art department and I collaborated on an exhibit celebrating historic highlights of the CCSF campus. We called the show Art and Architecture: The Marriage of True Minds, after Shakespeare's Sonnet 116. We featured several of Timothy Pflueger's architectural drawings, some easel works by Diego Rivera, and various pieces of Dudley's.

In 1985 City College arranged to move *Goddess of the Forest* from the park to the campus for restoration. Sculpture instructor Roger Baird consulted with Dudley to determine the best method to salvage the carved sections of the giant tree, since its interior and other parts had rotted beyond repair. Roger worked resolutely as a volunteer during his spare time for five or six years, saving the ornamented portion of the work. Though quite diminished from its original height of thirty-two feet, the sculpture—now just over thirteen feet tall—stands in the lobby of the Diego Rivera Theater opposite Rivera's fresco *Pan American Unity*.

When I visited Kobe, Japan, I was delighted to see one of Dudley's fanciful creations, *Bird Defying Man's Invasion of Space*, based on Indian lore. Edmonds Community College, north of Seattle, purchased the sculpture in 1990 for their Kobe Campus. Their original plan was to have Dudley go to Kobe to sculpt a bicultural pole he had modeled for them in his studio. Unfortunately, the Japanese sponsor got cold feet. He had two concerns. First,

Bird Defying Man's Invasion of Space, 1989
Red cedar, 14′ × 10′ × 5′
Sold in 1990 to Edmonds Community College and sent to their Kobe, Japan, campus
Photograph courtesy Dudley Carter

he was advised that given Dudley's age the risk was too great, and if something should happen to him blame might be placed on the Japanese. Second, the sponsor experienced financial losses and was hard-pressed to meet his operating expenses. One of the first areas to suffer cuts was the budget for art. Dudley was as disappointed as the college officials that he was unable to go to Kobe to work on site. He thought the bicultural pole would have been an ideal monument to the college's hopes for their Kobe

Meeting the Man in the Mural 169

campus. Instead of having him come to the campus to carve the bicultural pole, the college purchased *Bird Defying Man's Invasion of Space*. They treasured the sculpture and were relieved that it was not damaged in the devastating earthquake of 1995.

The last time I saw Dudley was in 1991. He was celebrating his one-hundredth birthday at various locations in the Northwest, but time conflicts allowed me to join him only at the gala in Portland where he was demonstrating his skill with an axe at Clackamas Town Center. I had just retired from teaching and was happy to help commemorate the life and work of this outstanding artist. Roger Baird drove up from the Bay Area, and the three of us celebrated our respective May birthdays in a nearby restaurant. Dudley, partaking of his usual vegetarian fare, was still the same lean and agile sculptor that Rivera had portrayed in his mural at the fair some fifty-one years earlier.

Dudley's memorable birthday celebration was a form of closure for me as less than a year later he died. The man I first met in painted form in Rivera's *Pan American Unity* had returned to eternal nature. I consider it a privilege to have journeyed even briefly with the living and breathing Dudley Carter.

Masha Zakheim (1931–2014) pictured with Dudley in 1983. Zakheim, a San Francisco native, taught English and humanities at City College of San Francisco for nearly thirty years. Inspired by Rivera's mural, she set up a San Francisco arts course at the college offering on-site tours of mural art in the city. She wrote extensively about art, publishing her book *Coit Tower San Francisco: Its History and Art* (Volcano Press, 1983). She gave lectures and tours under the auspices of her company, Articulate Art: San Francisco 1930s. Zakheim's appreciation of wood sculpture came to her honestly from her father, San Francisco muralist Bernard Zakheim.
Photograph courtesy Masha Zakheim

Chapter 39

Restoration and Reward

From a conversation with Roger Baird

Dudley Carter's surprise visit to San Francisco in 1981 afforded me a long-awaited opportunity to meet the sculptor of the *Ram*, City College's mascot. As an art instructor at the college, I was well aware that Dudley had carved *Big Horn Ram* decades earlier at the San Francisco fair and donated the sculpture to the college after Diego Rivera told him about the school and its choice of mascot.

But few students at the college knew that their school's symbol was the work of a famed artist. The *Ram* stood outdoors and was subjected to a succession of coats of paint—generally in the school's colors, red and white, but sometimes in the colors of rival colleges—applied by students infused with misdirected school spirit. By the time of Dudley's visit the sculpture had thirty or forty coats of paint splashed on it.

It took Dudley a couple of years to make room in his schedule, but he returned to San Francisco to restore the *Ram*. He checked it over and determined that the paint was almost a quarter inch thick in some areas, but he observed that it wouldn't be all that much trouble to eliminate the pranksters' handiwork. He insisted on restoring the *Ram* himself with his axe—no sandpaper, no paint remover—in order to preserve the texture and character of the wood. Carter amazed us all when he climbed atop the piece of art, axe in hand, and began chopping

The Goddess in Golden Gate Park as she awaits long-overdue attention, 1985
Photograph Emmanuel Montoya

off the layers of paint. I was much younger and I wouldn't attempt that. I knew then and there that I wanted this timeless human being as my friend.

I worked along with Dudley on the *Ram* in the bustling lobby of Conlan Hall, where students would pause to observe the restoration as they changed classes. The work was like cleaning up a cherished piece of antique furniture. Every coat of paint told a story. One burned and charred layer spoke of the sculpture having survived a fire sometime in its past.

One Sunday, in the midst of the *Ram's* restoration, Dudley took time to go with me to visit the *Goddess of the Forest* in Golden Gate Park. He had carved the work in 1940 at the Golden Gate International Exposition just after completing the *Ram*. Dudley was disturbed to find the *Goddess* sadly neglected and deteriorating rapidly. He quickly fired off a letter to Mayor Dianne Feinstein suggesting the sculpture warranted repair and relocation. Perhaps he felt he owed it to the city to restore that work of art. Dudley may have assumed he had an in with the mayor as she had extended him a warm civic welcome when he arrived at the college two weeks earlier.

Officials, faculty, and students of City College got behind Dudley and launched a campaign to bring the *Goddess* back to life. After a three-year effort, we convinced the San Francisco

> "Warren White has informed me of your generous offer to restore the superb redwood 'Ram' which you carved more than 40 years ago, and which has long been our City College's mascot. This is certainly a splendid gesture and one that I can assure you all San Franciscans deeply appreciate."
>
> Mayor Dianne Feinstein, an excerpt from her letter to Dudley

> "May I make the suggestion that this could still be corrected and successfully repaired and relocated much better than it ever was and contribute to the visual arts and education. It would be a great asset to this beautiful park."
>
> Dudley Carter, from his letter to Mayor Feinstein proposing the restoration of *Goddess of the Forest*

172   *The Master Carver*

3075 Bel. Red. Rd.
Bellevue, Wash.
98008

Oct. 18/83

Dear Emmanuel —

Glad to have heard from you yesterday and wish you luck with the "Goddess of the Forest" project. It looks like I may be able to salvage the front carved half, but it would take working it down to about 6" of wood if there is that much which is sound and then a very thorough job of reinforcing it to stand moving. It would require laying it on this side so it could be rolled back and forth and go to work on it with a chain saw axes and adze to hollow it out. If the park wish to give it to me it looks like I should stand the cost of the work on it, after they placed it in position. If they go along with it, it looks like I could take care of it early in January. Of course if they wished to cooperate a little a little help would help a lot.

I forgot to mention yesterday, I am scheduled to be on TV Oct 30 at 7 PM (channel 4 here) on "Ripley's Believe It or Not" program, you and some of the others may like to see it even if you dont Believe it.

I return to my Summer Camp at Gibsons in the AM, where I have a 28' long Bird underway so I can work under its wings, with a fire in a 50 gal. oil drum, can no doubt work outside all winter if the bird dont take off.

The very best regards to you and all.

Sincerely
Dudley

Letter from Dudley to Emmanuel Montoya, CCSF student and project coordinator for the restoration of *Goddess of the Forest*

Top left, top right, middle left: Moving day for the *Goddess*. Monument is carefully removed and lowered. Evidence of interior decomposition is obvious. Middle right, bottom left: San Francisco Park and Recreation employee performs initial chainsaw amputation of lower portion of sculpture. Bottom right: Prized cargo arrives at City College of San Francisco, ready for restoration and preservation. Photographs Emmanuel Montoya

Arts Commission and the Recreation and Park Department to relinquish the sculpture to City College. Once funds were raised, some $10,300, I took it as my personal project to see that the *Goddess* was rejuvenated.

The sculpture arrived on campus, and Dudley came down from Washington to help me determine what needed to be done. Makeshift scaffolding was erected around the piece so Dudley could do the boring needed for his evaluation. He questioned the stability of the staging but gamely climbed atop it anyway. The unthinkable happened. The staging collapsed, pitching Dudley to the floor. We rushed the ninety-two-year-old artist off to the hospital, expecting he had suffered numerous fractures. Amazingly, he didn't break any bones, but bruises slowed him down for about three months.

Dudley was more concerned about his deteriorating sculpture than his own aches and pains, and it wasn't long before he was back on the job analyzing the condition of the sculpture. I watched him drill depth holes, pull out samples, and make immediate pronouncements about the state of the wood and what it would take to restore it. I was sure that few people in the world commanded such knowledge of wood. I could learn a lot from that man.

When Dudley was satisfied that we had settled on a reasonable method of restoration, he returned home. For the better part of the next six years I didn't have to wonder what I would do with my spare time. Following Dudley's instructions, I saw the project through to completion.

In the spring of 1991 I attended Dudley's one-hundredth birthday party in Clackamas, Oregon. There in the shopping center, amidst a crowd of well-wishers gathered around the colossal cedars he had carved ten years previously, officials of the center presented Dudley with a golden axe, which he took and cut—ever so precisely—into a huge birthday cake. Then with a big grin on his face, he licked the axe clean!

A few months later, hoping to gain a better sense of Dudley's background, I traveled with my family to Alert Bay where Dudley had lived with the Kwakiutl Indians during his youth. We also visited Gibsons, on the Sunshine Coast of British Columbia's Sechelt Peninsula, where Dudley had his summer camp—his cabin and studio.

On our return to California we stopped to see Dudley at his place in King County's Slough House Park by the Sammamish River in Redmond, Washington. I found him to be doing well, as busy as ever, but he took time to visit. We had a good talk and he was pleased to know that I had been checking out his Canadian stomping grounds. Just before we left, he handed me something he had written about an Indian named Memaloosa Sam. It is a story about an old Indian Dudley met on a cruising trip into the Nitinat Lake country. It tells of Sam's last celebration on this side of the Great River, the River of the Big Sleep, the River of the Dead. To me the tale

> "I find a great deal more decay than at first expected. The test holes bored with a fourteen inch (14") bit indicated the surface wood was the most sound, but deteriorated toward the center. The center may be nothing but rot. The lower half of the sculpture seems to be decayed beyond any possible chance of repair. It is possible that the carved area on the front of the upper half may be hollowed out at the back, repaired, and reinforced with metal, and some use made of it that way. However there is every indication that the deterioration has reached a point where this would represent a great deal of time and expense to restore it. The only way to determine the exact amount of decay is to open it up and work on it."
>
> Dudley Carter, from Dudley's report to San Francisco's Recreation and Park Commission manager regarding the condition and restoration of *Goddess of the Forest*

"Goddess of the Forest"
Preparing to work — ACCIDENT Nov. 17/86

Material had been delivered for stageing to work on. Helper from park with chain saw had put two horses together (horses approx. 5' high x approx. 30" at base) and laid planks (approx. 1½" x 10" x 12') Helper and I had only worked about 10 minutes when the stageing collapsed. Not sufficient base to horses and not fastened to log, nor was there any other bracing. I had mentioned there was some defect in stageing. We both fell, it was about 7' from point of contact on paveing to the point on my back which was injured — Result paralising agony over entire back affecting nerve system, which in turn made more dificult hearing also making it impossible to continue work.

I was promptly rushed to Emergency Hospital, Xray showed no bones broken. Dr Willis Kirk gives me the best of care and takes me to French Hospital for Treatments Fri. Nov. 21, Sat. Nov 22, and Mon. Nov. 24 However these treatments did not seem to help. They did not use the heat lamp I had found very beneficial in a similar accident 60 years ago, nor did they apply osteopathic masage as was used at that time which produced good results. I have had the very best care from all the good people I have been associated with here, sorry I have not been able to do more myself.

DCC.

Dudley's notes regarding the fall he experienced when preparing to rework *Goddess of the Forest*. Courtesy Emmanuel Montoya

is especially poignant for, after he gave me that story, I never saw Dudley again.

Clearly, three significant factors influenced Carter's plenteous and unique art. First, there was his exceptional experience as a woodsman, which set the stage for the work. Additionally, he had an aesthetic style formed by his association with gifted Northwest Indians. Finally—and perhaps most important of all—he was so committed to and so enjoyed his work that he could keep on creating even to the age of one hundred. I've known no one else with such passion.

O nce, when Dudley set about to sharpen his axes, he asked me to help. He watched me closely for awhile and then walked away. Dudley regarded those tools most highly—as if they were the lifeblood of his existence. He kept them sharp as razors, their blades covered for protection. And he trusted me to work on them! That is when I knew I'd become his friend.

It is satisfying—inestimably rewarding—to know that I played a part in preserving *Ram* and *Goddess*, important examples of true North American art that can never be duplicated. Equally rewarding is the knowledge that Dudley Carter considered me his friend. I had hoped that would transpire from the time I first met him.

Roger Baird began teaching metal arts at City College in 1969 and was influential in having the State of California recognize the metal art form as a component of the fine arts education. He developed the CCSF sculpture program along with colleague Richard Moquim. Baird's administration of the restoration of the CCSF Dudley Carter works and his involvement as one of the founding members of the Diego Rivera Mural Project was instrumental in the establishment of the City College Art Gallery. Baird served as chair of the college's art department for the six years prior to his retirement, after which he continued to work as an artist. He is pictured here with the aged *Goddess*, remarkably restored.
Photograph 'Lyn Lambert

Restoration and Reward   177

Chapter 40

A Sanctuary for Sanctuary

From a conversation with Dick Cooley

Dudley captured my attention at an art show in a local shopping mall while I was serving as chair of the department of environmental sciences at the University of California, Santa Cruz. Being an amateur artist myself and married to an artist, art shows were a favorite diversion.

In many years of frequenting such shows I had never seen anybody use an axe to render objects of art. To me the axe is the tool of a pragmatist. I did wood carving myself, smaller pieces of course, so Dudley's Paul Bunyan approach interested me. Watching Dudley work with his axes and adzes was exhilarating. He worked so comfortably, so freely, so rhythmically, fully appreciating the shape and grain of his medium. Occasionally, Dudley would stop work to speak with onlookers, telling of his early introduction to the axe and to Native culture. It became obvious why his creativity would be expressed in such a manner. He explained that his permanent studios were in Washington State and British Columbia, but he migrated to California's sunshine during winter months.

A small hand-lettered sign posted by the carver's workbench caught my eye. It offered art instruction in exchange for accommodations. I queried him about that. He told me he and his wife Teresa were presently staying in a motel close to the beach, but were looking for something more suitable.

I put two and two together. I told him I would like to learn to carve with an axe and that I had a studio he could use and space where he might live. I invited him to visit my wife and me at our home.

Wanted APARTMENT or share HOUSE for two by- INTERNATIONALLY KNOWN ARTIST. WILL GIVE FREE ART INSTRUCTION IF DESIRED

DUDLEY G. CARTER
EL VIEW LODGE
810 3rd St.
SANTA CRUZ, CALIF.
95060
Phone- (408) 423-0873

Looking for housing in Santa Cruz, Dudley posted this sign offering art instruction in exchange for lodging. Courtesy Dudley Carter

Dudley and Teresa came over, found things to their liking, and in no time at all we became good friends. We welcomed them as our guests for many winters.

I learned so much about how to work with wood from Dudley; he knew wood better than anyone. The redwood he used in California wouldn't allow cuts across the grain as cleanly as did the cedar he used up north, but he could work with that.

Dudley worked for quite some time with failing eyesight. Before undergoing cataract surgery in his mid-nineties, he couldn't see well at all. We have a picture of him studying one of his sketches through a pinhole to sharpen his focus. The aged, cloudy-eyed artist whose mind's eye still possessed its youthful vision so intrigued Woody Carroll, a film student at UCSC, that he made a film of Dudley. Woody was one of several UCSC students who accepted Dudley's invitation to become an apprentice carver.

Dudley Carter often worked his apprentices more like servants, if they'd let him. He would have them squiring him around, running errands, and performing all kinds of personal tasks. His family and I tried to encourage him to hire help. He had the money, but he could always find willing apprentices, many of them women. He was benignly flirtatious, but always a gentleman—a straightlaced sort of a guy. Even around men he never used the language of a lumber camp.

Dudley liked to seek the advice of ladies when naming a work. He believed a title helped sell a piece. A work he originally called *San Lorenzo Tower of Life* became *Sanctuary: Preservation of Wildlife* because a young sociology student of mine had an interest in wildlife and suggested that more affective name.

Dudley had a number of idiosyncrasies. He frequently bought his clothes at flea markets and would

Dudley Carter with *Sanctuary: Preservation of Wildlife*
Photograph courtesy Dudley Carter

buy pants with a thirty-two-inch waist. I'd point out to him that they would be too big, but he insisted that he had worn size thirty-two all his life. He must have been about a size twenty-six at the time, but he would just cinch them up with his belt, heedless of all the pleats around his waist.

Above: Detail of *Sanctuary: Preservation of Wildlife*
Photograph courtesy Dudley Carter

Opposite page: Dudley Carter with *Sanctuary: Preservation of Wildlife*, work in progress, 1985, redwood, 14′ × 6′ × 3′. Dudley's description for this photograph: "Dr. Cooley's outdoor studio, Santa Cruz, California. The man with the axe has a little more carving to complete hatching bird at lower right side. D.C.C. with axe on left. This was a natural hollow redwood shell, salvaged from the beautiful beach at the mouth of the San Lorenzo River at Santa Cruz."
Photograph courtesy Dudley Carter

Dudley generally kept to a strict diet, but when he had a party he would have a bourbon or whiskey. And he could scarf down food like he was starving. He loved to go out for Chinese food, devouring all the sweet and sour pork on his plate and some of ours too. My wife, Alice, often made him oatmeal cookies, and they were usually pretty dry when she gave them to him. Nonetheless, he would put them in the oven and dry them crisp. Dextrinizing, he called it. Dudley credited his diet for his longevity. But he had relatives who lived to advanced ages, so I think genes had a lot to do with it.

It was difficult, next to impossible, to get Dudley away from his work. Every morning he would get up early, exercise for an hour or so, eat breakfast, and start to work—work all day, every day. I'd try to get him to break away from his routine every now and then, but rarely was I successful.

On one occasion, I managed to convince him to show me his first Haida house, which he built in 1935 and lived in with his family for a number of years before selling it to S.F.B. Morse. Morse's daughter Mary and her husband, Will Shaw, eventually inherited the Haida house and moved it to a lovely setting in Big Sur that they donated to UCSC. That parcel was designated as a nature preserve.

Though slight of build, Dudley was incredibly strong. He had an amazing ability to manipulate huge logs. He was hauling logs off the beach even in his eighties. He and a friend, also in his eighties,

"**Sanctuary speaks to the sacredness of the forest, nature, and the environment. Condor, King of the Skies, is perched on top, while stylized plant forms boldly work their way up the central redwood column. A gentle, nurturing forest maiden stands slightly recessed, protected by a concave redwood slab.**"

Anna Vaughan Hanson

retrieved one such log while walking on the beach in the Monterey Bay area. Dudley turned it into *Birds and Waterfall*, a handsome piece displaying a mother owl sheltering her chicks under her outspread wings. A great American eagle perches nearby, presiding over a tumbling waterfall. Dudley loaned that sculpture to the Santa Cruz Museum and it stood for many years in the museum's grounds overlooking the picnic area. Museum staff and members were disappointed when Dudley's family reclaimed the work, selling it to settle his estate.

In Dudley's later years his art went through a notable transformation. Rather than carving one huge log, he would combine several independently worked sections. They were more manageable for him that way and could be dismantled for transportation. Clever.

Dudley filled our yard with an array of wood sculptures, making it quite a fantasyland. My favorite was the head of a maiden he had carved from a root. Most of the sculptures were sold or returned to the family following Dudley's death, but I am delighted to say that his family gifted me with the head of the maiden.

Dudley's daughter, Mavis, and her husband, David Vaughan, had their home designed around Dudley's work. My wife and I visited the Vaughans when they sponsored an art show at their estate in Gibsons, British Columbia. The home was breathtakingly beautiful. One could look down from the bedroom on the top floor to the living areas below and see marvelous totems and walls full of art.

Dudley was as atypical as his art. Artists often tend to be rather selfish and jealous—not Dudley.

Birds and Waterfall, 1974, redwood, 8′ × 6.5′ × 20″
Loaned to City Museum of Natural History, Santa Cruz, California, returned to Dudley Carter estate, 1993.
Purchased by Marvin Boys and donated to the Redmond Library, Redmond, Washington.
Photograph Sue Winters, courtesy Anna Vaughan Hanson

He was infinitely generous and eager to share his techniques and knowledge. He delighted in the accomplishments of others. Artists can be impressed with their own importance. It still seems incongruous to me that this unassuming man, so at home demonstrating his skill in our local mall, was an artist of international acclaim with works exhibited at the opening celebrations of two major West Coast museums.

Dudley became known as a monumental wood sculptor. The word monumental fits Dudley's work perfectly, for it speaks of distinction, of lasting importance. A monumental work can be, but need not be, massive. It can be quite diminutive and yet possess monumentality. In the art world, the word monumental describes a work of powerful effects achieved through sharp contrasts, noble in concept yet simple in execution. Monumental. That was Dudley.

Dr. Richard A. Cooley (1925–1994), teacher, public policy researcher, and founder and longtime head of the environmental studies program at University of California, Santa Cruz. Born in Silver City, New Mexico, he served three years in WWII. Cooley received a doctorate in resource conservation from the University of Michigan and taught at the University of Washington prior to moving to Santa Cruz in 1970. He did conservation work in Alaska for many years, authored numerous books and articles on natural resource conservation, served on editorial boards of scholarly journals, and advised a wide array of government and private conservation organizations. Cooley was also an accomplished sculptor who exhibited his work in Alaska, the Pacific Northwest, and California.
Photograph courtesy Brigham Cooley

Chapter 41

Yes, Dudley, there is a Santa Claus

From conversations with Bertil Valley

I often wondered if it had been foreordained that I would eventually play a role in Dudley Carter's life.

It began when a downturn in business resulted in my being laid off in midlife from a job with a logging equipment manufacturing company. I found myself picking apples and cherries at a farm on Bel-Red Road, not far from Dudley's place. Sights and sounds indicated that something interesting was going on at that woodsy site. I really wanted to investigate it, but my Swedish reserve prevented me from hiking up the hill to check things out.

Later, in the spring of 1976, my wife Edith and I went to Vancouver, Canada, which was hosting a United Nations Conference on Human Settlements called Habitat. The conference brought together such visionaries as Margaret Mead and Buckminster Fuller, as well as Imelda Marcos and Kurt Waldheim, but the real heart and soul of the event was Habitat Forum. The forum was a wonderfully optimistic gathering of non-governmental types—artists and dreamers. Much to my delight, I discovered Dudley was one of the artistic dreamers invited to take part in the forum. He and his Northwest art certainly added flavor to the affair.

Dudley and his works at Habitat Forum, Jericho Beach Park, Vancouver, British Columbia, 1976
Photograph courtesy Bertil Valley

Advance the calendar nearly ten years to the autumn of 1984 when Edith and I were living on our farm in Issaquah and a newspaper story informed us that Dudley Carter had to vacate his beautiful Bel-Red Road property. I didn't like the idea of that. With the eviction deadline fast approaching, I decided to visit Dudley, who was in the midst of his one-man exhibition at Bellevue Square, and see what was up.

Ninety-three-year-old Dudley, working in the center court at Bellevue Square—his majestic cedar sculptures all around him—attracted quite a crowd. He had attached a small sign to one of the carvings stating his need for housing. However, he showed no sign that he was concerned about losing his home and workplace of nearly thirty years. But I was concerned!

We had six acres out in the country and a fifth-wheel trailer we weren't using. Thinking maybe we could help him out, I approached Dudley and explained what I had in mind. Dudley thanked me, but said he had some other offers to consider. I gave him one of my business cards so he could contact me. At that time, playing Santa Claus professionally allowed me to indulge my alter ego. With my long white beard and hair, even without my red suit, children were apt to take me for the old gentleman himself. Looking at the card that bore a picture of me decked out in full Santa regalia, Dudley chuckled and said, "Santa Claus, eh? Might not be a bad idea to move in with Santa Claus!"

Finding a place for Dudley also interested Susan Hoare, Director of King County's Arts Commission. The arts commission had awarded Dudley the commission for *Legend of the Moon*, the outstanding sculpture at the entrance to Marymoor Park, and Susan recognized Dudley as a national treasure. Upon hearing that he was considering moving to California or to his place in Gibsons, BC, and wanting to keep him in the area, Susan thought that Dudley should be set up to work and live in Marymoor Park. Dudley's Haida house could be reassembled at Marymoor, and King County Parks could assume ownership of the studio in return for Dudley living in the park as artist-in-residence. Dudley was agreeable, but the deal fell through—a political situation, Dudley called it. The county did agree to move Dudley's knocked-down studio, equipment, carving materials, wood supply, and several large sculptures to the maintenance yard at Marymoor and said he could work there—in the maintenance yard.

Bertil Valley's Santa Claus business card

When it became clear that he would not be permitted to live in the park, Dudley remembered my offer and came out to look over our place. Seeing the magnificent trees on the property he exclaimed, "This is it!"

We struck a deal and Dudley said he'd move in after his winter stay at Dick Cooley's place in Santa Cruz. Meanwhile, the county moved all his paraphernalia over to Marymoor.

In February we received a letter from Dudley informing us that he expected to return to the Northwest about the first of April. He enclosed a sketch of a cabin he wanted to build on our property that resembled a huge bird. Dudley figured this birdhouse could serve as his home and studio. With a portable toilet of the sort that building contractors use, that would be all he'd need.

Edith and I were sure that our neighbors would never accept that. I wrote to him suggesting that if he would forgo the idea of a birdhouse he could rent

Yes, Dudley, There is a Santa Claus

Above: Dudley Carter with *Celestial Intruder*, 1986, the inspiration for Dudley's proposed cabin, red cedar, 16' high, 37' long, carved at Gibsons, BC
Photograph courtesy Bertil Valley

Left: Dudley's sketch for a cabin he would live in on the Valley's property
Sketch courtesy Bertil Valley

our seventeen-foot trailer instead and use the shower and bath facilities in our home. We didn't hear from him again until one day in April or May when I wasn't home. Dudley showed up on our doorstep with his suitcases. Though taken by surprise, Edith invited him in and the two visited until I returned. By then they were getting along like old friends. And Edith, thoroughly smitten, was delighted when he agreed to move into our trailer.

Dudley had been at our place for about a year when Edith and I decided to go on an extended trip. Dudley could hardly manage there in the country on his own, so before we left we helped him move to a trailer park where he rented space from an elderly woman. Shortly thereafter the woman had to go to a nursing home, so Dudley found another place with a young couple and their child.

Dudley came to call his work site at Marymoor "the garbage pail," for he was confined to a fenced area of the park's maintenance yard along with refuse bins, stored picnic tables, and assorted equipment—hardly conducive to creative sculpturing. Sales of his sculptures dropped off drastically as there was no place to attempt to conduct business. It disturbed me to see him working under such conditions.

The circumstances behind Dudley's move from his property interested me. I couldn't understand why he would leave that property—land he bought in 1947 when the area was just a wilderness—a place where he was so much at home. In time Dudley explained that when his wife Teresa died he didn't need that much space, so he rented out their home. He moved into an addition he had made to the Haida house studio, expecting to finish his days living and working right where he was. In the late 1970s, Allied Stores abandoned their plans to build a shopping center next to Dudley's land and sold all the property they'd acquired for the project. The new landowners wanted to expand their holdings there—an area some called the golden triangle—and they made overtures to Dudley and his neighbors. Others were anxious to sell, but Dudley wanted to stay put. However, at the urging of his family in Canada, he sold the property with the understanding that he could lease it back from the purchasers for what he expected would be the rest of his life. Dudley continued to live and work there until September of 1984 when the property was resold. The new owners notified him that he must vacate and gave him thirty days to clear out.

Dudley was in the midst of preparing for his one-man exhibition at Bellevue Square. Recognizing how difficult it would be for Dudley to move his buildings and sculptures, the owners ultimately let him stay until the end of November. Interestingly, and somewhat ironically, the beautiful evergreen forest that was home to Dudley for so long became a high-tech jungle, the headquarters of Microsoft.

Bottom left, top left, top center, top right, bottom right: Art awaiting audience in the maintenance yard, Marymoor Park
Bottom center: Dudley takes a power nap while on the job in the maintenance yard at Marymoor Park
Photographs courtesy Bertil Valley

Yes, Dudley, There is a Santa Claus

Back when I was picking apples and cherries I had been reluctant to even approach Dudley Carter, but as years passed I found myself acting as his spokesman and assisting him in a variety of ways. I just couldn't tolerate watching him try to make a go of things in the maintenance yard at the park. King County owned a residence known as the Slough House, a livable little 1950s-style home in a park-like setting along the Sammamish Slough river, just north of Marymoor Park. I knew it would be an ideal spot for Dudley. A group of us got together, circulated petitions, and did what we could to convince the county to do the obvious.

In October of 1987 the manager of King County Parks, Russ Cahill, notified us that the way was clear for Dudley to move into the Slough House. Halleluhah! Park employees and volunteers pitched in to help with Dudley's resettlement, putting in over 200 hours, and Dudley Carter became the first ever artist-in-residence for King County Parks. In January 1988 the county held a public ceremony giving Dudley use of the house and grounds for the rest of his life. In return King County acquired a remarkable tourist attraction: an internationally acclaimed artist who made himself available to the public from dawn to dusk, seven days a week.

At ninety-six years of age, Dudley arrived at the Slough House envisioning projects that would take him forty years to complete. His business picked up right away, and he set about accumulating a serious supply of wood.

High on his agenda was a trip to Verlot, near Granite Falls, Washington, to check on his *Maid of the Woods* tree. Dudley had carved an image of a maiden on the living tree in 1947. The owners of the property had given him the mammoth cedar. Struck by lightning not once but twice, the property owners were anxious to have the cedar removed, and Dudley was just as eager to take possession of the huge tree. The lightning strikes served to harden the cedar, so it contained vast amounts of prime carving wood.

Although I had the misfortune to suffer a stroke after Dudley moved to the Slough House, I was still game to take him up to Verlot to oversee the harvesting of his tree. We drove to within about a third of a mile of the tree and hiked the rest of the way, both of us with walking sticks—Dudley using his traditional wooden pole and I my newly acquired four-pronged cane. As we hiked up the trail Dudley proclaimed, "Bertil, this is

Harvesting the *Maid of the Woods* tree, 1989. Photographs courtesy Bertil Valley

Fantail Bird, 1989, red cedar, 8′ × 14′, commissioned by the City of Redmond, Washington, for the Redmond Senior Center. Photograph Lisa Lambert

what we should be doing every day."

I'm sure he was right; there is something therapeutic about a walk in the woods. Those majestic hemlock, cedar, and silver firs are medicine for the soul.

Retrieving that huge tree, a tree Dudley estimated to be two thousand years old, was a major undertaking, but it was accomplished to Dudley's great satisfaction. He had the tree hauled to the Slough House Park, where it provided him with fine carving wood for myriad projects and plenty to share generously with his apprentices. Following Dudley's death, the remainder of the *Maid of the Woods* tree was sold to appreciative carvers. Who knows how many works of art owe their existence to that wonderful old cedar?

My memory is full of images of Dudley Carter. One that immediately surfaces occurred in 1985 when Dudley was living at our place. In recognition of his contributions to the visual arts, the City of Bellevue was honoring him at a public ceremony and sent a police car to pick him up. Since Dudley's hearing was poor and his speech rather indistinct to unaccustomed ears, I rode with him to act as interpreter. After they presented Dudley with a handsome engraved crystal piece, the arts commission

> **An excerpt from a newspaper article on the occasion of Dudley's new role as King County's artist-in-residence:** "They were gathered to do something we don't do a very good job of in our brave new world: They were about to honor an artist while he's still living; and they were going to do it with something more gratifying and more useful to him than flowery speeches and citations suitable for framing."
>
> Joe Mooney,
> "A refreshing tribute to an unusual artist,"
> *Seattle Post-Intelligencer*, January 28, 1988.

Yes, Dudley, There is a Santa Claus

expected him to make an acceptance speech. "Oh no!" I thought, as Dudley was quite difficult for most people to understand. But he squared his shoulders and rose to the occasion, speaking so clearly, so appropriately. It was the first time I heard him speak before a large group, and he gave a grand speech, outstanding.

In 1989 Dudley accepted a commission to do a carving for the new Redmond Senior Center. Ninety-eight and a generation older than most of the folks who would be using the center, he came up with an imaginative design he called *Fantail Bird*. He incorporated relief carvings of youthful faces in the bird's great tail, figuring that the seniors would prefer to see something of their childhood rather than the troubles of old age. Edith and I went with Dudley to the dedication of the artwork at the grand opening of the center. Dudley didn't hesitate to express his displeasure over the placement of the sculpture over the doors of the auditorium, above the sight line of most visitors where light and shadow did not play well on the work.

Dudley was a rare man. I may have been cut out to portray the spirit of Santa Claus in my old age, but Dudley Carter, even at a hundred, radiated the very spirit of life itself, making the most of every day and every opportunity.

Bertil Valley (1913–2004), born in Sweden and reared in California. Valley spent many of his early years transporting cargo on a three-masted schooner around Europe and Africa, then working at sea for the fishing industry in Alaska and later aboard a US Geological Survey research vessel out of Redwood City, California. He found his land legs and settled in the Pacific Northwest, enjoying a successful career in the building business and raising his family. Valley's joy in retirement was his role as Santa Claus. For twenty-five years he delighted children of all ages, playing Santa for numerous Seattle-area charitable organizations and the Seattle Seahawks. In 1989 a major stroke slowed him down a bit, but didn't diminish his volunteer spirit. For years Valley participated in support groups, visiting and encouraging hospitalized heart and stroke patients. A studious use of complementary therapies and a healthy diet, which he claimed was largely inspired by Dudley's example, kept Valley active until he died at the age of ninety-one.

Photograph 'Lyn Lambert

Dudley and Santa Claus, alias Bertil Valley, Christmas, 1985. Photograph courtesy Bertil Valley

Part V
Legacy

"While I may never become a great artist, there is a happiness and satisfaction in dealing with beauty, in trying to create sculptured forms. The work itself is its own recompense."

Dudley Carter
As quoted in the *Seattle Times*, May 3, 1931, after winning first prize in a soap-carving contest

Dudley Carter at work at the Heritage Festival at Marymoor Park, July 1987
Photograph courtesy Bertil Valley

Chapter 42

The Washington Centennial Hall of Honor

By 'Lyn Lambert

Washington State reached its one-hundredth year of statehood in 1989. Eight years prior to the celebration, the board of curators and director of the Washington State Historical Society considered how they might best mark the centennial. They decided to establish a hall of honor featuring one hundred eminent Washingtonians representative of the first century of Washington statehood.

Nominations came in from every part of the state and every field of endeavor. Honorees were persons who helped make Washington what it is. All were individuals who made outstanding contributions of national or international significance, while giving other Washingtonians a sense of pride and an impetus to achieve.

In 1985 Dudley Carter received word that his accomplishments had earned him a place among the Washington State notables. In 1989, when all one hundred honorees had been selected, eleven were designated in the arts and letters category. Dudley Carter was in very good company. His friends and colleagues George Tsutakawa and James Washington, Jr. were also among the artists honored. Dr. Richard Fuller, founder of the Seattle Art Museum and perhaps the individual most responsible for providing Dudley Carter's jump start into the art world, was acknowledged for all he did to provide an audience for the state's artists.

Dudley Carter's inclusion in the Washington Centennial Hall of Honor left no doubt that he had indeed mastered his art and established a legacy.

According to Dudley, the "great tribute" of being selected for the hall of honor made him "feel a . . . responsibility to the state to keep up a high standard of work and not let it down."[1]

Dudley C. Carter as pictured in the gallery of one hundred notable Washingtonians marking the centennial of Washington State, showing the artist at work on a clay model
Photograph "Hall of Honor" (1989), Washington State Historical Society

Named a Hero

In June of 1988, Washington State Representative Rod Chandler, recognizing Dudley Carter's significant contributions to the community, presented the ninety-seven-year-old artist-in-residence with Chandler's first Heroes Award. Chandler praised Carter for the time and care he devoted to his work and encouraged more senior citizens to follow Dudley's example by remaining active.

Photograph Bertil Valley

---

[1] Patricia F. Carpenter and Paul Totah, *The San Francisco Fair Treasure Island 1939–1940* (San Francisco: Scottwall Associates, 1989), p. 53.

The Washington Centennial Hall of Honor

Chapter 43

Transcending the Wave

Reminiscences of Geordie Tocher

It's hard for me to accept the fact that Dudley isn't around anymore. There were a lot of good sculptings remaining on his agenda. One of those is the marvelous concept for *Riding the Transcending Wave*, designed to mark the centennial of Washington State.

The monuments program, a project dreamed up by the 1989 Centennial Commission's Arts Committee, called upon Washington's artists to imagine an image that best symbolized Washington State. Artists from all over the state submitted proposals. The jury commissioned four to produce scale models, one of those four was Dudley. Dudley made two models of *Riding the Transcending Wave*. One resides with the Washington State Historical Museum, the other belongs to Dudley's family. But, sadly, the work was never commissioned.

From his youth Dudley possessed a drive to do something extraordinary—I would say, to be transcendent. That drive stayed with him till his dying day and is clearly evident in *Riding the Transcending Wave*, a work full of Dudley's hope and spirit. He was ninety-eight years old when he conceived that sculpture. Dudley used a large canoe, a primary means of transportation when the state was young. In the proposal Dudley explained that he used the canoe "as the vehicle, the symbol by which ideas, knowledge and the search for the objective may be transported, also it demonstrates how far we have come from the starting point to the super sophisticated age of today."

Native paddlers propel the canoe. Standing prominently in the bow of the canoe is the bowman with his ceremonial robe—representative of the

Model of *Riding the Transcending Wave*, 1989, collection of the Washington State Historical Museum
Photograph Neil House for the Washington State Historical Society

Transcending the Wave

The Bowman, 1989, red cedar, 6′2″ × 4′10″ × 16″
Photograph 'Lyn Lambert

primitive West Coast culture. His right hand shades his brow as he looks into the rising sun. A typical Dudley Carter owl sits atop the bowman's hat—perhaps a symbol of higher wisdom, clairvoyance, prophesy?

Some expressed concern that Dudley would take and use—solely for the purpose of art—the great trees that once grew abundantly, were for years the source of major industry, and are now on the decline in Washington State. Dudley was considerate of that attitude, expecting that through his work the great trees would be celebrated and their numbers increased. Dudley knew that when Indian carvers took a tree for their own purposes, they would speak to the spirit of the tree, promising to use its flesh wisely and thanking it for its sacrifice. Yes, Dudley believed it was fitting that a Washington State centennial work be hewn from cedar.

Co-chairs of the Washington Centennial Commission, Jean Gardner, then the governor's wife, and Secretary of State Ralph Munro, appealed to the public for financial assistance in creating the monument. They were unsuccessful, but Dudley went ahead and carved the paddlers and the bowman, expecting funds to materialize. He estimated the work would cost about $125,000.

I offered to supply the log for the canoe and to carve it if Dudley would do the rest. Dudley had taught me a lot about carving canoes. One trick to building canoes that Dudley and I particularly enjoyed disproved the adage that you can't put a square peg in a round hole—the Natives did that all the time. They understood that a surefire way to pin one piece of wood to another is to drill a round hole

Detail of a paddler from *Riding the Transcending Wave*
Photograph Sam Pemberton

in each piece and then drive a square peg into the holes. The corners of the peg are crushed and bind snuggly in the hole. Subjected to the stresses and strains of pounding waves, a canoe held together by round pegs in round holes would soon become flotsam.

Dudley intended the centennial sculpture to be about thirty to thirty-two feet long and twelve to twenty feet high. In his proposal he suggested that it "be installed on a miniature man-made island pointing to the rising sun, with the water provided by a

Detail of a paddler from *Riding the Transcending Wave*
Photograph Sam Pemberton

related fountain. The pool created by this would reflect the sculpture . . . "

He suggested that motion could be added; the canoe could be made to rock back and forth on rubber cushions. He considered adding changing colored lights and sound, concealing bells or other mechanisms in the canoe for the figurehead or the bowman to emit a sound—rather fanciful for a man nearly one hundred years old. That was Dudley for you—dispelling another common belief. He was living proof that imagination grows by exercise and can be mightier in the mature than in the young.

Ever mindful of sound engineering, Dudley carefully considered structural matters of the work.

His plans called for the canoe to ride the crest of a wave carved from a natural curve of a large cedar. The wave would be locked into a section of a tree trunk, probably seven or eight feet in diameter, and supported on other sections of smaller trees. All would be securely bolted and reinforced with concealed aluminum or steel, giving the project stability and resistance to high winds and earthquakes.

When Washington State failed to come up with the money to see the carving through, I tried to sell the idea to the Vancouver, BC, airport. They opted for a Bill Reid sculpture instead.

Contemplating Dudley's grand design for the centennial work, it is easy to see that Dudley was a man who managed to transcend the wave of commonality. He was a man apart. It's a shame *Riding the Transcending Wave* was never completed. The three paddlers and *The Bowman* were sold to individual collectors, but I believe *Riding the Transcending Wave* should be realized. Other artists could do it—it would still be Dudley's work.

Geordie Tocher (1927–2007) and *The Bowman* at the Slough House, Redmond, Washington, 1989. See page 39 for Tocher's bio. Photograph 'Lyn Lambert

Transcending the Wave

Chapter 44

An Emerging Vision

From the writing of David L. Vaughan

Dudley C. Carter was at work on a dream—a dream he'd had for years. The woodsman, engineer, timber cruiser, big game hunter, guide, canoe man, and famed heroic wood sculptor hoped his dream of carving a giant living cedar would crown a host of magnificent achievements.

His two-bitted axe arced through the sunlight, one hundred feet above the ground, high upon a mountain top in Washington, biting into the living wood of a giant cedar. Again and again its razor-keen blade struck.

Slowly the big cedar seemed to shake off the slumber of centuries. Subtly the expressionless wood softened. Then magically, in place of the shapeless tree, there appeared the face of a maiden. The busy two-headed axe gave place to a smaller one, and beauty began to take shape in the rough features of the maiden.

The axe-hewer would pause to glance at a tiny clay figure then step back to scan the tree maiden.

He stood on a scaffolding of small trees and rough cedar boards hand-hewn from fallen timbers on the mountain slope and circling the girth of the great cedar.

Dudley Carter dreamed of shaping a huge living tree. When finished, the spirit of the dawn would gaze from its tip and at her feet would be the animals and flowers of the forest. Tumbling over the maiden spirit, a waterfall would follow the natural contours of the tree to its base.

Dudley found the tree he wanted, with its thirty-foot circumference, at the crest of a mountain overlooking the untamed Pilchuck River Valley. He bought the tree and set about clearing the surround-

Dudley Carter in 1947, hewing a relief figure of a maiden on a 120-foot-tall living tree in the forest near Mount Baker National Park, some eleven miles east of Granite Falls, Washington. Living red cedar, 120′ tall, 15′ in diameter, carving 30′ high. Photograph courtesy Anna Vaughan Hanson

ing trees to permit light to fall upon it. Next he built platforms in nearby trees from which he could view his work as it progressed. Finally, he built the working scaffolding.

Carefully following a clay model he had made on rainy nights in his studio in the valley, he set about with several axes as his only tools to block out his great work. Unfinished and unnamed, it stood like a mountain spirit overlooking the valley.

Dudley Carter, born at Queen's Park, New Westminster, on May 6, 1891, made a handsome living as a forestry engineer and one of the West Coast's top timber cruisers. But he had a passion for this new art form and for complete freedom from regulation by other men. He would tell you that his family tree included John Bunyan, Sir Isaac Newton, Florence Nightingale, and Stix Stober Carter of pirate fame.

This was Dudley's own description of himself: "Height, 5 feet, 9 inches; weight, 135 pounds; black hair; color, Indian red; likes two creams in coffee, huckleberry pie, also fond of smoked salmon, raw meat."

His father, one of British Columbia's pioneers,

was owner of a logging camp in the Stave River country. In the wild backwoods Dudley grew to love the outdoors and to understand the mood and power of the Canadian forests. When his family moved to Alert Bay on the rugged coast of Vancouver Island, Dudley Carter came in contact with the art and culture of the Indian people. He saw their rituals and learned the legends that were to come to life in his later sculptures.

At the age of thirty-eight, he won a scholarship on which he attended the Seattle Art Institute. In 1944, at fifty-three, he was head of the department of sculpture at the University of Washington.

To those who viewed his huge works at the 1940 Golden Gate International Exposition and in museums of the West Coast, it was quite evident that varied skills went into their creation. They were the result of a combination of the techniques of the woodsman, the engineer, and the artist. His youth in the woods gave him the skill of an axe man; his training as a young man in forestry and engineering enabled him to select suitable timbers from the forest; and his natural genius and training as a sculptor enabled him to turn these timbers into works of art.

His great unfinished work was more than one man's lifelong ambition. For the people of North America, it was the growth of a phase of art truly unique to their continent.

NOTE: Excerpted and adapted with permission from an October 11, 1947, feature story entitled "New Age Art," published in the *Vancouver Daily Province* and authored by the late David L. Vaughan.

Dudley Carter never completed that lifelong dream. The great cedar upon which he began his vision of what he came to call the *Maid of the Woods* was struck by lightning—twice. The carved maiden was destroyed by the resulting fire. However, much of the tree remained. Dudley had the huge cedar felled and transported to his studio in Redmond, where it provided him and his apprentices with valuable fire-hardened carving material for years to come.

David with his wife, Mavis, pictured shortly after their marriage in 1944
Photograph courtesy Anna Vaughan Hanson

David L. Vaughan (1922–1990), Dudley Carter's son-in-law, prominent international lawyer, senior partner with the Vancouver firm of Farris, Farris, Vaughan, Taggart, Wills & Murphy. Vaughan and his wife, Mavis, who met in 1939 in Gibsons, BC, where their families spent the summers, were enthusiastic patrons of the arts, supporting talented, usually struggling, artists. They arranged and hosted sculpture exhibitions on the grounds of their West Vancouver home where the Sculptors' Society of BC, of which Dudley was a member, often met. David Vaughan died tragically in a highway accident in Novia Scotia.

Chapter 45

The *Maid of the Woods* Tree

From the notes of Dudley Carter

The great cedar, the largest I had ever found in Washington, grew near Verlot some eleven miles east of Granite Falls. Northern Mills, a logging company, gave me the tree as payment for some extra work I had done for them.

Best guesses put its age at about a thousand years, but upon removal of the tree we were able to count the annual rings, almost microscopic in places. We discovered that the tree was twice as old as we had imagined. It must have been a seedling about the time our calendar began, the time the Bible gives us as the birth of Christ.

This great tree bore a scar on its best side, the side free from limbs. The scar indicated that Indians had peeled the bark when the tree was about thirty years old, around the time of Christ's resurrection. The Indians made good use of cedar bark, peeling it off the trunk before the tree grew too large. The inner bark, the quarter inch next to the sap, provided material for clothing, baskets, mats, sails, and other necessities of everyday life. The peeling of the bark causes a dry side, damage that timber cruisers call a cat face. Interestingly, it was the habit of the Indians to make a conscious effort at conservation, removing only part of the bark and allowing the tree to recover and continue to grow. Only rarely did they peel a tree completely.

The area where the tree stood was originally timbered with a dense stand of cedar, as indicated by the many large stumps nearby. The timber had evidently been logged early in the 1900s when shingle bolts were in great demand and, as springboard holes in the stumps indicated, before the advent of chain saws. The *Maid of the Woods* tree was spared, probably due to its numerous burls and its enor-

Maid of the Woods with Mark Oestreich in foreground, red cedar, maiden figure 30′ tall
Photograph Jane and Kurt Oestreich

Dudley Carter supervising removal of the *Maid of the Woods* tree in 1989
Photograph courtesy Bertil Valley

mity—fourteen feet in diameter, which at the time made it difficult to fell. After the site was harvested, the whole area reforested with a dense stand of hemlock and white fir. The cedar did not reforest.

Having been given the giant cedar, my initial idea was to carve the entire trunk of the living tree. In 1947 I went to work on the forty-foot-high[1] *Maid of the Woods* in her forested setting. A family of great horned owls nested in the treetop, coming out frequently to display their size and form. They didn't seem to give a hoot, provided I let the tree stand.

[1] Dudley's other records indicate the carving was thirty feet high

The Maid of the Woods Tree

There was no trail to the site, and I thought it best not to let the exact location be made public. The mountain of dry chips from the carving presented an extreme fire hazard. However, eventually someone discovered the carving, and it became the subject of a documentary film, a *Life* magazine piece, and numerous newspaper articles. The publicity prompted the US Forest Service to build a trail to accommodate the spectators who came from home and abroad to see and photograph the maiden as she continued to cling to the tree. As interesting as the effort was, plans to make the site into a park failed to materialize, and I didn't complete the carving.

In 1978, some thirty years later, Allied Stores considered buying the tree for a planned major shopping center. I went to Verlot with some officials from Allied to check the tree and to assess the possibility of a sale, but we mutually determined to leave the tree in the woods for public viewing. Forest service personnel informed me that they had plans to improve the trail to the site. Then, strange as it may seem, shortly following our decision to leave the tree where it had stood for untold centuries, it was struck with a bolt from the heavens. Eight forest service firefighters worked for two days to extinguish the blaze, and the carving was left in pretty bad shape.

I was eighty-seven years of age at the time, but after evaluating the damage I determined I could resurrect the maiden. The fire had burned decayed wood in the heart of the tree, but what was left was very good. I figured I could salvage it using steel cables and guy wires to reinforce it while we worked on it, and if I could find some support for fixing it up, the sculpture could be better than ever. But that was not to be. In the mid-eighties lightning struck the great tree again—and again the fire was extinguished. The greater part of the tree was left standing, but most of the carving was obliterated.

The twice-burnt tree held a huge volume of the finest seasoned cedar, ideal for the growing demand for monumental wood sculpture. I was able to have the tree removed with the help of some contacts in the logging industry who actually had to build a road so logging trucks could get into the site. They transported it to the Slough House Park in Redmond where I was living at the time. I envisioned in the remnants of the tree a magnificent sculpture, a sculpture I would name *Riding the Transcending Wave* to commemorate the upcoming Washington State Centennial. Like the legendary Phoenix of old, the great cedar could rise to new splendor and glory from the ashes of its past.

The State of Washington was unsuccessful in finding a sponsor for *Riding the Transcending Wave*, Dudley's award-winning centennial design. On speculation, Dudley used portions of the *Maid of the Woods* tree to carve several major segments of his centennial project. The bulk of the salvaged cedar Dudley dedicated primarily to his apprentices. Following his death in 1992, the parts of *Riding the Transcending Wave* were sold separately to individual collectors. Dudley's grandson Michael inherited his grandfather's supply of fine carving wood and sold what remained of the tree to appreciative carvers.

Chapter 46

Art and Moralizing

From the writing of Richard S. Beyer

Dudley Carter was not the product of an art school but a man drawn to carving by his own recognition of his talent. Without contact with the larger recognized traditions, he built his art from the Northwest experience: big trees, Indian designs, logging heroics, and the art nouveau fashion of his times.

He looked locally for the meaning of his work, thus it embodies the values of Seattle before it became a big town. I never met Carter, but I have a vivid impression of him from a video that was made about him when he was in his late eighties and working on a shopping center commission in Oregon.

Back in 1931, exploring his art ideas, he made a small composition in a bar of soap, setting a realistic woman off against a cubist figure—the old against the new. Dudley would reject the new.

In the local artists file in the Seattle Library I came across a picture of Diego Rivera's huge mural with Dudley Carter in the center, hewing on a great log. I imagine Carter's excitement in being recognized by Rivera and Rivera's delight in sharing his vision and his energy with this strong idealist, a son of the working class. As was common in public art of that time, the mural design pictured a better tomorrow.

Carter carved a totem pole in the Westlake Mall. The scaffolding was erected around the great log, which was standing on end, and Carter worked with his woodsman's axe from level to level. Up there, with one stroke of the axe, he would define

the brow of a spirit face. He coordinated his vision and his hand in service to a better world. The vision lingered in Seattle until a former mayor sold the town out to the feds.

    Before this change, Indian design had been a living and public presence in Seattle. Many creative

Menace de Modernisme, 1984
Red cedar, 8.5' × 5'2" × 32"
A design Dudley transfigured from his 1931 award-winning soap carving
Donated to the City of Bellevue by Marvin Boys and installed at the North Bellevue Community Center
Photograph 'Lyn Lambert

people felt it: Bill Holm writing sensitively, Guy Anderson marvelously universalizing the line of the spirit eye, the Hauburgs spending generously, and Ivar collecting hungrily.

Debates arise periodically around the subject of non-Native American artists using Native American iconography. Indians have charged that others who took inspiration from their carvings were stealing their sacred heritage. Dudley Carter was not of the Northwest Coast Indian culture, but he grew up in it, was inspired by it, and was always respectful of it. As a talented sculptor, he was appreciated by Natives and non-Natives alike for incorporating the indigenous spirit into his art for the public's enjoyment.

Dudley Carter's regionalism inspired me. I don't think I would ever have started out in the carving business if, on coming to the Northwest in the late 1950s, I had not discovered the totem poles and the stories that were told about them. The level of abstraction and curious man-animal imagery loosed my way of seeing from the thrall of the impossible inside-out and outside-in Greek/Roman/Renaissance art of the schools and museums of the East Coast.

One afternoon, I sat alone in the well of the Burke Museum asking, as it were, the poles around me to say what they were about. They responded that they were the cautionary demons of a ritual society. Their presence moralized, and I think art should moralize.

The contrast of the old poles in the museum with Carter's poles in the public view gave me insight into how public art works. His work is of a time and people very different from our time and ourselves now.

Richard S. Beyer (1925–2012), a self-taught sculptor, created Seattle's much-loved *People Waiting for the Interurban* and over eighty other public sculptures. He graduated from Columbia University, earned a master's degree in education in Vermont, and moved to Seattle in 1957 to work on a PhD at the University of Washington. In 1964 he left a career as an economist with the Boeing Company and began making sculptures of people and animals, very often playful and mischievous. Beyer worked in brick, wood, and metal. He established a foundry in Seattle's Fremont district where he produced bronze and aluminum castings until 1988, when he moved his foundry to Pateros, Washington. His sculptures are highly interactive, eliciting hugs and often being dressed up and accessorized by an admiring public. Beyer's art and life are featured in the book *The Art People Love* by Margaret W. Beyer, Richard's wife, (Washington State University Press, 1999).
Photograph Stan Morse

Chapter 47

Life in the Fasting Lane

From the writing of Steve Johnston

In the spring of 1986, my job with the *Seattle Times* took me to Marymoor Park in Redmond where Dudley Carter had set up shop. Dudley sat me down on a log, turned off his hearing aid, and started talking. I couldn't break in with questions. He talked for four hours nonstop. The result was a lengthy story, but Dudley called me after it appeared to say it wasn't long enough.

Dudley Carter approached his life story like he did a forty-foot tree he was preparing to carve into a work of art. It took time. He worked around the edges of his life, taking a piece here and another there until it started to take shape. Finally he was ready to show it. Or, in this case, ready to reveal the secret of his long life: fasting.

"Fasting. It's nothing new," said the sculptor. "It's been done for years. Animals do it. My mother used to have chickens and when one of them got sick, the others would stop eating until the sick chick got well. You can fast whenever you need it. You can have a water fast or a vegetable fast or a fruit fast."

His favorite, he said, was the apple fast. Apples gave him something to chew on.

Carter thought he had figured out what's wrong with us today and, in his words, "The problem with people is they don't eat good food. They eat sugar, starch, and fat and they don't get enough exercise. There are dozens of little things that you do wrong

Bear Post Patio Wall Divider #2, 1986, red cedar, 7' × 13.5' × 18"
Carved at Marymoor Park and sold through the Dudley Carter estate
Photograph courtesy Anna Vaughan Hanson

and they aren't harmful by themselves, but you put them all together and they can kill a man."

Sitting on a clear cedar plank, Carter stated, "The automobile has robbed man of his greatest cure—walking and exercise."

Carter figured out his nutritional philosophy before he figured out he was a wood sculptor. During the time he was growing up in Queen's Park in New Westminster, BC, in a backwoods logging family, "either you took care of yourself or you died," he said. There was no medical help.

He told me he'd been given up for dead nine times. The first time was in 1892 when he was less than a year old and a cholera plague swept through the community, nearly wiping out the entire infant population of New Westminster. Carter lived because he had very good care. He said, "My mother carried me on a pillow for almost eighteen months because I was just a little bag of bones."

"Being ill affected me the rest of my life. I read an article that said if you're hit by cholera when you're young, you will have physical problems all your life. But it may have been the best thing that ever happened to me. If I was to live, I had to learn to live right."

Four years after recovering from cholera, young Dudley came down with rheumatic fever, and along with it, the beginning of his hearing problems.

Then when he was nine years old, he had an appendicitis attack. At the time he was chief skid greaser with the family logging business. The job required him to be bent over most of the time as he ran ahead of the team hauling logs, sloshing oil on the skidway to make the oxen's job easier. It was fortunate he had to be bent over so much, Carter said, because his "stomach hurt so bad, he couldn't stand

Life in the Fasting Lane

up anyway."

The pain stopped him from eating, and it was then that he discovered the benefits of fasting. He said he recovered in ten days, although later in life he lost his appendix.

Illness followed him for the next twenty-five years—pleurisy, pneumonia, and scurvy. In 1924 he was in Vancouver, BC, trying to recover from scurvy, a result of living in remote logging camps.

"Logging companies would feed you anything you want, as long as it came out of a can," Carter said. "There was no fresh food. Milk came from a can and it was a sweet thick mixture."

The doctors treating him for scurvy put him on a baby food diet. Carter found himself a new doctor.

"He put me on a regular diet and told me to stay away from doctors and pills," Carter said. "That was the last time I saw a doctor. I haven't been to a doctor since, except for injuries."

He concluded that having multiple physical problems might have been the best thing that ever happened to him. They forced him to learn to live right. He was sure that if he hadn't learned to live right, and that included fasting sensibly, he'd be dead and gone like his brothers instead of being alive and well in his nineties.

When I tried to bring him around to the subject of art, Carter shrugged as if to dismiss his work. Some of his sculptures were lined up against the fence around his workshop in the park's mainte-

Dudley with *Adventure on Western Waters*, 1986, red cedar, 6′ × 12′ × 4′
Shown in the maintenance yard at Marymoor Park. Sold in 1990 to Northwest Hospital, Seattle Washington.
The carving represents an incident in Dudley's own life, an encounter with a killer whale. He found the giant animals to be playful rather than hostile, but said, "When they play, they play rough."
Photograph courtesy Bertil Valley

nance yard where he worked seven days a week when he was in town. He was working on a panel made out of hand-split planks and posts he titled *Bear Post Patio Wall Divider #2*. He figured he could sell it for $6,000 or $7,000.

A piece called *Adventure on Western Waters*, showing an Indian in a canoe crashing through the waves, towered above him. Carter said he didn't know what it would be when he first saw the wood in the form of driftwood on the beach in British Columbia.

"I didn't see it until I started working on it," Carter said. "I think that's the way it is with most artists. They don't see it until they start working on it."

"It's like my life," he said. "There have been many adventures in it."

But the point he wanted to impress upon me that day was that without fasting, most of those adventures would never have been ventured.

Steve Johnston (1946–2010) grew up in the Northwest and served in the US Navy during the Vietnam War. After leaving the service, he studied journalism. He retired in 2001 after twenty-four years as a reporter and columnist with the *Seattle Times*. His popular *Just Ask Johnston* column offered Seattleites the real nitty-gritty about their city. He lived for years with multiple sclerosis and wrote eloquently about the way MS was limiting his life. In a series of columns entitled *Getting Around*, he described challenges of living with a disability. Even in retirement, Johnston tackled prevailing attitudes about our human condition in his *Sunday Punch* column, which appeared periodically in the *Pacific NW Magazine*, published by the *Seattle Times*.

Photograph courtesy Steve Johnston

Dudley carved *Adventure on Western Waters* from Western red cedar salvaged from the beach at his summer camp at Gibsons, BC. The driftwood had been worked over by the sea then left on the beach above high-tide level, seasoning for about six years before Dudley began the carving. He completed most of the work at Gibsons before bringing it to Marymoor Park, a move that involved a large crane, a boat, and a truck.

NOTE: "Life in the Fasting Lane" was compiled from notes provided by Steve Johnston.

Chapter 48

Healing Art

From a conversation with Kathy Conner

It was Independence Day weekend 1987 when I headed to Marymoor Park in Redmond for the annual Heritage Festival. Dudley Carter's towering sculpture, *Legend of the Moon*, graces the main drive to the park. The powerful work is an imaginative interpretation of the Snoqualmie legend known to many as Moon the Transformer.

I spent some reflective time with *Legend of the Moon*, drawn to thoughts of heaven and earth, before venturing into the festival. Among the mix of arts and crafts booths and displays, I was delightfully surprised to come upon Dudley Carter at work on another cedar creation. I stood in awe, transfixed by Dudley; he was so focused on his work that he seemed oblivious to anything around him.

Seated by Dudley was a gentleman of considerable distinction. His snowy white hair and flowing beard made me think he could be Santa Claus in his civvies. But this gentleman was long and lean, so if he was Santa he must have gone through a major weight loss program! After a while Santa spoke to me. He introduced himself as Bertil Valley, and in a gentle and most sincere manner, he explained that Dudley Carter was, at the age of ninety-six, looking for a home and a place to work. Bertil presented a petition he was sponsoring. His plan was to convince King County to do something unprecedented and designate Dudley Carter as their first artist-in-residence. He wanted to see Dudley in a home and studio on some county property just north of Marymoor Park. So taken was I by these two remarkable elderly gentlemen and so unthinkable did it seem to me that an artist of such renown should be without a place where he could comfortably carry on his art, that I enthusiastically and hopefully signed the petition. I also had my picture taken with the two gentlemen, not realizing how significantly they would soon figure in my life.

Bertil Valley's petition was successful, and in October 1987 Dudley Carter moved into his new home in Slough House Park. The following January he was officially installed as King County's first ever artist-in-residence. Thereafter, every time I had occasion to go to Redmond I would stop at the park to watch Dudley at work and to study the sculptures he had arrayed in the yard. Our two younger children, David and Susan, usually came along. Their youthful enthusiasm for Dudley's art added to my own enjoyment.

I took advantage of every opportunity to observe Dudley Carter at work. When the Bellevue Art Museum announced a fundraising exhibition at Bellevue Square and that Dudley Carter would appear at the event, I was there for another fix of my favorite sculptor. Again, thoroughly entranced, I watched Dudley at work in the busy shopping mall. The museum was offering a Dudley Carter sculpture for sale to raise funds for their operations, and with very little deliberation, *Bird Watcher's Dream #1* became a wonderful addition to our home.

Stops at Dudley's park became even more

The Beast That Was, 1982, red cedar, 8′ × 10′ × 20″, carved at Gibsons, BC, purchased by the Conner family, Issaquah, Washington. Photograph courtesy Anna Vaughan Hanson

significant to us after Susan, three years of age at the time, was diagnosed with a particularly belligerent form of cancer. A visit to Dudley's always boosted her spirits. One sculpture especially caught her imagination and charmed her at every visit. Dudley had named it *The Beast That Was*, but to Susan it was the magic unicorn from her favorite poem, *If I Found a Wistful Unicorn* by Ann Ashford. It was easy for Susan to see her mystical unicorn in the regal horse-like figure that Dudley had artfully combined with smaller residents of the forest—a bird, a frog, and wildflowers. I think Susan related to the creature's aura of majesty and playfulness.

For nearly three years our family devoted the best of our energies to helping Susan through her brave struggle, but in January of 1990 when Susan was six, we lost the battle. I plunged into a number of endeavors, trying to fill the void left by Susan's death. I devoted myself more to the rest of the family, attempting to make up for all they had missed while I attended to Susan during her illness.

Some years earlier I had received carving tools for Christmas, and my exposure to Dudley Carter re-awakened my earlier interest in wood carving. I had a granddad and an uncle who worked with wood professionally, and as a little girl I watched them for hours on end as they applied their woodworking talents. Perhaps they imparted to me an interest in the wonders of wood carving and a sense of the fulfillment to be found in the craft.

In the summer of 1991, I came across a flier announcing the appearance of a "Hundred-Year-Old Woodcarver" at an arts fair in Old Bellevue. Here was another opportunity for me to observe the master at work. At the fair a student apprentice acted as interpreter for Dudley since his hearing wasn't up to snuff. I visited with the apprentice and told her of my appreciation for Dudley's work and my desire to improve my carving skills. She suggested rather emphatically that I consider joining Dudley's group of carving apprentices and offered to set up an appointment for me to meet with him at his studio, urging me to bring along some of my carvings.

The idea of working with Dudley Carter was to me an impossible dream. In all my visits with him at the various shows and at his outdoor studio, I had said scarcely a word to him. His talent so intimidated me.

Apprehensively, I followed the apprentice's suggestion and called her to arrange an appointment. A few weeks later, I presented myself along with an assortment of my carvings to Mr. Carter. Welcoming me warmly, he started me out the way he did each apprentice, giving me a wooden form, an armature on which I was to shape some clay. I could practice his particular techniques in the clay before attempting to carve the likeness of a human head in cedar.

A typical sampling of heads sculpted in clay by Dudley Carter apprentices and stored at Dudley's outdoor studio preparatory to replicating them in cedar
Photograph 'Lyn Lambert

Carving lessons with Dudley Carter were uniquely experiential, probably not ideal for every wood-carver wannabe. Dudley was about as deaf as the bumps on the logs he worked on, and his speech was difficult to comprehend. But I soon realized that words were not necessarily Dudley's main means of communication. If students couldn't learn through

Suspended Fantasy Planter, drawing by Olemara Peters, 1991

observation and sensation, then perhaps they might be wise to find another teacher.

Dudley's apprentices were an interesting mix of personalities, ages, and backgrounds. They were all intent on their own work, yet at the same time interested in helping each other. Apprentices who had been part of the program for some time explained to novitiates what to expect when working with Dudley and what Dudley expected of us.

Dudley informed all prospective carvers that his apprentice program involved no money. In return for lessons, apprentices performed a variety of tasks unrelated to carving—anything from shopping, typing, and chauffering to doing yard work and repairing equipment.

My husband also got caught up in the action. He wasn't interested in carving lessons—he's a surgeon and not inclined to pursue any other form of carving. But I convinced him to become involved in the construction of Dudley's Haida house studio. My surgeon-husband also has a degree in electrical engineering, so he offered to install the studio's electrical service. The first order of business involved digging a ditch to carry the wires underground from the main residence to the studio. The irony of a doctor digging ditches wasn't lost on Dudley, and he often expressed his amazement over that.

Dudley's apprentice program turned out to be more than just an opportunity for me to pick up carving techniques from a master. Working with Dudley and other carvers who came to his studio to work and to learn was truly therapeutic and remarkably restorative.

Associating with the many interesting individuals attracted to Dudley Carter turned out to be a blessing too. People like Bertil, dear Bertil, whom I mentioned looked like Santa Claus. Well, Bertil was truly the spirit of Santa, all year 'round.

On Susan's fourth birthday, which fell on St. Patrick's Day, Bertil appeared at Swedish Hospital's Bone Marrow Transplant Unit in his Santa suit. He passed out gifts to all the children in Susan's ward, helping them see the magic and hope in life. Imagine, if Santa can arrive on your birthday, on St. Patrick's Day, what other magic can this old world offer? Over the three challenging years of Susan's illness, Santa Bertil visited her often, loving her and encouraging her—encouraging me.

In the years following Susan's death, my association with Dudley also heartened me considerably—his art, so full of spirit; his tenacity and humor, abundant; and of course, his carving counsel, priceless. In my time as one of Dudley Carter's apprentices, I learned much—much about art, about life, and about death.

Shortly before Christmas of 1991, it became apparent that Dudley needed a medical doctor's professional attention and not for his ditchdigging skills or wiring abilities. For years Dudley had kept what he described as a "healthy distance from doctors," watching his diet, exercising regularly, and fasting on the few occasions when he did become ill, but we were sure that medical advice was called for this time. Dudley was reluctant—to put it mildly—to see any doctors, but at my husband's urging, he finally agreed to do so. He thoughtfully considered their diagnoses, but agreed to accept only palliative care, rejecting all suggestions of surgery and medication.

I had been a nurse, so it was natural that my apprentice duties began to center on Dudley's medical needs. He accepted my help so graciously, not having any qualms at all when I traded my carver's hat for my nurse's cap.

Likewise, Dudley didn't hesitate to dispense healthcare advice, even to a doctor and nurse. At Christmastime our young son David became ill, and Dudley, ailing himself, gave us precise instructions for a diet he was certain would speed David's recovery. It called for an apple fast, followed by some non-starchy vegetables and dextrinized bread. He also suggested that, since it was Christmas, David would want to eat some special foods. He advised us to fix some red or green gelatin with a bit of whipped cream and a cherry on top, so David wouldn't feel left out of the Christmas feasting. And you know, David went along with Dudley's prescribed treatment and had a speedy recovery.

Dudley delighted in telling others how, like the proverbial cat, he managed to defeat death nine times. It appeared to us there would be no tenth lease on life, but Dudley continued to do business as usual, never complaining about the complications that ill health visited upon his life.

My family shared my love for Dudley and his work. We knew we would soon say our last goodbye

Suspended Fantasy Planter, 1991
Red cedar, 10′ × 18′ × 3′
Carved at Slough House Park, purchased in 1992 by the Conner family, Issaquah, Washington
Photograph 'Lyn Lambert

to this dear friend, so we determined to spend as much time as we could with him. We also decided to obtain our own collection of his carvings. I spoke earlier of Susan's favorite, her unicorn or Dudley's *The Beast That Was*. It was quite naturally the pièce de résistance. We told Dudley of Susan's love for that work, and he felt good about it becoming a memorial to her. He came to our Cougar Mountain home to select the site that would best fit *The Beast* and even supervised its installation, satisfied that it was set just the way he envisioned it.

Our next choice was a wonderful large constructed piece called *Suspended Fantasy Planter*. It depicts a grasshopper, a dragonfly, and a frog in a symbiotic relationship, held in equilibrium with a mythical bird. I see a happy interdependence, a balance of nature, expressed in the work.

The final piece we settled on Dudley called *The Last Frontier*. Attached to it when we purchased it was a sign, hand-printed by Dudley, reading "Work Not Completed." That is significant to me. To my mind the work appears finished, but in Dudley's mind more remained to be done. Perhaps, like so many things we set out to accomplish or conquer, it's hard to know when enough is enough. If Dudley were to live two hundred years, I think he would still feel that his life's work was not completed. I treasure that attitude.

Dudley's spirit visits me frequently, not only through our own treasured examples of his art, but in various and sundry places, always delighting and inspiring. Photographs of Dudley Carter carvings appear in an official Cub Scout woodworking handbook I used for a carving project with my son's Cub Scout den. When I visit Children's Hospital in Seattle to entertain young patients in the recreational therapy playroom, Dudley's *Legend of the Sea* meets me at the entrance. I enjoy seeing his other works displayed around the Seattle area, and whenever I meet with former apprentices or friends of Dudley Carter, there is always a sense of Dudley's presence.

I spend a lot of time carving, continuing to study with noted Northwest carvers and tackling increasingly ambitious projects. Dudley's encouragement and example set me on that path. His appreciation of the wonders of creation and his understanding of the magical, mystical interdependence of all that is and ever was, is truly inspirational, truly therapeutic. It's been very good medicine for my soul.

Kathy Conner and Dudley Carter in 1992 with *Bird Watcher's Dream #1* by Dudley Carter, 1988
Red cedar, 2.5' × 20"
Photograph courtesy Kathy Conner

Kathy Conner, a native of Indiana, moved to the Pacific Northwest in 1980, became enamored of Northwest Coast art, and continues to indulge her interest and to expand her inherent talent through her studies with other notable carvers. Conner trained and practiced as a nurse and devotes herself to her roles as wife, mother, and enthusiastic volunteer for local charities.

Catch the Wind
By Kathy Conner

A contemporary fable inspired by a loving and beloved child and by *Fawn and Bird*, a work of art by Dudley Carter

A beautiful, innocent fawn, loving life, frolics in the sun in a meadow of fragrant grass and wildflowers, a delicate wildflower herself—a joy giver.

But Hunter comes, and with no reverence for life, no eye for grace, no heart to care, he pursues her.

Fawn looks to the heavens and sees Raven. Raven, loving all creation, will never let her beauty be tarnished. Raven soars with wings outspread, five full circles over the tiny fawn, and sends Wind to rescue her. Wind catches the gentle soul, taking her to infinitely more beautiful meadows where she is forever safe.

Hunter is vanquished.

"I see in this sculpture my beautiful, delicate daughter, who was diagnosed with cancer when only three. The cancer had no respect for this joyful little angel, and when nearly six, she escaped its unrelenting ravages forevermore. She dearly loved Dudley Carter's whimsical sculptures, her favorite being *The Beast That Was*. She determined that the mythical beast had to be a magic unicorn. I fancy she now plays with that magnificent creature in the beautiful meadows to which Wind has taken her. Perhaps it is Raven, creator of life and governor of the spiritual realm, who keeps her so alive and close in my heart."

Kathy Conner

Fawn and Bird, 1979, red cedar, 9′ × 3′ × 16″
Carved at Gibsons, BC, eventually situated in the sculpture garden of the Redmond Public Library
Photograph 'Lyn Lambert

Legend of the Sea
By 'Lyn Lambert

The sea and her creatures figure largely in numerous North American Indian myths and legends. Dudley Carter's *Legend of the Sea*, portraying the sanctity and preservation of life, is his interpretation of one such legend.

In Dudley's work, a mermaid, a mother figure symbolic of creative and protective forces, holds a baby otter, representative of young beings, out of the reach of a sea serpent, a symbol of sickness and evil.

Ironically, ancient Greeks and Romans portrayed their god of medicine, Asclepius or Aesculapius, as a serpent. Asclepius healed by means of dreams and is often depicted in ancient sculpture in the form of a snake touching a man's shoulder with its mouth. The serpent was known to heal simply by biting the patient where it hurt, effecting a vaccination of sorts with its immediate, potentially poisonous contact. Dudley Carter shows his sea serpent administering its attention to the mermaid's shoulder.

George Thomas purchased *Legend of the Sea* for Bay Shore, a lakeside apartment complex he owned in Kirkland, Washington. The apartments were converted to condominiums in 1984.

Legend of the Sea, 1964, red cedar, 8.5' × 5'10"
Photograph 'Lyn Lambert

Thomas, a personal friend of the artist, retained possession of the sculpture. He wanted the work to have a new home where the public could have access to it and donated it to Seattle's Children's Orthopedic Hospital and Medical Center, now known as Seattle Children's. Thomas had an emotional attachment to COHMC, having been a patient there as a child, and his infant daughter died there in the early 1940s. He chose the hospital setting because of his past connections to the institution and because he felt the theme of the sculpture related to their mission.

Hospital records indicate *Legend of the Sea* was valued at $16,000 at the time of its donation. Seattle Children's maintains it as part of their sculpture walk on hospital grounds.

Chapter 49

As Light Illuminates the Darkness

From a conversation with Dean Fredrickson

For the life of me, I cannot understand why I hadn't seen my way clear to stop and meet Dudley Carter earlier. I had driven by his place countless times and noticed the carvings displayed there. Then one day, feeling somewhat at loose ends, I stopped. A hand-lettered sign attached to the chain-link fence caught my interest: "Apprentices Wanted."

When I was a child I watched my father occupy his winter evenings carving exquisite wooden images of animals, so I knew carving could be a productive time filler. I'd always had a yen for art, but I had not found a meaningful way to express that side of myself. Maybe I could be a wood-carver's apprentice?

The gate was open, so there was nothing to keep me from entering the woodsy yard. I took my time walking among the carvings, some young and fresh, others showing signs of advancing age. After a while I went over to watch the carver as he worked alone outside his workshop. Before too long, he looked up and spoke to me. He seemed eager to gain another recruit, insisting he could teach me in six weeks what it would take someone years to learn in art school.

I assumed he was seventy-five or eighty years old, yet he was still turning out extraordinary work. A man like that must have some secret. It seemed to me that working with such an individual would be a rare opportunity. I might discover what kept him going—tap into some of his wisdom. I decided to join the ranks of apprentices, learning later that the old master was actually ninety-seven years of age!

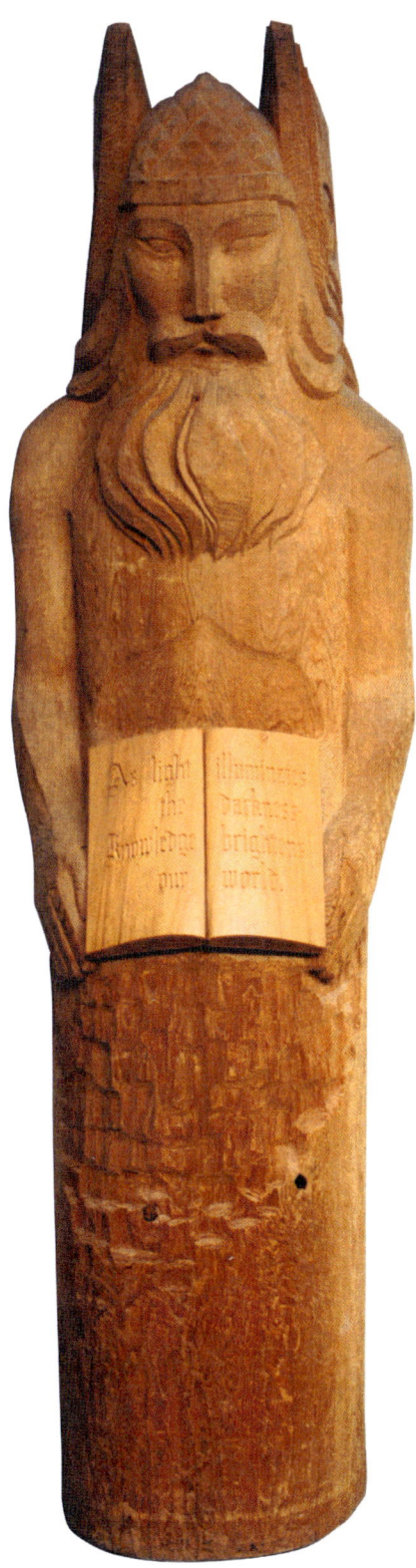

Mr. Carter started me out literally at ground level—cleaning up the grounds, mowing the lawn, moving logs, whatever he needed. Soon he showed me how to use an adze so I could help smooth out logs, readying them for him to carve. I chopped into my foot only once. As I gained Mr. Carter's confidence, he gave me more technical work to do. I soon found myself having the time of my life.

Respectful of the artist's age and stature, I addressed him as Mr. Carter until he asked that I call him Dudley. At first I felt somewhat uncomfortable being on a first-name basis with such a man—a man I admired as mentor or sage. Another difficulty was my tendency to be soft-spoken. I had to work at overcoming my reluctance to shout, especially at an older person. That was a must in Dudley's case due to his near deafness.

Dudley never ceased to amaze me. He received a commission from the University of Idaho to carve an image of their mascot. I wondered how many ninety-seven-year-old artists ever received such commissions. Dudley just took it as a matter of course. He selected a cedar log from his seemingly inexhaustible supply, had me set it outside the garage that served as his workshop, and then went to work.

He considered the wood in its entirety, measured it precisely, studied the grain of the wood, and got down to business in the manner in which he encouraged his apprentices—slowly and deliberately. He made definite, methodical chops with his axe or taps with his mallet on the handle of a chisel. As slow as the process seemed, it wasn't long before a Viking figure began to emerge. Dudley worked for hours at a time, tirelessly. He emphasized by word and example that wood carving is not a race.

The Viking, 1989, red cedar, 7' × 3'
Mascot, University of Idaho, dubbed Joe Vandal by the students
Photograph Shelly Hanks Photography, Moscow, Idaho

As Light Illuminates the Darkness

Details of *The Viking*, 1989. Photographs Shelly Hanks Photography, Moscow, Idaho

Nearing completion of the University of Idaho commission, Dudley asked me to help him with a book the Viking would hold. The design called for a quotation to be carved on the book's open pages. Dudley knew that I had worked as a calligrapher and figured I could help lay out the lettering. In keeping with the aim of a university, the words would proclaim, "As light illuminates the darkness, knowledge brightens our world."

Dudley always called that piece *The Viking*, but I learned later that the University of Idaho mascot is a vandal, and the students know Dudley's *Viking* as Joe Vandal.

Dudley spoke nonchalantly of his artful profession, referring to it as "making chips." After a time-out, say for a brief nap in his easy chair or an "apple break," he'd often say, "Well, I better go out and make some chips."

But Dudley was justly proud of his stature as a sculptor. His business card read "Sculptor and Forest Engineer."

At the time that I got to know Dudley, I was a commercial truck driver, but I had graduated from theological school and served as a minister in North Dakota. Dudley read his Bible every single day. He was no Bible-thumper, but he was deeply religious. His religion appeared to involve a healthy balance between his reverence for scripture and his reverence for nature. I had heard it said that Dudley Carter carried his environment around with him like a blanket. It seems to me that it was his balanced nature that made him comfortable in whatever environment he might be. He told me our human nature is a trinity—physical, mental, and spiritual—and they are inseparable. He maintained emphatically, "If any one of these gets out of balance, then we're in trouble." He was determined to keep his three human natures in balance.

Dudley kept his mental faculties as sharp as the blades of his axes. He studied his newspaper daily; he said all the world's affairs influenced his work and he had to be on top of things. With his hearing so limited, radio and TV were essentially useless to him, so the newspaper kept him informed.

He always knew exactly what he was going to do next and had little patience with anyone or anything that interfered with his agenda. If he expected you to show up at a prescribed time to help him, you'd darn well better keep your word and show up. If you let him down, he would show his displeasure without uttering a word.

His delight could be equally apparent. I remember showing up at his studio early one morning and receiving an enthusiastic welcome. Dudley, full of energy and excitement, told me he had been up until three-thirty in the morning sketching designs and making models. He always had a half dozen or so pieces in various stages of development, taking shape in his mind, sketched out on paper, modeled in clay, or in the carving or assembly process.

As for the physical side of things, Dudley knew he had to keep exercising. One might figure he'd get enough exercise in the course of his work. But he had arthritis and went through a vigorous exercise routine every morning while still in bed, to get his joints moving. He also knew just what to eat to fuel his system. He felt we should eat only what the body needs. At least one apple a day was a given, of course, and often for dinner he'd put together a substantial one-dish meal, no recipe required. He'd cut up fish or chicken, put it in a pan, heap on a variety of non-starchy vegetables, and smother it all with a pile of parsley. Then he'd cover it all with foil, pop it in the oven, and head outside to "make chips." After a few hours, dinner would be ready. In regard to his eating habits he said, "I love food as much as anybody!" He and I would occasionally go to a local buffet-style restaurant, and it surprised me to see him load up his plate. He would eat anything, even junk food, and he'd eat a lot. He seemed almost like an alcoholic falling off the wagon, but normally he ate very little. As for alcohol, he was known to enjoy a regular ration of rum—just an ounce.

Dudley felt so strongly about keeping vital that it disturbed him to meet up with people on the decline. One time a group of senior citizens, residents of a retirement home, scheduled a visit. The busload of seniors arrived and received a polite but brief welcome from Dudley, who immediately went to work, leaving me to show the folks around and answer their questions. As the bus pulled out, Dudley sputtered, "They walk around like a bunch of zombies. People who sit around old people's homes playing cards and bingo are literally committing suicide," stressing the last two words.

Then Dudley became ill. At his age his skin was quite thin, and his work made him vulnerable to scrapes and cuts. A log had rolled against his lower leg causing a wound that just wouldn't heal. Dudley thought he could let nature take its course, but finally he acquiesced to his family's pleadings and went to see a doctor. The doctor prescribed antibiotics, which Dudley was determined not to take. After more pleading from his family, he finally agreed, but the antibiotics didn't agree with Dudley's system. He broke out in an angry red rash from head to toe. As miserable as the condition was, it never kept Dudley from his work. When his skin was at its worst and he couldn't wear shoes, he'd wear stocking slippers, even when working outside.

Dudley decided that the medication was killing him. He resolved to take no more antibiotics and cure the problem his own way. He began an apple fast. He also found another doctor who agreed that antibiotics weren't necessary and gave him a cream to treat the weeping leg wound. Believe it or not, the rash went away and his leg healed beautifully. But I never heard the end of "those damn pills."

For the rest of his life Dudley groused to anyone who'd listen to him about the dangers of antibiotics. He claimed that they had further impaired his already minimal hearing and upset his sense of balance.

Following pages: A letter from Dudley to his sister Eltheen mentioning his completion of *The Viking* for the University of Idaho. Dudley comments on the damage done by the antibiotics. Courtesy Ethleen Carter King

"The Stough House"
7447 159th Pl. N.E.
Redmond Wa. 98052

Hi Theen Dave and Family — Dec 16/88

Just a note to say I had just written Gene to forward this to you (not knowing where you were) at the last minute got your letter.

I had written giving you each duplicate cheques $1,500.00, $1,000.00 for you each personally and $500.00 to help any you find in need. I am just finishing a commission for the U. of Idaho, it pays $6,500.00 as soon as I'm paid up I expect in Jan or Feb. I expect to contribute about $1,000.00 to the Ecclesia hall they expect to build at Maple Ridge. This way I can help some of you out a little without disturbing the bank account.

I have several large prospects here and two in Calif. which may materialize, if they don't, I keep on making sculpture for the Collectors and sell from time to time. Two large pieces just about ready to set up now. I am one of the sculptors selected to make a proposal for the Washington Centennial that would pay off pretty good if it comes my way. I have several apprentices who work for free which helps to speed things up.

The physical damage done by the antibiotic pills is gradually clearing up the doctors responsible for it finally admitted they did not know enough about it. I found a new skin specialist who treated it externally no pills, with good results. The enclosed article explains how far off the medical profession has drifted

The case they give Dr. Mary Calderone is a duplicate of mine, only due to my greater age my case is much worse. I thank the Good Lord I have been directed in the ways to cope with it — and it looks like I will come out of it better than if it hadn't happened. The medical profession have drifted away from the way man was designed to live.

Mike came down from Gibsons today and will help a little preparing the set up of a large sculpture (16' hi) "Bird Defying Mans Invasion of space" over the week end. He also brought a large burl piece about a ton. So there will be some chips to make, some of my apprentices are away over the holidays, so it helps. I am now finishing the commission for the U of Idaho at the CROSS ROADS shopping mall. Just had a call from Anna she and Lex are coming Monday with a chicken dinner and will stay over night. I will probably go to Gibsons for a day or two at Christmas.

Hope you all can find your way and time for a visit to the "Slough House" soon

Love in the One Great Hope

Hadley

The very best wishes for Christmas and the Bigger and Better New Year.

Dudley at work on *Celestial Adventure*, 1991, with Roy Wagner and Olemara Peters in the background
Photographs 'Lyn Lambert

A diminished sense of balance was not apparent to those of us who worked with him. Asked by the Redmond Chamber of Commerce to be grand marshal of the city's Derby Days Parade shortly after his hundredth birthday, Dudley came up with a curious creation he called *Celestial Adventure* to enter in the parade. The magnitude of the creature required Dudley to do much of the work while balanced on a makeshift platform. Most people at any age wouldn't even think of working atop such an arrangement of planks and sawhorses, but Dudley clambered up and down it like a mountain goat.

The following winter, I learned that Dudley had potentially serious prostate problems and it hit me extremely hard. I didn't want to lose him and feared that hospitalization would kill him more certainly than would any disease. I was relieved that he didn't have to be hospitalized. He kept right on working. After his hundredth birthday, he began the reconstruction of his Haida studio. It seemed as if he willed himself to live long enough to see the studio standing once again.

A group of apprentices and Dudley's grandson,

Celestial Adventure, red cedar, 8'3" × 16' × 6'10"
Dudley and his intriguing sculpture were featured in the City of Redmond's 1991 Derby Days Parade. The centenarian artist served as the parade's grand marshal.
Photograph 'Lyn Lambert

Redwood rounds of Haida house floor prior to the additon of aggregate concrete infill
Photograph 'Lyn Lambert

226   *Legacy*

Michael Vaughan, worked with Dudley to set up the Haida house. Dudley assigned me the job of preparing and laying redwood rounds for the floor. At one point I reshaped some of the smaller segments so they would better fit the configuration. Dudley didn't like that. He wanted all the pieces round unless they were naturally skewed. Apart from a few details, the Haida house was pretty well completed before Dudley died.

Having been a student of Dudley's, I became all fired up to emulate his work, and I did a number of Native-style carvings. I love the art form, but I see now that it isn't my style. My spirit seems determined to express itself through more realistic designs. I am not following lockstep in the groove of the old master carver, but I've been imprinted with an enhanced sense of form and design and have a greater appreciation of monumental sculpture.

Dudley illuminated my view of the world at a time when I very much needed it.

Dean Fredrickson (1943–2014) pictured carving a figure for *Ring Around the Rosie*, a commissioned work for the Redmond YWCA Family Village. A native of North Dakota, Fredrickson graduated from Northwest Bible College, drove trucks professionally for many years, and pursued art as an avocation. He created numerous fine works in both wood and bronze.
Photograph 'Lyn Lambert

The distinctive head of *Celestial Adventure* gazes over Elliott Bay while situated at the Shilshole Bay Beach Club, a private event venue in Seattle.
Photograph Ronald Holden

As Light Illuminates the Darkness

Chapter 50

Windsong

Excerpted from "A Patient Hand" by Ronald Holden

In the summer of 1990, a delegation from the Medina Parks Board came to call on Dudley Carter, as potential patrons often did, with a view toward purchasing a sculpture, this one for Medina Park.

The board's landscape consultant and Eloise de Butts, who spearheaded the project, settled on a work that Carter had carved about a year earlier and labeled simply *Suspended Head*. An S-shaped piece of red cedar, it was a delicate female face whose hair was represented by the natural striations of sun-bleached driftwood. *Suspended Head* was exhibited at the Medina Days festival in August; a contest was held to find a more elegant name and a fund drive was held to raise the $5,500 purchase price. Janet Sandvik, a former teacher, thought the sculp-

ture's hair looked like "music floating in the wind" and suggested it be called *Windsong*. Carter selected Sandvik's proposal from some 250 entries.

A gravel path meanders through Medina Park, studded with fitness stations where urbanites can pause to tone their muscles. *Windsong* hangs from a roughly hewn post and beam in a grove of pine, alder, birch, and Oregon grape between the park's two ponds.

An original composition dedicated to Dudley Carter was performed at the dedication ceremony for the

Detail of *Windsong*, 1990
Photograph courtesy Anna Vaughan Hanson

sculpture in April 1991. Titled "Shey Manido," which means Great Spirit in Chippewa, the song was written and performed by Dent Davidson, director of the St. Thomas choir, and Esther "Little Dove" John, a musician from Sultan who is part Blackfoot Indian.

Windsong, more a grace note than a thundering public monument, seems to embody Carter's vision: a wise face, an expression neither mirthful nor stern but infinitely tolerant.

Opposite page:
Windsong, 1990, Red cedar, 9′ × 5′ × 18″
Pictured at Medina Park, Medina, Washington
Photograph Mary Sikkema

Shey Manido
By Dent Davidson

Shey Manido, gentle spirit moving over waters
Hand of God: formless chaos takes form
Face of God: image of all winging birds
Forest trees, wild beasts, water, life, breath
   of God
Windsong: your children awake from sleep of clay
Great Manido: we give you thanks, source of all
   creation
Mighty Windsong: feed the flame of your wisdom
   within us
Shey Manido

 **Ronald Holden** is a Seattle-based freelance writer who specializes in gastronomy and the arts.
Photograph courtesy Ronald Holden

NOTE: This story was excerpted and adapted by permission from "A Patient Hand," by Ronald Holden, *Eastsideweek*, May 1, 1991.

Chapter 51

Ingrained Difference

From the writing of David Marshall

I met Dudley in 1955 at the University of Oregon's first exhibition of Pacific Northwest sculptors, which was sponsored by the university's school of architecture and allied arts.

Sculptors from British Columbia, Washington, and Oregon were invited to provide an example of their work for an exhibition in the Little Art Gallery and participate in a three-day conference on the university campus. Out of this event grew the Northwest Institute of Sculpture and a series of conferences and exhibitions hosted each year by a different state or province. The annual events offered sculptors in the north-south corridor of Western North America an opportunity to become aware of one another, exchange ideas, view one another's work, and present their art to the public in various cities.

The 1956 conference was held in Vancouver, BC, and the exhibition at the Vancouver Art Gallery. David and Mavis Vaughan, Dudley Carter's daughter and son-in-law, invited conference sculptors to a party at their West Vancouver home. This became the beginning of my long friendship with the Vaughans, who supported sculptors of this region. It also provided me the opportunity to visit Dudley Carter whenever he came to Gibsons to work at his studio on the beach below the Vaughan's home on Gower Point.

Many artists in Europe and North America over the past 150 years absorbed the influence of cultures beyond their own. Paul Gauguin incorporated elements of the art of the French Polynesian Marquesas Islands into his paintings, and by the beginning of the twentieth century, other artists

Indian Legend, 1938, redwood, 8′ × 4′ × 18″
So ingrained was Dudley's appreciation of Coastal Indian folklore that he created works like *Indian Legend*, which portrays a story of a young Indian who takes his beloved to the seashore to show her the wonders of creation.
Photograph courtesy Anna Vaughan Hanson

in Paris viewed with serious interest the work of so-called primitive cultures. Picasso, Braque, and other cubist painters discovered the virtues—the magic geometry—of African wood carvings, which they encountered in shops dealing in secondhand objects and ethnographic collections. These African works bear an interesting similarity to the simplified geometric forms of late Cézanne paintings.

Dudley Carter made use of West Coast Indian art in a similar way, incorporating that influence into his work. However, there is one important difference. The cubist painters discovered African sculpture in museums and shops. They knew little of the land, the beliefs, and the lives of the people who produced those works. But Dudley lived and worked in our forests, experienced the weather, climbed over the mountains, and developed an intimate understanding of the trees. He had a more sympathetic admiration for Indian art of the coastal region than can those who have not lived among them. He absorbed the coastal environment as well as the expressive and formal lessons of Indian art and synthesized them with other elements of his own spirited nature. He did not set out to copy but developed a parallel expression in terms of his unique West Coast experience.

Carter was more appreciated in the State of Washington than in his native British Columbia. King County, Washington, where he lived for many years, provided him a home in the woods with workspace in natural surroundings appropriate to his work and life experience. He was viewed as a state treasure and respected for his remarkable, continuous production of fine works of art.

 **David Marshall** (1928–2006) was born to a farming family in Islay, Alberta. The family moved to Toronto where Marshall, at the age of twelve, became infected with the art bug when visiting an art museum. Educated at Ontario College of Art, Vancouver School of Art, Heatherly's School of Art, London, England, and University of British Columbia. Instructor of sculpture at Capilano College, North Vancouver, BC, for seventeen years, where he put his friendship with Dudley Carter to advantage by arranging for Dudley to meet with his students at every opportunity. Marshall was an internationally exhibited sculptor working in stone, wood, and bronze. His works are found in public and private collections around the world, and several are displayed in Big Rock Garden Park in Bellingham, Washington.
Photograph courtesy Carel Marshall

Ingrained Difference

Chapter 52

"It would be better if..."

From conversations with Michael Vaughan

In the winter following my grandfather's one-hundredth birthday he began to show signs of aging, and I remember my mother lamenting, "I'm not ready for my father to be old!" I never thought of my grandfather as old. Rather, I think that having a lifelong purpose and the wherewithal to pursue it prevented the passage of time from robbing him of youth.

My earliest recollections of my grandfather go back to my days as a very young boy out in a dinghy with him, reeling in driftwood logs and towing them to his cabin on the beach at Gibsons. My grandfather was an eagle-eyed scavenger, and together we searched the beaches, foraging for wood. In later years he would tell me what wood he needed and trust me to find it.

Today I can look at a piece of his sculpture and tell you, for example, that *Firebird* came out of the forest, that *Abstract #2* he carved from beach slabs, and that *Sea Life*, *Ravenchild*, *Feathered Companions*, and *Mythical Bird* are all driftwood.

We called Grandfather "Ducko," the family's term of endearment that came about years ago in a rather convoluted way. As a kid I combined the name of a character called Dudley the Duck from a TV cartoon with some popular song lyrics, "Mommy-o, Daddy-o," and began calling Grandfather "Ducky-o." My baby sister, Anna, picked that up as "Ducko." Soon Mum and Dad were calling him Ducko too. It stuck.

If I were to select any artworks that best tie Ducko to me, the Haida houses would likely top the list. Childhood memories of visits with my grandfather in his first Bel-Red Road Haida house studio are so clear. There was no other place like it. It seemed to take me to another dimension. I consider myself fortunate to have spent the last months of Ducko's life working almost under his thumb, reconstructing his final Haida house studio in Redmond, Washington. We were close to completion at the time of his death in 1992.

During the Great Depression, Ducko moved his family to the San Francisco area, where he made some advantageous connections. One of those connections was Sam Morse, an heir to the telegraph fortune. He owned just about the whole Monterey Peninsula and became known as the Duke of Monterey. I gather he was a powerful, politically savvy person and also a patron of the arts. He would use any method he could think of to support the artistic community—donations, trades, whatever—and Sam and Ducko worked out a trade.

Ducko offered to do some work for Sam in exchange for permission to erect the ancient equivalent of a house trailer, a Haida house, on property that Morse owned. Traditional Haida houses were conceived with transportability in mind. The Natives designed these houses to be easily dismantled and moved from place to place. Their construction involved no nails or hardware, which of course they did not have. They relied on the dwelling's low-slung design and gravity to keep things in position. Ducko said that he did not adhere to all the traditions of the Haida when replicating their dwellings—to do so he would have had to bury a freshly killed slave under each corner post!

In 1935 Ducko traded his services to Sam Morse for the use of some land right near the mouth of the Carmel River, where he built his first

Mythical Bird, 1980, yellow cedar, 11′ × 5′7″ × 3.5′
Purchased by the Mercer Island Arts Council in 1996 and installed on the southwest edge of Pioneer Park, Mercer Island, Washington
Photograph copyright David Friedman
Reprinted by permission of the *Mercer Island Reporter*

Playful Coyote appears to be keeping an eye on things as Raven, the mythical bird, is shown intermingled and becoming one with four contemplative, almost beatific, human countenances. Raven and Coyote are creatures around which there is much lore and mythology, often contradictory. Both play similarly significant roles in many traditions as creator, teacher, and keeper of magic.

"It would be better if..."

Haida-style dwelling. Trading was second nature to Ducko. He learned the skill during his logging days with his father and uncles. Most of their early business transactions were trades. Ducko told me his family had owned a twenty-dollar gold piece that sat on the mantel for years during his childhood. They never spent it. They generally traded logs for their provisions. Part of his payment to Sam Morse consisted of canoe lessons for Sam's daughter Mary. Mary Morse wanted to learn to paddle a canoe and Ducko took her out on the Carmel River. He had gained quite a reputation as a canoe man, navigating timber-cruising crews through Death Rapids near the source of the Columbia River.

Ducko worked deals for the redwood and other materials he used in that first Haida house. His only out-of-pocket expense was seven dollars and fifty cents for salvaged auto glass for the windows. The house served as his studio and family home for some five years. Sam Morse bought the Haida house when my grandparents moved back to Seattle at the beginning of World War II. Sam's daughter Mary and her husband, Will Shaw, eventually inherited the Carmel Haida house. They moved it to Big Creek in the hills above Big Sur, land they deeded to the University of California at Santa Cruz. I understand that the Shaws maintained a ninety-nine-year lease on the land. Not so many years ago, on a trip to the area, Anna and Mum stayed overnight in that Haida house.

When my grandparents returned to the Northwest in 1941, they rented a succession of homes in Bellevue. One, in the vicinity of the Catholic church on Main Street in downtown Bellevue, came with acreage loaded with fruit and nut trees and grapevines. Grandmother put her legendary skills as a vintner to good use while they lived there.

In 1955 they moved to property they had purchased on Bel-Red Road, where Ducko built their home and a second Haida house studio. It attracted considerable attention and soon became a landmark in the area, recognized as a work of art. Ducko's business really took off. In addition to selling his monumental sculptures and smaller carved works, he ran a profitable cedar products operation. There are houses in the Bellevue area today still fenced with rails hand split by my grandfather.

In 1958 Ducko built a third Haida house replica on tiny Reef Island in the San Juans for a family named Hart. Bellevue businessman Ron Sher, his wife, Eva, and his sister, Abby, bought the island in 1979. They found the house in a state of disrepair but recognized its value and wanted to have it restored. They tracked Ducko down and were delighted when he agreed to do the work himself. He camped on the island for the time it took him

Dudley pointing out details on façade of Haida house to grandson Michael Vaughan
Photograph 'Lyn Lambert

Dudley confers with Michael Vaughan and Dean Fredrickson during construction of *Replica of a Haida House #4*
Photograph 'Lyn Lambert

Dudley Carter's Reef Island Outhouse, 1978
Photograph Wally Gudgell

Grandmother made a rather unilateral decision to sell the Haida house studio to Bill McNae with the understanding that he would take possession of the building when they moved. Well my grandmother moved, but my grandfather did not. Ducko stayed put, continuing to use the Haida studio until the early 1980s when Bill McNae wanted it transported to Whidbey Island. My grandfather had to let it go.

Ducko then set to work building a replacement Haida-style studio on the existing concrete pad. The replica of the replica was a bare-bones cousin of the earlier models. It had no carvings to adorn it, and apart from the frame, Ducko used no old-growth cedar. It had walls of plywood and the roof was covered with ordinary roofing paper. But it served the purpose. Ducko attached an eighteen-by-eighteen-foot lean-to onto the studio, plumbed it, and lived in the lean-to.

When my grandmother died in 1975 her half

to bring the structure back to life. He even built an outhouse—he made it a true work of art. The Shers became good friends and patrons of Ducko's. They later sold the island and all the artwork on it. I understand the island went up for sale again for a mere seven million dollars. Of course, that included a genuine Dudley Carter outhouse!

Sometime in the 1970s, my grandparents talked about moving from their property on Bel-Red Road.

Michael Vaughan fitting totem on *Replica of a Haida House #4*
Photograph 'Lyn Lambert

"It would be better if..."

Completed *Replica of a Haida House #4* as it appeared when used by Haida carver Ralph Bennett. *Owl Post*, 1979, red cedar, 8′9″ tall, appears in right foreground.
Photograph 'Lyn Lambert

of the estate was to be distributed to her heirs. In order to accomplish that, Ducko sold the Bel-Red property. He continued to live there, doing business as usual and leasing the land from the buyers until 1984, when the new owners of the property decided to develop it and ordered him off. Ducko considered moving to Gibsons or California, but people on the King County Arts Commission wanted to keep him in Washington. Their idea was to dismantle his studio and move Ducko, his sculptures, and a rebuilt authentic Dudley Carter-style Haida house, improved and adorned, to Marymoor Park. Ducko disassembled and bundled up the Haida house. He moved it and almost everything else he owned to the maintenance yard at Marymoor, went to California for a visit, and awaited the action of King County Parks. Then came the kicker: the arts commission's plan did not fit with the park department's basic policies—people cannot live in the park.

Eventually, arrangements were made for Ducko to move—lock, stock, and Haida house—to Slough House Park. That was in 1987. In 1991, at one hundred years of age and needing more indoor workspace, Ducko decided to set up the Haida house. He did not want to simply reassemble the beams and plain posts of the Bel-Red Road reconstruction. He wanted a beautiful place that would be more like an authentic Haida dwelling. It would be a work of art. He dealt with all the red tape of obtaining building permits and county park approvals, and we set to work, enlisting the help of Ducko's legion of apprentices.

Ducko had in his possession some carved house posts that were commissioned in the mid-1980s by Bill Minor, an entrepreneurial fellow living in Issaquah, Washington. Bill had an ambitious plan to construct a Haida-style village on waterfront property he owned in Lund, BC, about a hundred miles north of Gibsons. Ducko and I went up there—I guess it was in 1986—to survey the site. It is at the end of the road, and they call it Land's End because you cannot go any farther without getting your feet wet. It is a beautiful, picturesque area. Ducko and I took measurements and gathered all the information we needed to proceed with the project.

Bill claims to be a descendant of Bill Miner, legendary train robber of Ducko's Stave Lake days. Ducko used to tell us grandchildren about hearing the whistle of the train when Miner, "Canada's Gentleman Bandit," robbed it in the early 1900s. Bill Miner became a folk hero, and the movie *The Grey Fox* was made about him. It is a marvelous yarn—one that I always enjoyed.

Bill, the train robber's progeny, bought and paid for the corner posts. Ducko went ahead and carved a door and overhead totem on speculation. But Bill's project never got off the drawing board. Ducko decided to use the carvings in his own studio, and he bought the posts back from Bill. The door design is similar to those of Ducko's other Haida houses—a mother and child, a prominent theme in the art of the matriarchal Haida culture.

The Haida house floor is composed of redwood rounds like those used in the original Carmel River Haida house. We had the structure up and the floor nearly complete when Ducko died. With the help of a number of apprentices, I was able to finish the construction some months after his death.

Since my grandfather's death I have often contemplated just how he managed to be so prolific in his work. How could he turn out hundreds of time- and energy-consuming major artworks? Of course, his career spanned a lot of years, but it was more than that. It was not apparent to me in my youth, but after having thought about it over the years, I

Teresa and Dudley Carter pictured at the time of their fiftieth wedding anniversary. Photograph Adonis Studio, West Vancouver, BC, courtesy Evelyn Balko

Loving grandparents Dudley and Teresa Carter Photograph courtesy Anna Vaughan Hanson

"It would be better if..."

realize that there appeared to be an emotional distance or independence separating my grandparents, at least in the later years of their marriage. I think it could be that he directed his passion—that creative energy that many would express as sexual energy—into his work. Marriage was, however, enormously important to Ducko and my grandmother, and they were deservedly pleased and proud when we celebrated their golden anniversary. My grandmother died about five years later.

Another idiosyncratic aspect of my grandfather's life was the amount of work he turned out after his wife died. I have observed that when one spouse dies, often the other loses interest in life, becomes less productive. The opposite was true of Ducko. After my grandmother died, he became busier than ever.

His golden wedding anniversary had been cause for celebration, of course, but I think Ducko may have been equally proud of his two golden axes. The first came from the US Navy in 1960 in recognition of his having carved the Sand Point Naval Air Station totem. At the celebration of his one-hundredth birthday at Oregon's Clackamas Town Center, where he had carved three massive works ten years earlier, the management of the center presented him with his second golden axe. Ducko used those golden axes too, but never on anything tougher than cake.

In the spring of 1992, when it appeared that my grandfather was dying, all the family in Canada who were able to travel, including his sisters Eltheen and Aene and my cousin Earl Carter, came down to the Slough House. Earl had worked with Ducko on *Mythical Bird* and became sort of a protégé, going on to do some outstanding construction work, most notably with the First Nations of Canada, in a number of educational centers. Earl suggested we should build a casket for my grandfather. We selected some of the best cedar Ducko had stored on the property and roughed it out together. I finished it up on my own and did not use any nails in its construction. I adzed the surface to give it the texture Ducko liked so much. We buried him with a graveside ceremony in a cemetery in Mission, BC, where his parents are buried.

In the years after my grandfather's death, I found it a challenge to establish my own individuality. I think I had become lost, in a professional sense that is. I had spent many years as my grandfather's part-time administrative assistant and several extremely intense months working closely with him on the Haida house. It was a demanding experience, working in the shadow of a man of that magnitude. And Ducko was hard to please. He would say to

Dudley Carter—the man with the golden axes—and *The Bowman*, a significant figure in Dudley's design for the Washington State Centennial *Riding the Transcending Wave*

The Bowman, 1989, red cedar, 6′2″ × 4′10″ × 16″
Photograph Eddie Davis

my sister and brother and me, "Don't rest on your laurels. Do better. Push yourself to the limit!"

He had what my sister and brother and I called his "it-would-be-better-if" attitude. We would show him something we had done, and he would check it over and invariably say, "It would be better if...." Those words tended to be more a burden than the encouragement I expect he meant them to be.

As years pass I appreciate more and more my time with Ducko. I know how honored I am to have worked with him and am surprised to see the extent to which his influence manifests itself in my own work. I build cedar furniture now, and along with the valuable woodworking techniques I gained from my grandfather, I am making use of his life lessons—lessons about the joy of accomplishment and the idea that when you work hard you will have contentment at the end of the day. And I am working through the "it-would-be-better-if" precept.

Ducko read scripture every day, and there is a passage in Isaiah 65 (NRSV) that tells us, "... like the days of a tree, so shall the days of my people be, and my chosen shall long enjoy the work of their hands." It also says, "... one who dies at a hundred will be considered a youth, and one who falls short of a hundred will be considered accursed."

I can almost hear Ducko saying, "More of us could make it to a hundred if we would just live better, live closer to the way nature intends us to live." I have come to believe that my grandfather loved us the same way that God loves us—just the way we are, but too much to let us stay that way.

Michael Vaughan, eldest of Dudley Carter's three grandchildren, makes his home in Gibsons, BC. A graduate of the University of British Columbia with a degree in Sociology, Vaughan was a longtime assistant to his grandfather. He also worked as an entrepreneur, distributor of Alaska yellow cedar, designer, and craftsman, producing rustic cedar furniture.
Photograph 'Lyn Lambert

"In the woods too, a man casts off his years, as the snake his slough, and at what period soever of life, is always a child. In the woods, is perpetual youth . . . In the woods, we return to reason and faith. There I feel that nothing can befall me in life—no disgrace, no calamity, . . . which nature cannot repair. Standing on the bare ground—my head bathed by the blithe air and uplifted into infinite space—all mean egotism vanishes. I become a transparent eyeball; I am nothing; I see all; the currents of the Universal Being circulate through me; I am part or parcel of God."

Ralph Waldo Emerson

Chapter 53

A Sister Remembers

From the writing of Aene Carter Ferguson

My memories go back nearly eighty years. I was just a child, but these memories of my dear brother, as old as they are, are clear as crystal.

Dudley was seventeen years older than I. When I was growing up he was away working, coming home only for short visits whenever possible. I was very fond of him, and he always made a big fuss over me as I was his only sister at that time. Eltheen is five and a half years younger than I am.

When he came home he'd have a bristly beard, and he would grab me and say, "A whisker rub for you!"

My face would be stinging and red, and I would yell for help. Even at that, I was always beside him or on his knee.

Dudley would often bring me a beautiful doll when he came to visit. I finally had many dolls. When I was thirteen he gave me an especially lovely one and said it would be the last.

One time when he had been home awhile, he

Dudley and his sisters, Eltheen King and Aene Ferguson, March 29, 1992
Photograph 'Lyn Lambert

240   *Legacy*

Dudley Carter sketching on the day his sisters visited. Nine days later, on April 7, Dudley died. Photograph 'Lyn Lambert

noticed Mother's dinner set getting smaller. A few days after he left, along came two barrels of dishes. A full set of twelve of everything, with veggie dishes and platters—such a surprise for my mother.

Another time he was working at Stave Falls. I was about ten years old. It was a beautiful day and I was outside skipping when I heard a horse coming down our private road. I hurried in to tell my mother that there was an old Chinese man in a covered wagon coming. But who do you think it was? Dudley! He had gone hunting and bagged a deer, so he rented a wagon to bring the carcass to my parents. He stayed a few days and made a smokehouse to cure the meat. It was a big job, but that was the only way at that time to keep it. My brother loved smoked venison.

Dudley always remembered our birthdays—the four younger brothers', Eltheen's, and mine. He made sure we had something to enjoy on our birthdays and at other times too. My parents produced a large family, seven boys and two girls, and they did not always have the money to do special little things in a big way. But Dudley did.

NOTE: Dudley's sister Aene Ferguson died in June of 1996 at the age of eighty-nine.

A Sister Remembers

Chapter 54

Voices of the Spirit

From conversations with Ralph Bennett

I never met Dudley Carter, but I know Dudley Carter as surely as one man ever knows another. I know him through his art. I know him by virtue of living with and caring for his art. And I know him by living and working in the place where he lived and worked and died.

I am Haida, born to a long line of chiefs on both sides of my family, a nephew of chiefs. Chief is a white man's term. The Haida have no word for chief. Big Slave fits better for a leader of the Haida. Incidentally, Haida—like the names of many Native tribes—simply means people. In a sense we are all Haida, and perhaps we are all meant to be chiefs.

In the fall of 1993, encouraged by a group of people in the Dudley Carter Foundation and with permission from King County, I moved to Slough House Park. The foundation hoped to reestablish the artist-in-residency program that had begun and seemed to have ended with Dudley Carter. Having heard of my work, they thought I might be able to enliven Dudley's Haida house and resurrect an active arts program there. I told them I didn't mind being "an Indian in a box."

My responsibilities included taking care of the Dudley Carter artworks that remained in the park following his death. Dudley's family arranged with King County to keep a number of his monumental works there while they settled his estate. I agreed to take care of the artwork for the family and the park property for the county in exchange for living in the residence there.

As a fifth-generation carver, I took it as a great privilege to carry out my work in Dudley Carter's Haida house studio. It is a wonderful setting for spirited teaching and creating. The Haida house is, for me, a spiritual place—a spiritual place in the midst of a complex urban setting.

Inspiration for the design of the Haida dwelling is the whale. The doorway is the creature's mouth, the beams are its ribs, the walls and roof are its skin, and the smoke hole is its blowhole. The whale, and in turn the Haida dwelling, reminds the Haida of the Great Spirit, the architect of all that is.

Walking into a Haida dwelling is entering into myth. In the tribal world the house can be understood to be the iconic embodiment of the word, the divine story. It is for the Haida like reading scripture is for literate believers. The Bible, the Torah, the Koran, and other sacred books remind believers of their Creator, remind them of what their Creator expects of them. The ancient Haida used no written language, so their highly symbolic art carried the message of scripture. Symbolism is the voice of Spirit. Symbolism spoke truth to the ancients—truths of our roots, of the seasons, of property, of relationships, of responsibility—all that is important.

When working in and around the Haida house, I didn't hear voices that were not there. I didn't see things that were not there, but I sensed a great presence. And I understood that my presence there was a gift. I had been given a gift, and the only way I could gain value from that gift was to give it away. In my time there I became more widely recognized as a source of Native lore, a teacher of Northwest Coast art and culture. King County granted me the title of Artist-in-Residence, and as such I could further extend my gifts. People of all ages and inclinations came to the Haida house to learn of Native ways, to learn of Dudley Carter's ways, and in many cases, to learn ways to develop and use their own gifts.

Alert observers entering the Haida house notice that Dudley Carter left what American painter and art educator Robert Henri would call his impress— his footprint, his trace—on the inward side of the door. When I saw and touched the interior side of

Feathered Companions, 1982
Red cedar, 5'7" × 4'7" × 2'
Photograph 'Lyn Lambert

In this work, Ralph Bennett's favorite Dudley Carter sculpture, Ralph sees a raven protectively nurturing three chicks, behavior atypical of the raven, which would raise its young by intimidation. Ralph suggests that Dudley used *Feathered Companions* to indicate that one species can acquire beneficial qualities from another. Close examination of the young birds shows that these are not birds of a feather that flock together. Note the difference in the eyes and the beaks of the chicks.

Voices of the Spirit

the entrance door, I recognized that Dudley went to a great deal of trouble to carve it in a manner that has the complexity of the inside of a whale. He didn't need to do that, but it indicates that to him what is on the inside is as important as what is on the outside. He knew what he was leaving. It took more effort to carve the back of the door than it did the front. It is abstract art, totally abstract.

Every day I would make a point of going out and touching one of Dudley Carter's carvings. They are the embodiment of his spirit, the manifestation of his spiritual expression. Although voiceless, they speak. They speak to another place in our existence, a place beyond the understanding of words.

One work, *Feathered Companions*, spoke most emphatically to me. It isn't large and it is not a complicated piece. But it is powerful and conveys a monumental message. It is, perhaps, one of the best things I've ever seen. Dudley Carter did many larger sculptures, many more highly acclaimed, but there is none that says more to me. *Feathered Companions* shows us an adult bird. From all appearances it is a raven, and this large raven shelters three young birds in its outspread wings. The work is beautifully executed, but what is unusual about this piece is the behavior of the raven. Ravens teach their young by intimidation, but this raven is protecting the young—it is acting like a chicken, adopting the nature of a chicken. Likewise, we have seen that Dudley Carter, although a white man, adopted and adapted much of the nature of the Indian.

The more I was around Dudley's work, the more I understood that art didn't come first for Dudley. People came first. I think Dudley cared about what happened in the lives of people around him, perhaps as a result of his influence. It is almost a sacrificial thing.

Dudley understood that it takes community to accomplish anything in this world, and he gathered an extended family around him. Dudley Carter's work shows us that he had grasped the tribal attitude—the "it takes a village" philosophy—that we hear of so often these days. It's a philosophy that seems difficult for literate societies to grasp. But no one can achieve Dudley Carter's type of art alone. It is possible to have at least the illusion of painting or writing in isolation, but totem poles and monumental sculpture, the likes of which Northwest Coast Indians and Dudley Carter brought forth, cannot be born of isolation.

I don't think that Dudley was especially concerned if everybody didn't get his message. I think he appreciated those who did understand. I believe his fundamental message had to do with interdependence, universal mutual reliance, and obligation—connection. Take his piece *Condor*, done in the 1930s. Back then the attitude was, "We can do any damn thing we want. And we can do it any way we want. We'll clear-cut the forest. We'll take the whole forest as long as it's economically feasible, whatever way we can make the most money." People were ignorant of what they were doing to wildlife in general. They were annihilating the condor. Aesthetically, the condor is an ugly creature. But Dudley was aware that the condor is a magnificent, magnificent creature. And he was aware that the condor is a symbol of what we are—not just the condor but also the salmon, the eagle, all the different creatures—where they go, we're going. *Condor* reminds us of that. Suffering bird, suffering people. Somebody had the foresight to place *Condor* right at the entrance to Slough House Park. You see it coming and going, and hopefully, you get its message.

The more I think about it, the more I wonder if my being influenced by the spirit of Dudley Carter could be likened to Dudley gaining by osmosis the nature of the Indian. He watched, he listened, and he learned from Indian master carvers. He learned carving techniques; he heard the myths, learned the symbolic importance of the animals; and he learned to speak through symbols. And then, when he came to a critical place in his life and his means of earning his livelihood was threatened, what did he do? At almost forty years of age, he turned to artistic traditions he had observed in Indian culture. And what are traditions? Traditions are guides, guides to progress—not anchors to the past. There were strong canons or rules about carving in the Native traditions. Do you stick with them or do you vary them? Do you copy or originate? That seems to be a big question today. Dudley did not copy. His work culminated from his own memories, his own experiences, and his own imagination. And to me, that's the way art should be.

Dudley Carter's life had many facets to it, and he wasn't afraid of any of them. He certainly didn't fear death. People who are afraid to die are not living. Robert Henri observed that "the reason so many artists have lived to great age and have been so young at great age is that . . . they have lived living, whereas most people live dying."

Dudley carved until a few weeks before he died at one hundred years of age. Just that fact says more than words can convey. It shows that he was in command of his destiny. And, judging from the work he was turning out toward the end, he excelled beyond any reasonable expectation. I understand what it takes to complete an imaging process. It takes an extreme amount of confidence to bring out your vision—not confidence in your technical ability—the confidence to expose your inner self. You know that not everybody will accept your vision. Controversies in the art world are constant. Dudley seemed able to shrug them off and just continue doing his sculpture.

Each morning as I walked out of the Slough House to begin the day, I would see the carved sign, "Dudley Carter, Sculptor." Holding up the sign was an owl. What does that owl mean? Does it mean that Dudley liked owls or that the owl is just aesthetic and easy to do? No! The owl is a messenger. A messenger! And the sculptor is a messenger. But the sculptor's message is often beyond the grasp of the intellect. Only a receptive heart can comprehend that message, for symbolism is the voice of Spirit and Spirit speaks only to the heart.

Ralph Bennett—Goo la'Slacoon—Haida artist, teacher, storyteller, and fifth-generation carver. Reared in Hydaburg, Alaska, by his grandparents, Bennett learned from them the spiritual and moral traditions of their tribe and clan, and his wood carvings reflect that heritage. As a young man, he earned his living in the high tech world of avionics. After serving as King County's artist-in-residence in Redmond for four years following Dudley Carter's death, Bennett continued devoting himself to art, carving, painting, teaching, and storytelling around Washington State and California. He has received many honors and awards, among them the Washington State Governor's Arts and Heritage Award for the year 2000. His work appears in galleries and museums nationally and internationally.
Photograph 'Lyn Lambert

Chapter 55

Legend of How Raven Put the Light in its Right Place

A version of the legend told by Ralph Bennett

Long ago, near the beginning of the world, all things were created. Raven made all things and gave all things to the people. He gave them first to the leaders. One of the leaders of the Haidas was Bear. Of all the gifts of the Creator, Bear liked light the very, very best. He liked the light so much that he decided to keep it all to himself.

He made a big box specially to contain the light, all the light in the universe, and he kept it in his lodge. Every now and then, but not very often, he would let the people of Bear Clan have a little glimpse of the light, but most of the time they groped about in darkness.

Raven knew that the light was to be for all people. He knew he must contrive a way to get Bear to give up the light, so the people would no longer be kept in darkness. Darkness was a terrible state of affairs. It was like nighttime all the time. It was worse than nighttime, for there were no moonbeams and no twinkling stars. The people stumbled around bumping into things, generally making a major mess of everything.

Even today we see that ravens like to have an overview of things. If we look for ravens, we look to the very tops of the trees, not in the middle of the trees, not down in the bottom branches. Way up in the treetops is where we will likely find a raven surveying the community. A raven is curious. A raven wants to know everything. He wants to see everything that is going on. A raven is very social too, always trying to talk to people. We often hear

Raven and Sun Totem, 1964
Red cedar, 15′ × 30″ × 12″
Photograph courtesy Jane and Kurt Oestreich

Inspiration for this totem is Raven and the Sun, a story important to many Northwest Coast tribal peoples, a story told in many versions with many titles.

Filling the center section of the pole is Raven clasping the Sun. On one wing of the raven there appears to be an ovoid sort of yin-yang symbol, a symbol of the harmony of opposites, the harmonious interaction of the female and male, and dark and light forces of the universe. A small, stylized raven appears on the raven's opposite wing.

The low men on the totem pole are shown encapsulated in darkness. Their faces and posture show great displeasure, grief, and sadness, the result of their miserable unenlightened existence. One figure wears a hat with many rings. The rings, according to Haida tradition, indicate an individual of importance. The plain hat shows the other to be a commoner. These figures tell us that the miseries of darkness are visited equally upon high ranking and common people alike.

The top figure clasps a raven and stands upon a circle. Dudley could be telling us that by embracing the spirit of Raven, the Creator, one will become enlightened and rise above the limits of the earth.

The legend of Raven and the Sun explains that the enjoyment of enlightenment comes only through the sharing of it.

Legend of How Raven Put the Light in its Right Place

Ravenchild, 1982, red cedar, 9′ × 6′ × 4′
Carved at Gibson's, BC, and purchased for Crossroads Shopping Center, Bellevue, Washington, in 1993
Photograph courtesy Anna Vaughan Hanson

him calling out, "Caw, caw, caw!"

So Raven flew to the top of the highest tree and sat in the all-consuming blackness. He kept constant watch on the lodge of Bear Clan, all the while trying to find a way to get the light to the people. And he detected, even through the pitch-black darkness, that the chief's maiden daughter bumbled and stumbled her way to the river every so often to fetch water. She carried animal skins to fill with water to take back to the lodge for the people. Raven observed that before the maiden filled the skins, she would cup her hand to sip from the waters of the stream. And that gave Raven an idea.

Now, Raven has transforming powers. He can change himself into anything at all, from a tiny, tiny fir needle to the grandest of mountains. So Raven transformed himself into a single tiny, shiny fir needle. He dropped into the river just in time to be caught up in the maiden's hand, and she drank him down. Raven floated into the maiden's warm insides and landed in a cozy spot where he transformed himself once more, this time into a very, very little human being. He went to sleep for a long, long time. As he slept, he grew.

Nine months later a baby was born in the house of Bear. This baby, like most human newborns if we dared to admit, was an odd-looking little fellow—really ugly. At least he would have been ugly if it had been light enough for anyone to see him. This little baby had a long beak-like nose and a few straggly feathers sprouting here and there. And he was noisy! His cry mingled the worst wails of a spoiled child with the raucous calls of an angry raven. Yet he could giggle and coo as melodiously as the wind as it whistles through the pine boughs.

And Grandfather Bear, like all grandfathers since the beginning of time, deeply loved the strange new member of the family. As months went by and the baby grew, his grandfather lavished the child with love and affection, playing with him and making toys for him.

Soon the little fellow learned to crawl and found his way to the box that contained the light. He pulled himself up and tried to push open the lid of the box. His grandfather watched with admiration at the strength and determination of his offspring and decided to let his grandson have a peek at the light in the box. Grandfather opened the lid just enough for a ray of light to shine forth on the Raven Child. Bathed in the warmth and light, he appeared beautiful—as beautiful as the most beautiful of all grandchildren. The old man, seeing the pleasure the child found in the light, raised the lid of the box, lifted the light in the form of a brilliant incandescent ball, and tossed it to his delighted grandson.

In a flash, quicker than thought, as the light traveled to the Raven Child, he changed from his human form to a huge, black, shining winged figure, its beak open, ready to catch the light. Raven snapped up the light, flapped his great wings, and flew up to the smoke hole of the house. He pulled and tugged the huge ball through the hole and threw the orb into the vast darkness of the sky where it broke into billions and billions of pieces. One large piece floated up and became the moon. Many, many small ones, too numerous to count, became the stars. The largest piece of all floated far beyond the rim of the world and became the sun.

Bear, angered at having been tricked and deceived, dashed to the door of his house, threw it open, and ran outside where he was at once greeted by a world transformed by the radiant light. He saw the people singing and dancing, overjoyed by the magnificent beauty of the Earth that had been hidden by the darkness. His anger turned to jubilation. He knew that Raven had done a good thing. He knew that, although Raven had tricked him, he had put the light where it belonged. And Bear knew that having a thing of beauty did not make it a joy forever. Only by letting it go could he truly possess it.

Dudley with *Ravenchild*, 1982
Photograph courtesy Anna Vaughan Hanson

Legend of How Raven Put the Light in its Right Place

Chapter 56

And the Story of Memaloosa Sam...

Introduction by 'Lyn Lambert

Dudley Carter crossed the River of the Big Sleep on April 7, 1992, but much of him remains ever with us on this side. My earthly time with the amazing centenarian spanned little more than a year, but I soon learned that our connection would endure. Death does not have the last word.

Shortly after Dudley's passing, I found among my collection of Dudley Carter materials a story he had written, typed by someone unknown, titled *Memaloosa Sam*. There was no indication of when Dudley had written the tale, whether it was derived from an Indian legend, or if it is simply a product of his fertile imagination. Regardless, the story *Memaloosa Sam* haunted me. It was a facet of Dudley's creativity that I had not previously experienced.

In the years since Dudley's departure, as my co-writer Mary Sikkema and I compiled the Dudley stories, we often pondered *Memaloosa Sam*. Why did Dudley write that story? What were his thoughts when he sketched Sam seated with his twelve friends? We'll let you decide...

> "Memaloosa Sam was one of three old Indians I had met on a cruising trip into the Nitinat Lake country from Clo-oose. I was there again several years later and was informed of the passing of Memaloosa Sam."
>
> Dudley C. Carter

Memaloosa Sam

By Dudley C. Carter, edited by 'Lyn Lambert

Dudley wearing one of his signature hand-knitted hats
Photograph courtesy Anna Vaughan Hanson

Memaloosa Sam, one of the old Indian whale hunters of the Nootka people of the west coast of Vancouver Island, lived at Clo-oose, where canoes put in from the storm.

Sam was showing young Quatsino James how to make a whale harpoon. The straight wood from the yew tree must be sharpened at the top, the small end, for penetration. Then it must be burned to make it harder—the whale has a thick, tough hide.

It was now ninety-nine summers and ninety-eight winters since Sam first saw the light of day. His twisted and gnarled hands moved slowly as he carefully worked the point of the harpoon. He moved in obvious agony with an injured knee as he explained to James that it was now many moons since the canoe log rolled over his leg. Sam's worn and wrinkled face beamed slightly as the boy spoke encouragingly of the wonders that the white man's medicine could do. Sam indicated that he still held strongly to the old ways and had faith in the words of the Nootka medicine man at Quatsino.

"It is the devil," Sam said. "The devil must out."

The white man's chuck and the white man's ways were not good for Sam.

Memaloosa Sam wanted Quatsino James to marry Gluk-wan, the daughter of his brother's son, but that was taboo. Quatsino James and Gluk-wan were of the same phratry, or clan, and so marriage could not be.

Gluk-wan was collecting salal berries in front of the big house, spreading them out to dry in the sun on skunk cabbage leaves laid on split cedar boards placed across logs just at high tide level. Sam said, "Gluk-wan, bring me a spike and a hammer."

She said, "No, that is not good. You have said that before. I know what you intend to do."

Gluk-wan had attended mission school at Metla-katilla, and she did not have the same faith in the old ways. Sam remained silent for a long time, and he slowly rocked back and forth on the beach in agony. Gluk-wan went to gather more salal berries.

Sam hobbled up to the big house making two stops on the way and got his spike and hammer from inside the door. In agony he repeated, "The devil must out. The devil must out."

He limped slowly back to the beach steadying himself on logs as he went. He placed his injured leg against the end of a log and drove the spike into his knee with the hammer. Rolling back onto the clear white sand between the logs at high tide level, he passed out, remaining there for a long time until revived by the rising tide to carry on for many more moons. Whatever happened to the devil, Sam had the satisfaction of being brave enough to give him a chance.

However, Sam was running out of summers and winters. But he still had one more trick to pull on the devil—he would go where the devil dare not go. Sam would cross the Great River. The River of the Big Sleep. The River of the Dead.

Memaloosa Sam was regarded highly by the Nootka people. According to tradition, his passing from this world

The Gambling Guessing Game of the Bones by Dudley Carter
Sketch courtesy Dudley Carter

to the Happy Hunting Ground called for great celebration.

This would be the last occasion to use the fine clothes of the white man, clothes that an old missionary had left to the tribe many years before—an old battered top hat, a scissors-tailed coat, and a white shirt befitting a gentleman of high rank. They had been used by the tribe on three other festive occasions: a chief's potlatch, a wedding, and the erection of the Big Totem. There were no pants to this fine suit, now green with age. It was taken from the big carved cedar chest where the chief's ceremonial masks and finery were stored. To complete Sam's costume he would wear the finely woven traditional fringed cedar bark aprons in place of the white man's pants. Shoes did not matter because he always moved by canoe.

Sam was one of high rank and had acquired wealth. He had at one time thrown a big potlatch. According to tradition, he had distributed most of his wealth in gifts to his people. The time had not yet arrived when his carefully selected guests would return the usual gifts with interest. The few possessions he now had were carefully gathered, placed in his canoe, and held in readiness for his departure.

The large carved feast dish was brought out and placed on the finely adzed split cedar planks that formed a great, strong table. There was much feasting and ceremonial dancing around fires. Although Sam was silent now, his personal songs were sung by the guests and by masked dancers who moved to the rhythm of Native drums and rattles. In the songs, Sam was extolled for his relations with the supernatural and his daring deeds of bravery, which included this last act, his greatest, his most daring clash with the devil. The last act that Sam was to take part in on this side of the Great River was now to begin—the exciting ceremony, the Gambling Guessing Game of the Bones.

Sam was placed in the seat of honor at the head of the table, wearing the apparel of one of the highest rank: the top hat, white shirt, coat and tails, and the beautifully woven cedar bark aprons with abalone buttons and fringe. His frail and wasted frame was held in place by cedar bark cords fastened to long split-cedar stakes driven in the ground. Beside him, firmly planted in the ground, was his carved ceremonial staff. The players took their places on opposing sides of the table and the game was underway.

Through the long dark night, the players waged back and forth in the firelight. At times the whispered word was scarcely audible. At times it was as silent as death. Again and again, like an uncontrolled orgy in the night, the players would become frenzied and wild, seemingly on the verge of destruction and violence. And the devil played his part. The noise dropped away as if due to the intense concentration of the players. It was almost silent except for a rustling sound like the shuffling bones of the dead. As the tempo of Sam's passing increased, the excitement, feelings, and commotion raged like the rising swells of the ocean until all the celebrants rose up with a terrific shout followed by a crash that almost broke the drum. The game was over. In the low, flickering light of the fire, a lone figure, like a shadow afraid of the light, passed out into the night. So went the Gambling Guessing Game of the Bones. The fires burned low and the stars were beginning to fade and lose their light before the rising sun.

Whether it was due to Sam's deadpan poker face or the supernatural powers he may have just acquired, the honored guests likely remembered the potlatch of former years when Sam had bestowed wonderful gifts on them all. And they may have realized that the time had come for them to repay with interest. So they passed the winnings on to Sam. The devil had lost and Sam had won.

Sam's earthly belongings had already been packed in his canoe, and just as he had sat at the table, he was now placed in the canoe. The last act was performed by the masked dancers to the sound of the drums and Sam's song. And with a strong push, he was set adrift on the outgoing tide—adrift on the broad Pacific where he had spent so much of his life as one of the top whale hunters of the Nootka people.

And so Memaloosa Sam crossed the Great River, the River of the Big Sleep, and left the devil behind.

Chapter 57

River of Life

By Anna Vaughan Hanson

As a young, emerging sculptor, I felt a strong urge to explore a variety of traditions and mediums other than wood. I sculpted in marble and bronze, creating several highly polished pieces.

But at the age of twenty-eight, I looked again through new eyes to see the dynamic strength and vitality of my grandfather's way of expression in wood. He captured so much that others missed. The original quality of the medium was preserved. As he often said, "No tool suited me more than the axe."

With his tree faller's tool, he became one with the medium. He sculpted with strong flowing planes—curvilinear forms. The natural undulations of the cedar, the spirit of the tree, guided him. Bold, stylized compositions emerged. The original character of the wood was never lost—nothing polished or sanded—the lively texture of the axe remained.

I have studied my grandfather's sculptures, from the monumental three-dimensional public works, such as *Goddess of the Forest* and *Wek Wek and the Holukmeyumko*, to smaller garden sculptures and reliefs. It is the carvings that are in our family collection—the ones that are part of our daily lives—that have moved me the most.

Easter Parade shows my grandfather's amazing wit and sense of humor. I can see how much fun he had with this piece. I can imagine the twinkle of his eye and the upward curl of his lips as he carved it—he just plain had fun. But on a scholarly note, it reveals his fascination with early cultures, whether Pre-Columbian, Inuit, or First Nations of our Northwest Coast.

This sculpture, although only three feet in width, seems so much larger. The openings, the play

Easter Parade, 1960
Redwood, 6' × 3' × 4"
Photograph Anna Vaughan Hanson

"Carved at Easter time, thus its title. Represents the merging of two cultures—Northwest Coast Indian and Pre-Columbian Mexican. Similarity in these two early cultures is shown in the headgear, the focal point of the composition. The interesting character of the wood, the pronounced grain, developed as the sculpture remained outside in the weather—wind and sand eroding the surface."

Anna Vaughan Hanson

and ornate Pre-Columbian headdresses accented with Northwest Coast symbolism, the U-form. But when asked about the theme, my grandfather merely stated that it represents Easter Sunday morning. Two women adorned in their Easter bonnets are bringing the reluctant man to church. Trapped in the middle, he is submissive, represented in a frontal pose with arms and hands positioned like the characters on Haida poles.

The three planks, untouched at the base, remind us of the origin of the sculpture. But cutting away material and creating openings transformed the rectangular planks, freeing them from their original format. The composition grew and seemingly expanded beyond its three-foot width.

Shaman with a Mask, 1964
Hollow yellow cedar, 8' × 2' × 2'
Photograph courtesy Jane and Kurt Oestreich

of negative and positive space, and the deeply cut, bold carving style give the composition its expansive energy. Hard to imagine, this sculpture was created from three salvaged planks floating down the Santa Cruz River.

With his double-bitted axe, Ducko began carving three figures into the thick planks. This eclectic piece portrays the figures with strong Mayan profiles

River of Life

However, an exciting transformation occurred following its completion. Carved in Palm Springs, it was exposed to high winds and sandblasting that brought the strong grain pattern to the surface. This greatly enhanced the sculpture, especially the facial features.

Shaman with a Mask is an intriguing piece. It was carved from a yellow cedar tree that grew hollow at the higher elevations. The mysterious figure is putting on his mask; one eye is human and one eye is animal. Arms and legs are carved with bold planes to fit the cylindrical totem shape. But one leg is replaced by the owl to add a mystical sense to the piece—further blending the human with the animal.

To give the sculpture a light, ethereal quality, openings were carved into the shell. The figure is no longer locked into the totem format. The shaman becomes more three-dimensional, more animated, almost alive. The asymmetry of the sculpture adds to this—the tilt of the mask and the expressive hands with one folding down and the other reaching upward. The shaman has been captured just as he begins to transform. It seems that he is just one step away from breaking out into our world.

Segment of Creation was carved from a small slab, barely two feet in width and five feet in length. The bold style, the strong curvilinear forms, carved to capture the highlights and shadows, give the sculpture a sense of drama—the miracle of creation. The oval forms expanding outwards from the chick are not symmetrical, giving animation and energy to the moment of creation.

Openings cut into the panel give the composition a strong three-dimensional quality. The upper part of the composition—the boldly sculpted ovals that envelop the chick—is the focus. Beneath this, a more subtly carved bird dives downward. Although depicted diving down, its abstract form has an upward energy embracing the ovals. The bird is very stylized—the legs, greatly enlarged, curve outward to

Segment of Creation, 1965
Redwood, 5′ × 20″ × 4″
Photograph Anna Vaughan Hanson

"Carter wanted to experiment with a pierced panel, with negative and positive forms, a more abstract sculpture for the growing market in contemporary design. The sculpture is a bold, stylized composition, carved with strong circular forms. Soon after it was carved a religious exhibition was opened. Ducko (his family nickname) was requested to enter it and thus gave the sculpture this title."
          Anna Vaughan Hanson

"The bird goes through several transformations as it emerges from its shell. This small piece captures the flow of Carter's life. It shows his appreciation of Indian legend, his insatiable urge to express himself, his skill with an axe, adze and chisel and his deep respect for wood."
          Jim McDowell, British Columbia historian, for whom this sculpture was a favorite

enwrap the upper ovals. The wings, in their abstract U-shape, direct the eye up and back into the composition. First we view the chick; then our eye catches the more subtle bird in flight. Within the body of the bird is an oval form. Could this be an egg? Which comes first—the chicken or the egg? The circle of life continues.

This sculpture, like the others, seems to expand beyond its borders. The openings, the boldly sculpted forms, and the lively asymmetry give his sculptures an exciting vitality.

Now in my 60s, I have just completed a composition for the Carter on the Park, an apartment complex near Dudley Carter Park in Redmond, Washington. The mural, *River of Life*, rises to twenty-eight feet on the wall of the lobby. I began carving the ferns on the right in a refined naturalistic style. As I delved deeper into the project, my approach evolved. Picking up my grandfather's tools—axe, adze, and slick—the forms became bolder.

The tall vertical column on the left was carved in a more stylized way with bold planes to catch the highlights and shadows. This column is topped with

---

River of Life, 2016, by Anna Vaughan Hanson, Dudley's granddaughter and noted Canadian wood sculptor. Anna's sculpture is prominently featured in the lobby of the Carter on the Park, an apartment building near Dudley Carter Park in Redmond, Washington.
Photograph William Wright Photography

an owl, a reoccurring symbol found throughout my grandfather's life. The wise owl with his all-seeing eyes represents my grandfather. He is gazing down as the river of life flows by.

Two birds swoop down over the water, the third turns to look back towards my mentor for inspiration.

Even though I have been carving for decades, I feel I still have so much to learn. My grandfather's strong, bold style is inspirational. Using simple hand tools—axe, adze, slick, and chisels—gives the surface more texture and character. Being true to the medium and preserving the natural character of the wood gives sculpture a dynamic vitality. Upon completing one composition, I am so eager to dive into the next.

My grandfather was often asked which project was his favorite. With a twinkle in his eye, his response was always, "I haven't done it yet."

> "I'm really enjoying tackling the Carter on the Park mural. I'm using Ducko's axe, adze, and slick . . . it feels great!"
>
> Anna Vaughan Hanson
> quoted while Anna was working on *River of Life*

Anna with her grandfather
Photograph courtesy Anna Vaughan Hanson

Anna Teresa Vaughan Hanson (1952–2018), born and educated in Vancouver, BC, graduated from University of British Columbia, Emily Carr University of Art and Design, and Capilano College with degrees in fine art and sculpture. Early in her career she worked as a graphic designer, a display technician, an interior designer, and a teaching assistant. But for over forty years, drawing inspiration from her grandfather, the focus of her career became wood carving. Like her grandfather, she carved with laser-sharp focus, using axe, adze, and chisels. Also like her grandfather, her pieces ranged from bowls to massive murals. Hanson's notable works can be found in Japan, Scotland, the US, and on BC's Sunshine Coast. Hanson was an adventurer. She competed in Swiftsure International Yacht Races, faced heavy weather in tug boats, endured blizzards at the timberline, and lived for years on boats and in isolated cabins with her husband, Lex. She remained positive throughout her fight with pancreatic cancer. She left behind a large unfinished commission in red cedar, a work that inspired her to keep carving right up until her final weeks, again, in the manner of her grandfather.

Epilogue

Never Say Never

By 'Lyn Lambert

I first visited Dudley Carter's studio in early 1991 when a fellow student in Dudley's monumental wood sculpture course at Bellevue's Sammamish High School asked Dudley if we could see his studio sometime. The old master promptly replied, "Yes. Why don't we do that today?" So we did.

As I wandered through the sculpture-studded, woodsy city lot that comprised Dudley Carter's outdoor studio, I was enchanted by what I encountered and surprised by the feeling of well-being and wonderment that came over me. It was magical. I felt so at home. And I wondered how I might spend more time there.

I had enrolled in the monumental wood sculpture class after spotting an item in our local paper informing that the master sculptor was offering a class open to the public. The course consisted of ten weekly classes, five dollars per session. When I called to enroll, the registrar advised me that Dudley was "really old."

"Somewhere in his eighties?" I guessed.

But the registrar corrected me, telling me that Dudley was ninety-nine. At that age he might not be able to guarantee that he'd be around for the entire ten weeks. So, we would pay our fee each week.

Creating monumental wood sculpture was never among my aspirations, but I was interested in knowing more about Dudley Carter. His artwork had impressed me since I moved to the Pacific Northwest in 1970 with my husband and our two

Seeds of Enchantment, 1987
Red cedar, 4′ × 16″ × 4″
Photograph Courtesy King County Library System

In 1987 Penny Rediger and her two young sons made frequent weekend visits to Slough House Park to watch Dudley Carter at work. The boys were fascinated by the old man with the axe and the stories he told them. Penny felt a powerful connection to the artist and to the beautiful woman she saw taking shape in the new and whimsical work of art he was bringing to life. The femininity of the woman appealed to Penny. Yet she also saw depth and strength in her, emphasized by the negative spaces in the work. Dudley explained that the fronds or stalks of corn represent the flow of life, one into the other. When the work was nearly finished, Penny dared to ask Dudley if he would sell it to her. He asked if she had fifteen hundred dollars. As a single mother and having just begun a new job, Penny proposed that she pay him five hundred dollars a month for three months. Dudley agreed to that arrangement and told her the name he had given to the piece—*Seeds of Enchantment*. Penny enjoyed the work for some twenty-four years, but after her children had grown, she decided on a change of lifestyle and wanted to sell the work. In 2011 'Lyn Lambert purchased the piece from Penny and loaned it to the Redmond Public Library.

young sons. I had enjoyed watching Dudley at work in Bellevue's Crossroads Mall on many occasions and thought that taking a class from the artist would be an opportunity to learn more about him. Predicting a large turnout for the class, I assumed I'd find a place in the back of the room, do my best to go unnoticed, and enjoy observing the master at work. To my surprise and dismay, enrollment in the class numbered only around two dozen—primarily artists and art teachers. It would be difficult for me to blend in with the woodworkers. However, Dudley had a way of making even one of little talent believe there was an artist in her somewhere. I came to enjoy plying my hand to the art.

Spending time at Dudley's studio was in the back of my mind as I enjoyed his classes at the school, but I wondered how that would be possible. Dudley regularly invited interested persons to become apprentices. My lack of talent, however, had me convinced that would not be an option for me.

Then, about halfway through the course, Dudley asked if anyone in the class could type. Instantly, a thought long buried in my mind popped to the surface: *Never admit you can type.* In days gone by I'd been advised that to admit one could type would assure one of being saddled with any group's most mundane and thankless tasks. But surely this situation would be different. I raised my hand—the only one to do so. Dudley took note of my offer, and some weeks later I received a call from Dudley's grandson Michael asking if I could come to the studio that afternoon and type. I was both elated and apprehensive.

I picked up my portable typewriter, a pack of paper, and a dictionary and drove off to Redmond. I had no idea what typing assignments Dudley had in mind. It turned out that he needed a number of letters typed—letters thanking politicians and other notables for the plaudits and favors he received on the occasion of his one-hundredth birthday and letters to timber companies requesting specific types of wood for sculptures that were taking shape in his mind. My typing skills proved acceptable to Dudley, and before long our association grew into a close friendship.

I was happy to think that I was performing acceptable typing and telephone duties for him, but when Dudley wanted to bestow upon me the title of secretary, I maintained that I hardly qualified as such. Dudley countered by pronouncing that I should be known as his "executive secretary, no—the secretary general!" Dudley was always generous in expressing his appreciation. I felt that a fitting designation for me was amanuensis—one who writes for

The sculptor's secretary, 'Lyn Lambert, comfortably perched on Dudley's *Bird Seat* in 1991
Photograph courtesy 'Lyn Lambert

'Lyn Lambert, Dudley's grandson Michael Vaughan, and Dudley's daughter, Mavis Vaughan, on the doorstep of *Replica of a Haida House #4* during its reconstruction
Photograph courtesy 'Lyn Lambert

someone else. But we agreed that Dudley could refer to me as his secretary.

At times Dudley called me his interpreter. He was extremely hard of hearing, and some people found his speech rather indistinct. Generally, he was able to understand me and I him. I also served as part-time driver—local runs only as I tended to be freeway phobic. Over time I became barber, shopper, wardrobe mistress, and stand-in when he had to deal with people in difficult situations, such as an IRS audit. Dudley's final tax return came under scrutiny because the IRS questioned some of his deductions. They assumed that a man of one hundred would have a hobby, not a business, and his deductions couldn't possibly be business deductions.

Never Say Never

A portion of Dudley's tools stored in the garage of the Slough House. His handmade notes indicated which tools were for his use only; others were available for his apprentices' use.
Photograph 'Lyn Lambert

Showing the IRS folks recent newspaper articles about Dudley convinced them that he was still in business and the deductions were legitimate.

Dudley Carter was a vigorous, ambitious, prolific, defiantly independent ninety-nine-year-old when I first got to know him. However, during our months together—while he carried out his demanding sculpture business, welcomed visitors to the county park, and worked with his group of apprentices— Dudley acquired what turned out to be an incurable illness. That alone would be enough to sap the strength and test the spirit of a man half his age, but he also experienced a number of other major difficulties or "areas of discontent," as his daughter termed them. Dudley graciously accepted my assistance and companionship while he matter-of-factly dealt with what life had in store for him.

He planned to treat his latest physical trouble in his usual manner, by fasting. But I was concerned that he may have a particularly belligerent problem, so I asked him what he would do if he had something that fasting wouldn't cure. His reply was swift and sure: "Then you die! It's a lot better to die that way than the way the doctors will have you die."

Although he remained supremely mentally competent to his final days, Dudley's remarkable physical strength and vigor waned. He honored me greatly by asking that I share, along with his daughter who resided in Canada, the power of attorney for his affairs. This was no small relinquishment as Dudley was known to guard his personal powers wisely and admirably. I assumed that mantle with a tremendous sense of responsibility and humility.

Dudley Carter passed away in his sleep just a few weeks short of his 101st birthday in the little rambler in Slough House Park where he had happily and commendably served as artist-in-residence.

Shortly after his death, a group of Dudley's friends, patrons, and apprentices formed the Dudley

Tucked among the tools of his trade is a paddle, the design inked and awaiting the sculptor's chisels
Photograph 'Lyn Lambert

C. Carter Northwest Arts and Cultural Foundation, a nonprofit corporation. Their mission was to keep alive the artistic spirit Dudley brought to that little gem of a park in Redmond. They envisioned Dudley's park as a mecca for wood-carvers in the way that Pilchuck Glass School is for glass artists. They connected with Haida carver Ralph Bennett. He was enthused about moving into the park and continuing an active carving program there. They hoped to see the park named for Dudley Carter and developed with a multipurpose art studio, a sculpture garden, and picnic areas. Unfortunately, the group disbanded. But fortunately, with wisdom of foresight, the City of Redmond, after inheriting the park from King County, granted the studio landmark status, named the park after Dudley, and installed a Dudley Carter sculpture. A landscape architect drew up marvelous plans for a sculpture garden, studio building, and picnic areas. All that is lacking at the time of this writing is the funding to develop the plan.

My time with Dudley and the decades that have followed have been more interesting than I could have imagined. I am exceedingly grateful that something prompted me to ignore that old dictum: Never admit you can type. My Dudley Carter experience has been anything but mundane and thankless. Dudley continues to send me typing assignments and arranges opportunities for me to meet wonderful people.

Never say never; say relatively seldom, if ever.

Apprentice Tim Kelly and his vintage tractor, grading the site for the reconstruction of *Replica of a Haida House #4*
Photograph 'Lyn Lambert

A meeting of the Dudley C. Carter Northwest Arts and Cultural Foundation in Dudley's Haida-style studio at Slough House Park. Left to right: Douglas Weber, Ralph Bennett, Pam Slyter, Kathy Conner, Foundation President Jim Moore, 'Lyn Lambert, Michael Vaughan, Jim Balkonen (partially hidden), Dean Fredrickson, Bertil Valley
Photograph Mike Hoonan

Never Say Never

Dudley Carter, at the age of one hundred, his hands as sure and as steady as ever, signing *Wolf and the Raven*, which he carved in 1978

Photograph 'Lyn Lambert

Following his centennial birthday celebration, Dudley was exceedingly anxious to resurrect and make use of his Haida-style studio, but he lacked ready funding to begin the project. His checking account had been drained due to some circumstances beyond his control, and never wanting to tap into what he called his "reserves," Dudley determined he had to sell a sculpture. He had some prospects in mind, but they didn't materialize. Knowing how disappointed he was and wanting to see Dudley's project come through, I told him I had been hoping to purchase a sculpture sometime in the future, so perhaps I could help. My purchase of *Wolf and the Raven* provided enough capital for Dudley to begin rebuilding *Replica of a Haida House #4*. Dudley had not signed the sculpture when he originally carved it, so he signed it for me at the time of purchase. He wanted to date the work but couldn't remember when he had created it. Not having the chronology of his sculptures available, he decided to date it the year of his signing. Thus, *Wolf and the Raven* bears the date 1991, although it was carved in 1978.

Afterword

To Preserve and Protect

From a conversation with Mayumi Tsutakawa

At the time of Dudley Carter's one-hundredth birthday in 1991, as director of the King County Arts Commission, I was invited to speak at the celebration hosted by King County and held at the park where Mr. Carter was artist-in-residence. Members of the King County Arts Commission wanted to acknowledge the sculptor as a very important contributor to Northwest art.

There are now many different kinds of artists and many schools of art within the art community of the Pacific Northwest. In the fledgling art community here, when Dudley Carter was finding his niche, indigenous Native American carving techniques and the use of wood on a monumental sculptural scale was not taught as art. He had developed an appreciation of those techniques. Through his work, he helped preserve and spread that body of knowledge. That is his unique contribution to the Pacific Northwest art community.

A public site should be designated for the preservation of his works. I'm not sure to what extent his pieces are still preserved, but existing pieces should be collected and displayed for the public view along with photographs of his art no longer preserved. The park, now known as Dudley Carter Park where Mr. Carter erected his Haida house studio, would seem to be the logical place for the preservation of his works and for displays honoring him and his unique contributions.

Mayumi Tsutakawa, shown here with her father, the late sculptor George Tsutakawa, is a native of Seattle and received her master's degree in communications and her bachelor's degree in Japan area studies at the University of Washington. An independent writer, editor, and art curator, Tsutakawa has been active in many roles in the arts and cultural world, including editor of a number of literary anthologies, executive director of the King County Arts Commission, independent curator and director of external relations for the Wing Luke Asian Museum, advocate for cultural democracy as chair of the Association of American Cultures, and grants manager at the Washington State Arts Commission.
Photograph 'Lyn Lambert

Dudley Carter speaking to dignitaries, patrons, students, and friends gathered at the party held by King County to celebrate his one-hundredth birthday. Dudley was on hand for the entire six-hour celebration to visit with guests.
Photograph 'Lyn Lambert

After Photographs

Afterthoughts. Everyday life often presents us with afterthoughts. Afterwords. Books frequently include afterwords, as does this book. But Dudley Carter's book warrants "after photographs."

With the compilation of the Dudley Carter stories and accompanying images accomplished, there remained in our collection a number of photographs of seldom seen Carter creations much too interesting to ignore. They didn't quite fit into our storytellers' tales, so we have placed these "after photographs" here for your enjoyment.

Unless otherwise indicated, all photographs in this section are courtesy Anna Vaughan Hanson.

Above: *Replica of a Haida House #1*, 1935, under construction
Redwood and native oak, 12′ high, 24′ wide

Right: *Condor, Coyote, and Eagle*, 1936
Redwood, 16′ × 4.5′ × 2′
One of several sculptures Dudley created for Federal Arts Projects from 1934–39

Opposite page: *Lake Wilderness Totem*, 1949
Red cedar, 35′ × 5′ × 5′
Photograph Lisa Lambert

Above: *Woman with Birds*, 1947
Acacia, 5′ × 4′ × 16″

Right: *Northgate Totem*, 1952
Red cedar, 59′ × 7′ × 7′
Newly restored and situated at
Clearwater Casino,
Suquamish, Washington in 2014
Photograph Lisa Lambert

Above: *Alaska Building Totem*, 1956
Red cedar, 22′ × 30″ × 30″
Carved for the Alaska Airlines Building in
Federal Way, Washington

Opposite page: *Bird Woman*, 1947
Red Cedar, 12′ × 4′ × 10″
As displayed in the Redmond Library,
Redmond, Washington
Photograph King County Library System

Above: *Feast Bowl*, date and measurements unknown
One of many feast bowls carved by Dudley

Left: *Spirit of the Western Waters* canoe, 1972
Red cedar, 4' × 3.5' × 23'

Opposite page: *Synthesis of Organic Forms*, 1969
Red cedar, 14' × 4' × 4'

Owl Patio Wall #1 with details (below), 1976, red cedar, 7' × 12', carved at Habitat Forum, Vancouver, BC

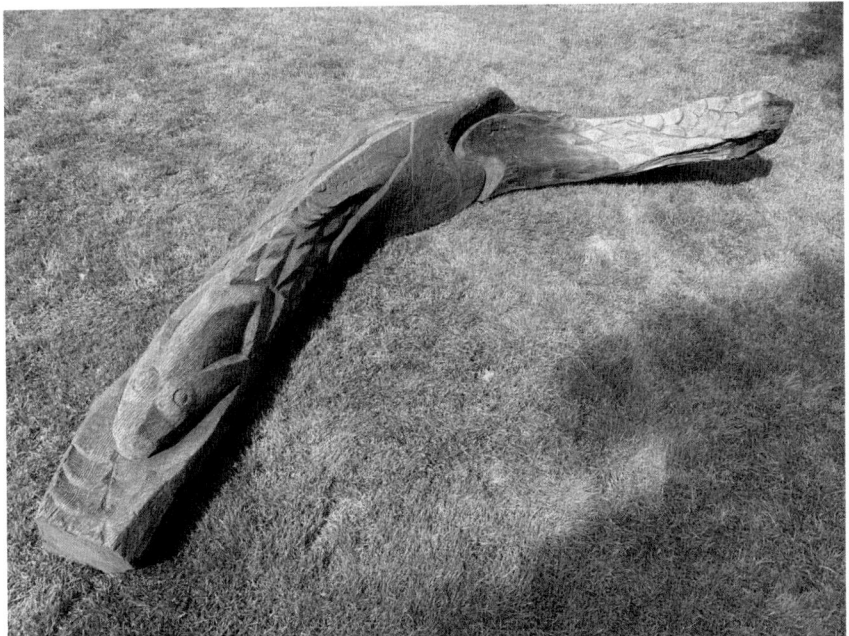

Above left: *Suntower*, 1976
Yellow and red cedar,
13′7″ × 3′2″ × 3′9″
Carved at Habitat Forum,
Vancouver BC

Above right:
Owl and Plant Forms, 1981
Red cedar, 7′ × 3′ × 20″
Carved at Gibsons, BC

Left: *Frog and Bird*, 1979
Red cedar, 12′10″ long
Photograph Lisa Lambert

After Photographs

Opposite page: *Wolf and the Raven*, 1978
Red cedar, 7′ × 3′ × 18″
Dudley carved *Wolf and the Raven* at his summer camp in Gibsons, BC. In Native lore, wolves are the epitome of the wild spirit and ravens are birds of mysticism and magic. Wolf experts have noted that wolves and ravens often display a playful relationship. Perhaps that is what Dudley has depicted in this work.
Photograph Lisa Lambert

Top left and right: Front and back views of
Sea Lion, Seaweed, Seahorse, and Sea Otter, 1986
Red Cedar, 8.5′ × 3′9″ × 2.5′

Right: *Ship's Figurehead*, 1985
Red cedar, 12′ × 3′ × 8′
Dudley's vision for this piece included a ship, total work to be 60′ long—price tag $60,000.

After Photographs

Opposite page: *Three Panel Abstraction*, 1989
Red cedar, 10′ × 6′ × 5′
Photograph Lisa Lambert

Above left: *Bird Watcher's Dream #2*, 1988
Red cedar, 2.5′ × 14″ × 11″
Used by Dudley to illustrate carving principles to students and apprentices

Above right: *Legend of the Deep #2*, 1982
Red cedar, 8′8″ × 3′8″ × 2′

Left: *Gift to the Wolf and the Raven*, 1991
Yellow and red cedar, 7′ × 3′10″ × 33″

After Photographs

Acknowledgements

Mary Sikkema and I embarked on this project in 1992, shortly after Dudley Carter's death. Mary was an accomplished writer, and we decided my role would be that of researcher and editor. We enjoyed several years of collaboration, gathering, writing, and revising stories, then sending them off to the storytellers for their review. Sadly, Mary suffered what proved to be a terminal illness, but not before she had accomplished what seemed to me a formidable task: organizing the stories into an enjoyable format. A chronological order seemed logical, but that turned out to be unworkable. The sequence of the stories as published here is very much a result of Mary's gift of organization. I give her high praise for that.

This book would not exist in its present form were it not for the storytellers who shared their remembrances of and their insights into this notable artist's life. They made the compilation of this book not only possible but a most enjoyable endeavor indeed. Storytellers' families contributed generously too, serving up tasty treats while Mary and I absorbed Dudley Carter stories. I regret so very much that Mary and most of our storytellers and their spouses died before they could see these stories in print.

Great gratitude goes to members of Dudley's family whose assistance and encouragement were invaluable, adding considerable material that only his family could provide.

Emmanuel Montoya, notable San Francisco artist and printmaker, generously shared material he gathered through his close association with Dudley. Emmanuel also offered his enthusiastic encouragement throughout the over quarter-century gestation period of this book.

And Douglas Weber! I wonder if Dudley Carter's book would have materialized had Doug not come into Dudley's life and most serendipitously into mine. Doug's enthusiasm for and understanding of Dudley and his work, coupled with his unstinting faith in my ability to tackle a book about such a legendary figure, proved to be just the stimulus I needed.

All of our reviewers gave much of their time and expertise reviewing drafts of the manuscript and helping refine it.

Mary and I were blessed with families who provided unending support and understanding while we devoted so many years to the Dudley project.

Speaking of families, Lisa Lambert, my daughter-in-law, brought her genius, her very good nature, and bushels of brilliance to the project, keeping it moving ahead when Mary's health no longer allowed her to continue our collaboration.

Combining the array of material we had gathered in a pleasing way was a daunting challenge. I am ever so grateful that designer Tim Young came on board to make the Dudley book not just another art book, but an example of what may be considered book art.

Ejaz Yusaf and the good-natured staff at Bellevue's Zebra Printing went out of their way to assist me in the Dudley book from the get-go, from the early days when they helped me with balky copy machines to providing fine quality proofs to help us prepare to publish. Over the years I spent so much time in their shop that I thought they might charge me rent. I owe them many thanks.

And Dudley! I am deeply, deeply grateful to Dudley for his friendship and for his most gracious appreciation of me throughout our extraordinary and all-too-brief time together.

Most of all, I thank the Almighty—the Creator, Sustainer, and Cherisher of all—for the gift of time with the remarkable man who was Dudley Carter and for the opportunity to meet so many other fine people who were a part of his life. So many Godsends! Blessings indeed!

'Lyn Fleury Lambert

A special note:
To any unnamed, uncredited contributors to this book whose words, photographs, or ideas we have been unable to properly ascribe, I extend my apology. I have tried to track you down, but I have to date been unable to connect. If you will get in touch with me, any subsequent editions of the book will be sure to convey due credit.

Chronology of Dudley C. Carter Sculptures

This list is far from complete as Dudley Carter was not particularly particular about such particulars. We have compiled this information from material provided by Dudley's family and through independent discovery. This partial record indicates the remarkable range of Dudley Carter's work and the variety of his clientele. It may be helpful in identifying Carter sculptures or providing provenance. Most of Dudley's significant sculptures are included here, but many minor works and most paddles, bowls, signs, and cedar products such as split rail fences are not recorded.

Works are generally listed according to their date of completion. Original purchasers and/or last known locations of sculptures appear when available. Dimensions are generally noted in order of height, width, and depth. We regret that the accuracy of some dimensions is dubious and that we have been unable to verify them. Page numbers indicate where photographs of sculptures that are included in *Dudley Carter: Tales of the Legendary Wood Sculptor* may be found.

1929	*Carved Book Cover*, yellow cedar, 10″ × 8″ × 1″. Bill Weigel, Supervisor of Forestry for Washington State
1929	*Bessy Lum*, plaster, 12″ × 4″ × 4″
1929	*Riding the Comb*, Britannia metal, 7″ × 5″ × 3″
1929	*Father, Mother, and Child*, lead, 7″ × 4.5″ × 2.5″
1930	*Passing of a Race*, soap, awarded second prize in Procter & Gamble–*Seattle Times* soap-carving contest
1930	*Assassin*, large, simple, axe-hewn carving
1931	*Menace de Modernisme*, soap, awarded first prize in Procter & Gamble–*Seattle Times* soap-carving contest
1931	*Pioneers of the Lumber Industry*, plaster, 6″ × 5″ × 4″, subject timber cruisers, Abby Sher, Santa Monica, CA
1931	*Rivalry of the Winds*, red cedar, 14′ × 4′ × 4′, purchased by the founders of the Seattle Art Museum in 1932 for display in the new museum, later placed outdoors in Volunteer Park, restored and eventually loaned to the Redmond Public Library, Redmond, WA. Pages 17, 32, 34
1932	*Sculptured Table*, red cedar, 3.5′ × 5′, table top supported by four cougars, Will Shaw, Big Creek, CA. Page 45
1932	*Mother of the Fawns*, red cedar, 8′ × 3.5′ × 4′, garden seat, Charles Orton, Orting, WA
1933	*Running the Rapids*, native yew wood, 5′ × 30″ × 10″, Dr. Leo Eloesser, CA
1934	*Ram Head*, redwood, 4′ × 2′ × 18″, Federal Art Project, CA
1935	*Replica of a Haida House #1*, redwood and native oak, 12′ × 24′, Will Shaw, Big Creek, CA, Landels-Hill Big Creek Reserve, University of California, Santa Cruz. Pages 47, 268
1935	*Condor*, redwood, 6′ × 5′ × 30″, exhibited at the opening of San Francisco Art Museum, purchased in 1975 by Allied Stores for proposed but abandoned shopping center project, acquired in 1995 by Marvin Boys to become part of King County Parks' collection. Page 53
1935	*Wek Wek and the Holukmeyumko*, redwood, 12′ × 5.5′ × 5.5′, exhibited in 1940 at the Palace of Fine Arts, Golden Gate International Exposition, San Francisco, CA; purchased in 1975 by Allied Stores for proposed but abandoned shopping center project; acquired in 1995 by Marvin Boys to become part of King County Parks' collection. Pages 55, 56, 89
1936	*Condor, Coyote, and Eagle*, redwood, 16′ × 4.5′ × 2′, one of several sculptures produced for Federal Arts Projects 1935–43, California School Board. Page 268
1936	*Head*, redwood root, 5′ × 2′ × 18″, Federal Arts Project, Monterey, CA
1936	*U.S.A. Coat of Arms*, sugar pine, 5′ diameter relief carving, Defense Language Institute, Presidio of Monterey, CA
1937	*Peciavish*, redwood, 15′ × 6′ × 3′, exhibited in 1940 at the Palace of Fine Arts, San Francisco, CA. One of 16 works purchased by Allied Stores, Seattle, WA
1938	*Indian Legend*, redwood, 8′ × 4′ × 18″, one of 16 works purchased in 1975 by Allied Stores, Seattle, WA, rumored to have been acquired later by one of Seattle's McCaw brothers. Page 231

1939   *Shasta Cascade Building Facade*, sugar pine, 32' × 26'. Golden Gate International Exposition, Timothy Pflueger and Otto Deichmann, architects, San Francisco, CA. Pages 45, 58

1939   *Nine Eagles*, sugar pine, each approximately 9' × 3.5' × 3', displayed in the courtyard of the Shasta Cascade Building, Golden Gate International Exposition, San Francisco, CA

1940   *Big Horn Ram*, redwood, 10' × 2.5' × 3.5', carved at the Golden Gate International Exposition. Presently serves as mascot for City College of San Francisco, CA. Page 59

1940   *Goddess of the Forest*, redwood, 32' × 7' × 7', 30 tons, carved at the Golden Gate International Exposition. Unsuitably situated in Golden Gate Park, San Francisco, for many years where it suffered decay. Moved in 1983 to City College of San Francisco where major portion of carving was preserved. Essentially a shell remains but the work retains its power and purpose. Pages 60, 172, 174

1943   *Female Head*, yellow cedar, 3' high, owned by the Earl Amick family. Page 69

1945   *Foreign Lady*, cottonwood, 3.5' × 2' × 12", purchased in 1975 by Allied Stores, Seattle, WA

1945   *Mountain Maid*, red cedar, 5' × 3.5' × 18", Vaughan residence, Gibsons, BC

1946   *Woman with Birds*, acacia, 5' × 4' × 16", Minor residence, Lake Sammamish, WA. Page 270

1947   *Bird Woman*, red cedar, 12' × 4' × 10", displayed at the Henry Art Gallery, Seattle, WA in 1949, purchased by the Long family, on long-term loan to the Redmond Public Library, Redmond, WA. Pages 67, 271

1947   *Forest Deity*, red cedar, 14' × 9' × 4', purchased by Miller Freeman for Pacific National Bank, Bellevue, and displayed for decades at various locations in Bellevue Square. Cover, pages 78, 79, 80

1947   *Maid of the Woods* or *Verlot*, red cedar, 120-foot-tall living tree, 15 feet in diameter, near Mount Baker National Park, 11 miles east of Granite Falls, WA. Relief figure of a maiden 30 feet tall, 10 feet from the ground. Tree struck by lightning in 1978, carving destroyed. 1988, artist salvaged tree for future use. Pages 27, 199, 202, 203

1947   *Head*, red cedar, 3.5' × 22" × 22", carved at Granite Falls, WA. Vaughan residence, Gibsons, BC

1947   *Big Horn Ram*, red cedar, 7' × 22" × 22", carved at Granite Falls, WA, Lloyd Logren, architect, Bellevue, WA

1948   *Archway*, luan mahogany, 8' high, 18" on each side, installed in a Seattle, WA, residence designed by Thomas Dunstan, architect

1948   *Ram*, stone, 14" × 6" × 5", Ray Egner, Lake Sammamish, WA

1949   *Pioneers of the Lumber Industry*, red cedar, 2 panels, each approximately 8' × 5.5', commissioned by the Schafer Brothers Logging Company, Aberdeen, WA, acquired by Hedda Schafer Shepherd, Fremont, CA. Pages 12, 13, 14

1949   *Lake Wilderness Totem*, red cedar, 35' × 5' × 5', commissioned by Gaffney's Lake Wilderness Resort, now owned by the City of Maple Valley, WA. Pages 82, 83, 84, 269

1950   *Air Hostess*, red cedar, 3.5' × 22" × 22", purchased in 1975 by Allied Stores, Seattle, WA

ca. 1950s   *Thunderbird*, red cedar, 12' with 6' wingspan, Earl Amick family. Page 70

1952   *Bird*, red cedar, 4' × 4' × 12", Steven Richardson, Seattle, WA, architect, Gaffney's Lake Wilderness Lodge

1952	*Northgate Totem*, red cedar, 59′ × 7′ × 7′, *Canoe*, red cedar, 32′ long, *Northgate Signage*, red cedar, commissioned by Allied Stores for Northgate Shopping Center, Seattle, WA. Pages 21, 81, 86, 270
1954	*Tikis*, red cedar, 2 sculptures, each 14′ × 2.5′ × 2.5′, commissioned for Trader Vic's restaurant, Cosmopolitan Hotel, Denver, CO
1954	*Old Man House Interpretive Center*, red cedar, 12′ × 20′, Suquamish, WA. Page 74
1955	*Mink and Wolf Totem*, red cedar, 46′ × 5.5′ × 5.5′, commissioned by Shell Oil Refinery, Anacortes, WA. Pages 94, 95
1955	*Bridlewood Sign*, red cedar, 10′ × 14′, M. W. Mylroie Construction Company, Bellevue, WA
1955	*Prince of the Grizzlies*, red cedar, 12′ × 28″ × 28″, Bon Marche, Seattle, WA. Page 87
1955	*Bird of the Air*, red cedar, 10′ × 7′ × 22″, Bon Marche, Seattle, WA. Page 87
1956	*Replica of a Haida House #2*, red cedar, 17′ × 30′, Dudley Carter's studio, Bellevue, WA, until 1980 when dismantled and transported to Whidbey Island, WA, by Bill McNae. Pages 120, 122
1956	*Alaska Building Totem*, red cedar, 22′ × 30″ × 30″, Alaska Building, Federal Way, WA. Page 270
1956	*Thunderbird "Oscars,"* red cedar, over 150 thunderbirds, each 3.5′ × 22″ × 6″, commissioned by Shell Oil Company for worldwide distribution
1956	*Progress*, red cedar, 9′ × 8′ × 2′, Rainier National Bank of Commerce (later Security Pacific Bank), then part of Seafirst Bank Art Collection. Page 63
1956	*Totem*, red cedar, 16′ × 2′ × 20″, Children's Hospital, Boston, MA
1956	*Feast Bowl*, red cedar, approximately 16″ × 4′, purchased by Allied Stores, Seattle, WA
1958	*Replica of a Haida House #3*, red cedar, 14′ × 22′, Reef Island, WA, commissioned by a Mrs. Hart, once owned by Ron and Abby Sher, sold in 1995 along with other Dudley Carter works on the island to Oakley Sunglasses principal. Page 139
1958	*Killer Whale*, red cedar, 9′ × 3′ × 16″, Bon Marche, Spokane, WA
1958	*Thunderbird*, red cedar, 8′ × 7′ × 30″, Bon Marche, Spokane, WA
1958	*Big Horn Head*, red cedar, 3′ × 26″ × 24″, gift from Sydney Gerber to the Bellevue Public Library, Bellevue, WA. Displayed outside, untreated, deteriorated
1958	*Flower Girl*, red cedar, 28″ × 16″ × 6″, dimensions uncertain, Kirkland, WA
1959	*Sequoia*, redwood, 5′ × 28″ × 16″, carved at Earl Neel's nursery, Palm Springs, CA, stolen from the nursery
1959	*Bride of Chief*, red cedar, 4′ × 20″ × 8″, carved at Earl Neel's Nursery, Palm Springs, CA, sold at Chi Omega Art Show, Seattle, WA
1959	*Gypsy*, red cedar, 3′ × 16″ × 8″, carved at Earl Neel's nursery, Palm Springs, CA, sold at Chi Omega Art Show, Seattle, WA
1959	*Leaping Whale*, red cedar, 5′ × 3′ × 8″, sold at Chi Omega Art Show, Seattle, WA
1959	*Owl Totem*, yellow cedar, 10′ × 34″ × 12″, carved at Earl Neel's nursery, Palm Springs, CA
1959	*Spirit Mask*, red cedar, 18″ × 32″ × 12″, with movable beak and cedar bark hair, Dr. Boone, Bellevue, WA

1959	*Seated Ram*, red cedar, 16″ × 12″ × 8″, Don McAusland, Bellevue, WA. Page 128
1960	*Post*, red cedar, 8′ × 2′ × 20″, corner post for the original Bellevue Clinic, later waiting room décor in new clinic, Bellevue, WA
1960	*Naval Air Station Totem*, red cedar, 46′ × 4.5′ × 4.5′, Sand Point Naval Air Station, Seattle WA, Pages 97, 98, 99
1960	*Desert Scout*, redwood, 18″ × 7′ × 6″, carved at Earl Neel's nursery, Palm Springs, CA. Purchased in 1975 by Allied Stores, acquired in 1995 by Marvin Boys, displayed in Redmond Public Library, Redmond, WA. Pages 89, 134
1960	*Easter Parade*, redwood, 6′ × 3′ × 4″, carved at Earl Neel's nursery, Palm Springs, CA. Collection of Anna Vaughan Hanson, Gibsons, BC. Page 255
1960	*Bird Carrying Message*, sugar pine, 20″ × 4′, carved at Earl Neel's nursery, Palm Springs, CA, Kurt and Jane Oestreich's residence, Redmond, then later, Camano Island, WA. Page 29
1960	*Grizzly Bear and Raven Totem*, red cedar, 10′ × 30″ × 8″, a school in Medina, WA
1960	*Thunderbird Totem*, red cedar, approximately 3.5′, Sammamish High School mascot, Bellevue, WA, stolen
1960	*Diving Girl*, red cedar, 4′6″ × 28″ × 28″, a candy shop in Issaquah, WA
1960	*Interior Doorway Panel*, sugar pine, Thomas Dunstan, Bellevue, WA
1960	*Seagull on a Post*, red cedar, 10′ × 5′ × 12″, Don McAusland, Bellevue, WA, donated to City of Redmond, installed in Dudley Carter Park, Redmond, WA. Page 127
1960	*Fawn*, red cedar, 10′ × 3′ × 14″, Redmond, WA
1960	*Faith, Hope, and Charity Triptych*, red cedar, 3 panels, each approximately 8.5′ × 3.5′ × 20″. Subjects: Fawn, Birds & Plant Forms; Fawn & Plant Forms; Bird. Bayview Manor Retirement Home, Seattle, WA
1961	*Sylvan Fantasy Stump*, red cedar, 7′ × 5′ × 2′, Redmond, WA
1961	*Diving Bird*, red cedar, 7′ × 3′ × 20″, church camp, San Juan Islands, WA
1961	*Dragon*, red cedar, 4.5′ × 30″ × 8″, Cressman residence, Mercer Island, WA
1961	*Chief Spokan Garry*, red cedar, 12′ × 4.5′ × 22″, St. Dunstan's of the Highlands Church Parish Hall, Shoreline, WA. Page 110
1961	*Fort Columbia Sign*, red cedar, 4′ × 41′ × 10″, Fort Columbia Historical Park, Naselle, WA. Page 74
1961	*Bird and Bear House Post*, red cedar, 8′ × 2′ × 12″, Fenton residence, Seattle, WA
1961	*Bus Stop*, red cedar, shelter with 3 columns, 18′ high. El Dorado Land Development, Mercer Island, WA, Thomas Dunstan, architect. Page 71
1961	*Little Big Horn (With Owls)*, black walnut, 4.5′ × 18″ × 18″, carved for Seattle World's Fair, Seattle, WA, Art Museum Pavilion. Later displayed at Pacific Science Center, Seattle Center, Building #2, entrance to Sea Monster House
1961	*Bear on Top of Post*, red cedar, 7′ × 28″ × 20″, Department of Anthropology, University of Washington, Whidbey Island State Park, WA

1961	*Last of the Sugarloaf Tribe*, red cedar, 3.5′ × 14″ × 10″, carved at Earl Neel's nursery, Palm Springs, CA. Albert Culverwell, Blue Jay, CA. Page 75
1961	*Springtime*, redwood, 11′ × 2′ × 16″, carved at Earl Neel's nursery, Palm Springs, CA. Purchased by Allied Stores, Seattle, WA in 1975. Donated to PONCHO Auction, purchased by M. Alhadeff, later sold to Bill Minor, Bellevue, WA
1962	*Music Hour*, walnut, 4′ × 7′, carved at Earl Neel's nursery, Palm Springs, CA. Vaughan residence, Gibsons, BC
1962	*High Mountain Companions*, redwood, approximately 6′ × 2.5′ × 2′, carved at Earl Neel's nursery, Palm Springs, CA. Purchased by Allied Stores, Seattle, WA, in 1975, acquired in 1995 by Marvin Boys. On 5-year loan in 1997 to Redmond Town Center, Redmond, WA. Page 133
1962	*Podium*, red cedar, 4′ × 2.5′ × 2′, West Seattle High School, Seattle, WA
1962	*Totem*, red cedar, dimensions unknown, Chicago, IL
1962	*Totem Mascot*, red cedar, 5.5′ × 3′ × 16″, Sammamish High School, Bellevue, WA
1962	*Thunderbird and Bear Totem*, red cedar, 5′ × 3′ × 16″, New York, NY. (DuPont House, 1964 New York World's Fair? Theme of fair: Peace through Understanding.)
1963	*Woman with Gift*, red cedar, 5′ × 2′ × 16″, Don McAusland, Bellevue, WA. Page 127
1963	*Wildlife*, redwood, 7′ × 26″ × 8″, 2 bears and a bird, carved at Earl Neel's nursery, Palm Springs, CA. Purchased in 1975 by Allied Stores, Seattle, WA
1963	*Thunderbird in Flight*, red cedar, 6′ × 5′ × 12″, a lodge in Glenhaven, WA
1963	*Primitive Park Sign*, red cedar, 12′ × 6′ × 12″, Stevens Pass Highway, east of Everett, WA
1963	*Owl and Ram Totem*, alder, 7′ × 18″ × 16″, Rotary Club, New Lynn, New Zealand
1963	*Door Panels, Winkenwerder Forest Sciences Laboratory*, red cedar, 3 panels, each 9′ × 22″, University of Washington, Seattle, WA. Page 131
1964	*Chinook Bear Totem*, red cedar, 14′ × 30″ × 28″, Chinook Middle School, Bellevue, WA. Page 119
1964	*Bear with Sign*, redwood, 7′ × 3.5′, Anderson residence, Santa Cruz, CA
1964	*Shaman with a Mask*, hollow yellow cedar, 8′ × 2′ × 2′, Vaughan residence, Gibsons, BC. Page 255
1964	*Legend of the Sea*, red cedar, 8.5′ × 5′10″, purchased by George Thomas for display at the Bay Shore Apartments, Kirkland, WA. Donated in 1984 by Thomas to Children's Hospital and Medical Center, Seattle, WA. In 1996, sculpture was situated at the north end of the hospital's herb garden. Page 219
1964	*Raven and Sun Totem*, red cedar, 15′ × 30″ × 12″, Vaughan residence, Gibsons, BC. Page 247
1964	*Bird Seat*, red cedar, 28″ × 3′ × 7″ (dimensions uncertain) purchased in 1975 by Allied Stores, Seattle, WA
1965	*Segment of Creation*, redwood, 5′ × 20″ × 4″, carved at Earl Neel's nursery, Palm Springs, CA. Vaughan residence, Gibsons, BC. Page 256
1965	*Bird and Plant Form Abstract*, sugar pine, red chalk coloring, 5′ × 2′, Bellevue, WA
1965	*Seabird*, sugar pine, 6′ × 2′, purchased in 1975 by Allied Stores, Seattle, WA

1965	*Semone*, red cedar, 7′ × 24″ × 2″, door, carved at Earl Neel's nursery, Palm Springs, CA. Sold to Bill McNae, Whidbey Island, WA. Page 123
1965	*Voice of the Waves*, red cedar, 5′ × 2′ × 10″, West Vancouver, BC
1965	*Totem*, red cedar, 20′ × 30″ × 26″, carved with the assistance of Phil Claymore, Blaine, WA. Originally attached to park superintendent's residence, later installed as a sign post, Peace Arch Heritage Park, Blaine, WA
1965	*Thunderbird and Dogwood Blossom*, red cedar, 7′ × 34″ × 22″, Hal Cook, Bainbridge Island, WA
1965	*Model Canoe with Figureheads*, red cedar, 30″ × 4′ × 16′ long. Later titled *Spirit of Western Waters #2*. Sold by Dudley Carter estate to Barney Granger, Kirkland, WA
1966	*Open Abstract Designs*, sugar pine, 6′ × 3′, pierced panels, carved at Earl Neel's nursery, Palm Springs, CA
1966	*Whale Post*, red cedar, 15′ × 20″ × 14″, Hyak School, Bellevue or Seattle, WA
1966	*Legend of the Deep*, red cedar, 9′ × 3.5′ × 10″, Chuck Wills, Vancouver, BC
1966	*Timber Industry—Boom Man and Faller*, red cedar, 2 panels, each 9′ × 5′ × 6″, installed on exterior walls at entrance to Peoples National Bank, later U.S. Bank, Hoquiam, WA
1966	*Woman and Child*, red cedar, 13′ × 30″ × 12″, Nalos residence, Bellevue, WA
1966	*N.W. Indian Abstract*, red cedar, 4′ × 3′, McKinstry residence, Bellevue, WA
1968	*Killer Whale Eating Seaweed*, red cedar, 6′ × 30″ × 8″, Jordon residence, Seattle, WA
1968	*Abstract*, red cedar, 6′ × 2′, red chalk coloring, purchased in 1975 by Allied Stores, Seattle, WA
1968	*Totem*, red cedar, 5′ × 20″ × 10″, Dr. Leo Vieth, West Germany
1969	*Two Totems—Bear and Thunderbird*, red cedar, *Bear*, 3.5′ × 12″ × 12″; *Thunderbird*, 3.5′ × 30″ × 12″, Catherine Pietromanacko (or Pietromonaco?), Italy
1969	*Synthesis of Organic Forms*, red cedar, 14′ × 4′ × 4′, abstract, Robert Van Aken residence, Bellevue, WA. Page 273
1969	*Driftwood Flower*, red cedar, 10′ × 4′ × 30″, vandalized at Crossroads exhibit, Bellevue, WA
1969	*Big Horn Ram*, red cedar, 7′ × 3.5′ × 30″, purchased by Allied Stores, Seattle, WA, in 1975
ca. 1970s	*Mountain Majesty*, red cedar, 5′ × 3.5′ × 6″, Marvin Boys residence, Bellevue, WA
ca. 1970s	*Wise Owl*, red cedar, 6′ × 18″ × 18″, Marvin Boys residence, Bellevue, WA
ca. 1970s	*Seashore Girl*, red cedar driftwood, 6′ × 18″ × 18″, Marvin Boys residence, Bellevue, WA
ca. 1970s	*Lady of the Sea*, red cedar driftwood, 6′ high, Marvin Boys residence, Bellevue, WA. Page 88
1970	*Bird*, red cedar, 10′ × 7′ × 13″, incomplete, Dudley Carter estate
1971	*Totem*, red cedar, 16′ × 30″ × 30″, George Ducey, Lake Stevens, Washington. Model owned by Bill McNae, Whidbey Island, WA
1972	*Driftwood Head*, red cedar, 4′ × 30″ × 8″, John Clark, West Vancouver, BC
1972	*Owl and Bear*, red cedar, 10′ × 2′ × 10″, Hal Cook, Bainbridge Island, WA

1972	*Spirit of the Western Waters*, red cedar, 4′ × 3.5′ × 23′ long canoe, Martin Goeslin, Tacoma, WA. Page 272
1974	*Birds and Waterfall*, redwood, 8′ × 6.5′ × 20″, loaned to City Museum of Natural History, Santa Cruz, CA. Returned to Dudley Carter estate in 1993. Purchased by Marvin Boys and donated to the Redmond Public Library, Redmond, WA. Page 182
1974	*Winery Panel*, sugar pine, 8′ × 5′, Field Winery, Fresno, CA
1975	*Killer Whale*, red cedar, 9′ × 5′ × 10″, carved at Dundarave Pier, West Vancouver, BC, Abby Sher, Santa Monica, CA
1975	*Bear and Mask*, red cedar, dimensions unknown, Justin W. Dart, Seattle, WA
1976	*Owl Patio Wall #1*, red cedar, 7′ × 12′, carved at Habitat Forum, Vancouver, BC, Ron Sher, Bellevue, WA. Page 274
1976	*Two Thunderbirds*, red cedar, each 2′ × 3′ × 12′ long, carved at Habitat Forum, Vancouver, BC, for Allied Stores, Seattle, WA. Acquired by Marvin Boys in 1995 for King County Parks. Pages 89, 184
1976	*Suntower*, yellow and red cedar, 13′7″ × 3′2″ × 3′9″, carved at Habitat Forum, Vancouver, BC. Purchased in 1994 by Pam Slyter for the Individual Progress Center, Redmond, WA. Page 275
1976	*Grand Prairie Totem*, red cedar, 17′ × 30″ × 30″, carved at Dundarave Pier, West Vancouver, BC, for Grand Prairie Composite High School, Grand Prairie, AB. Pages 114, 115
1976	*The Craft of Yakima Valley*, red cedar, 5′ × 2′ × 18″, Washington State Arts Commission, Yakima Valley College, Yakima, WA
1976	*Ram Head*, yellow cedar, 30″ × 22″ × 20″, gift from the artist to Marvin Boys, Bellevue, WA. Page 92
1977	*Riding the Comb*, red cedar, 4′ × 5′ × 22″, Don McAusland, Bellevue, WA. Page 129
1978	*Legend of the Moon*, red cedar, 35′ × 11′ × 6′, King County Arts Commission, Marymoor Park, Redmond, WA. Pages 100, 103, 104, 105, 107
1978	*Totem*, red cedar, 9′ × 20″ × 8″, Bruno Gerussi, Toronto, ON
1978	*Wolf and the Raven*, red cedar, 7′ × 3′ × 18″, carved at Gibsons, BC, purchased in 1991 by 'Lyn Lambert, loaned to MainStreet Property Group's Carter on the Park, Redmond, WA. Page 276
1978	*Nesting Birds*, red cedar, 10′ × 2′ × 16″, carved at Gibsons, BC, Peter C. Vaughan residence, Gibsons, BC
1978	*Abstract #2*, red cedar, 7′4″ × 4′ × 22″
1979	*Fawn and Bird*, red cedar, 9′ × 3′ × 16″, carved at Gibsons, BC, purchased by Chuck Skoor, Issaquah, WA, then by 'Lyn Lambert in 1993, donated to Redmond Public Library, Redmond, WA. Page 218
1979	*Sea Lion*, red cedar, 7′ × 30″ × 14″, carved at Gibsons, BC, purchased by Chuck Skoor, Issaquah, WA, acquired in 1993 by Dean Fredrickson, Burien, WA
1979	*Owl Post and Rails*, red cedar, Post 8′9″ tall, purchased by Chuck Skoor, Issaquah, WA, donated to King County in 1994 by the Dudley Carter Foundation

1979 *Frog and Bird*, red cedar, 12′10″ long, Chuck Skoor, Issaquah, WA, 1993 sold to 'Lyn Lambert. Page 275

1980 *Reflections of the Primitive Background of the West Coast*, red cedar, *Mythical Beast*, 39′ × 6′, *Primitive Woman*, 30′ × 8′, *Forest Garland*, 36′ × 7′, Portland's Clackamas Town Center, Happy Valley, OR. Moved to Columbia Gorge Interpretive Center Museum, Stevenson, WA.
Pages 154, 155, 156, 157, 158, 160, 161, 162, 164

1980 *Mythical Bird*, yellow cedar, 11′ × 5′7″ × 3.5′, carved at Gibsons, BC, 1996, Pioneer Park, Mercer Island, WA. Page 233

1980 *Sea Lion and Sea Horse*, red cedar, 11′ × 5′ × 4.5′, carved at Gibsons, BC, Sunshine Coast Art Centre, Sechelt, BC

1980 *Sea Lion*, red cedar, 4′ × 2′ × 10′ long, carved at Gibsons, BC

1980 *Forest Ensemble*, red cedar, 10′ × 2.5′ × 2.5′, Ron Sher, Bellevue, WA

1981 *Fawn and Birds*, red cedar, 12′ × 30″ × 16″, carved at Gibsons, BC, sold through Dudley Carter estate

1981 *Owl and Plant Forms*, red cedar, 7′ × 3′ × 20″, carved at Gibsons, BC, sold in 1988 to Bruce Paterson. Page 275

1981 *Bridge to Nowhere*, red and yellow cedar, 4′ × 7′ × 19′ long, Vaughan residence, Gibsons, BC

1981 *Sun and Moon*, red cedar, 5′ × 3′ × 16″, Michael Vaughan, Gibsons, BC

1982 *Ravenchild*, red cedar, 9′ × 6′ × 4′, carved at Gibsons, BC, purchased in 1993 for Crossroads Shopping Center, Bellevue, WA. Pages 121, 248, 249

1982 *The Beast that Was*, red cedar, 8′ × 10′ × 20″, carved at Gibsons, BC, purchased in 1992 by Conner family, Issaquah, WA. Page 213

1982 *Legend of the Deep #2*, red cedar, 8′8″ × 3′8″ × 2′, displayed at Crossroads Shopping Center, purchased by Marvin Boys in 1997, donated to the City of Bellevue, displayed at the Northwest Arts Center, Bellevue, WA. Page 278

1982 *Feathered Companions*, red cedar, 5′7″ × 4′7″ × 2′, sold by the Dudley Carter estate. Page 243

NOTE: Data pertaining to the below listed Carter works created following 1982 is unfortunately sketchy

Cougar, Wolf, and Bird, yellow cedar, 6′ × 20″ panel, unfinished, stolen from Slough House Park following Dudley's death

Entrance Door and Totem for Replica of a Haida House #4, red cedar, 2 segments, together 16′ × 3′, date carved possibly 1985. Installed 1992, Redmond, WA

Last Frontier, red cedar, 12′ × 4′, purchased unfinished by Conner family, Issaquah, WA

Owl and Plant Forms #2, red cedar, 8′ × 5′ × 2′, sold to Dr. Walker

Sea Lion, 9′ × 3′, for pool décor, sold sometime prior to 1991

Unfinished Lizard Paddle, cedar with sketched design, 5.5′ long. Page 51

1984 *Menace de Modernisme*, red cedar, 8.5′ × 5′2″ × 32″, purchased by Marvin Boys from the Dudley Carter estate, donated to the City of Bellevue, WA, installed at the North Bellevue Community Center, Bellevue, WA. Pages 91, 206

1984	*Frog Spiral*, red cedar, 2'3" × 23" × 8'11" long, sold through Dudley Carter estate to Pam Slyter, Individual Progress Center, Redmond, WA
1985	*Sanctuary: Preservation of Wildlife*, redwood, 14' × 6' × 3', carved at Dick Cooley's studio, Santa Cruz, CA, sold through Dudley Carter estate. Pages 179, 180, 181
1985	*Bird with Attributes of Man*, redwood, 4' × 4' × 16", carved at Dick Cooley's Santa Cruz, CA, studio, sold through Dudley Carter estate
1985	*Head on a Redwood Tree*, redwood, 9' × 4' × 4', carved at Dick Cooley's Santa Cruz, CA, studio
1985	*Ship's Figurehead*, red cedar, 12' × 3' × 8', displayed at Crossroads Shopping Center, Bellevue, WA, sold through Dudley Carter estate to owners of a waterfront estate in Medina, WA. Dudley's vision for this piece included a ship, total work to be 60' long and to sell for $60,000. Page 277
1985	*Abstract*, yellow cedar, 3'8" × 2' × 18", displayed at Crossroads Shopping Center, Bellevue, WA, sold through Dudley Carter estate
1986	*The Beast*, redwood, 6' × 3.5', a gift from the artist to San Francisco City College, CA. Page 168
1986	*O Time in Thy Flight*, red cedar, twin figures, not identical, each 3'3" × 4' × 10'5", one piece sold in 1996 through Dudley Carter estate, the other to Heidi Bohan
1986	*Sea Lion, Seaweed, Seahorse, and Sea Otter*, red cedar, 8.5' × 3'9" × 2.5', sold through Dudley Carter estate. Page 277
1986	*Adventure on Western Waters*, red cedar, 6' × 12' × 4', sold to Northwest Hospital, Seattle, WA, in 1990. Page 210
1986	*Celestial Intruder*, red cedar, 16' high, 37' long, carved at Gibsons, BC, intended for display at Canada's Expo, sold to a party in Canada in 1990. Page 186
1986	*Bear Post Patio Wall Divider #2*, red cedar, 7' × 13.5' × 18", sold through Dudley Carter estate. Page 209
1987	*Paddle*, sold to Leo A. Thomas
1987	*Seeds of Enchantment*, red cedar, 4' × 16" × 4", sold to Penny Rediger, later to 'Lyn Lambert, loaned to Redmond Public Library, Redmond, WA. Page 260
1987	*2 Corner Posts*, red cedar, 11' × 18" × 12", carved for Haida House replica ordered by Bill and Michelle Minor. Plans cancelled by Minors and Dudley Carter bought the posts back in 1991 for installation in *Replica of a Haida House #4*.
1988	*Owl Panel*, red cedar, 4'2" × 17", Robert Dickhoff, Jr.
1988	*Defiant Bird*, red cedar, 10' × 6' × 4", Robert L. Hass
1988	*2 Porch Posts*, carved for back porch of Slough House residence, sold through Dudley Carter estate
1988	*Paddle*, sold to Patricia Cook, Ray Egner's daughter. Egner purchased Dudley Carter's stone sculpture *Ram* in 1948.
1988	*2 Paddles*, 1 red cedar, 1 yellow cedar, for Salish Lodge at Snoqualmie Falls, WA
1988	*Bird Lover* or *Bird Watcher's Dream #1*, red cedar, 2.5' × 20", for Bellevue Art Museum, resold to Conner family, Issaquah WA. Page 217

1988   *Bird Watcher's Dream #2*, red cedar 2.5′ × 14″ × 11″, used by Dudley to illustrate carving principles to students and apprentices. Sold to apprentice Jim Balkonen through Dudley Carter estate. Page 279

1988   *Eagle, Beaver, and Salmon*, red cedar, 9′ × 3′ × 16″, for Bill Way, Sammamish, WA

1988   *Mythical Bird* (small), 5′ × 16″ × 10″, Dr. Wayne Ono, Redmond, WA

1989   *The Viking*, red cedar, 7′ × 3′, mascot, dubbed "Joe Vandal" by students at the University of Idaho, Moscow, ID. Pages 221, 222

1989   *Three Panel Abstraction*, red cedar, 10′ × 6′ × 5′, displayed at Crossroads Shopping Center, Bellevue, WA, sold through the Dudley Carter estate to the City of Redmond. Installed at Luke McRedmond's Landing on the shores of the Sammamish River, Redmond, WA. Page 278

1989   *Beachcomber's Bride*, alder, 2′6″ × 2′ × 18″, displayed at Crossroads Shopping Center, Bellevue, WA, sold through Dudley Carter estate

1989   *Hatching Bird*, red cedar, 7′ × 22″ × 14″, displayed at Crossroads Shopping Center, Bellevue, WA, purchased by Marvin Boys and donated to the City of Bellevue, installed in courtyard of North Bellevue Community Center. Page 91

1989   *Raven*, sold to Jean Tobin

1989   *Fantail Bird*, red cedar, 8′ × 14′, commissioned by the City of Redmond, WA, for the Redmond Senior Center. Page 189

1989   *Bird*, 33″ × 17″, sold to Robert Levin

1989   *Riding the Transcending Wave*, 1 of 2 scale models commissioned for the Washington State Centennial. Page 195

1989   *The Bowman*, red cedar, 6′2″ × 4′10″ × 16″, major figure in *Riding the Transcending Wave*, centennial concept, carved in expectation of receiving funding for the entire sculpture. Funding for the project never materialized. Figure sold separately through Dudley Carter estate. Pages 196, 238

1989   *Three Paddlers*, red cedar, each approximately 6′5″ × 3′ × 21″, created as parts of the centennial work *Riding the Transcending Wave*. One paddler sold in 1991 to Sam Pemberton, the other two sold through the Dudley Carter estate. Pages 196, 197

1989   *Bird Defying Man's Invasion of Space*, red cedar, 14′ × 10′ × 5′, sold in 1990 to Edmonds Community College, Lynnwood, WA, for their Kobe, Japan, campus that opened in 1990 and closed in 1997. Page 169

1990   *Windsong*, red cedar, 9′ × 5′ × 18″, suspended head with post. Sold to City of Medina for installation in Medina Park. Pages 228, 229

1990   *Firebird*, red cedar, 10′ × 3′, sold through Dudley Carter estate

1990   *Bird Seat*, red cedar, sold to Bill Henning, 1991. Page 261

1991   *Nature's Gift Planter*, red cedar, approximately 7′ × 3′ × 2′, sold to Bill McNae, Whidbey Island, WA

1991   *Suspended Fantasy Planter*, red cedar, 10′ × 18′ × 3′, sold to Conner family, Issaquah, WA. Page 215, 216

1991   *Gift to the Wolf and the Raven*, yellow and red cedar, 7′ × 3′10″ × 33″, sold through the Dudley Carter estate. Page 279

1991   *Celestial Adventure*, red cedar, 8'3" × 16' × 6'10", significant figure in Dudley Carter's entry in Redmond's 1991 Derby Days Parade, for which he was the Grand Marshall. Sold through the Dudley Carter estate to Joseph Roberts for display at the Shilshole Beach Club, Seattle, WA. Back cover, pages 226, 227

1992   *Replica of a Haida House #4*, red cedar, 18' × 30'. With redwood and aggregate floor. Final construction carried out after Dudley Carter's death by Dudley Carter's grandson, Michael Vaughan of Gibsons, BC, assisted by a number of dedicated apprentices. Donated to King County by the Dudley Carter estate, later transferred, along with the park property, by the county to the City of Redmond, WA. Pages 234, 235, 236

1992   *Bird Reaching for Morning*, yellow cedar, a work in progress at the time of the artist's death. Center segment sold as totem by the Dudley Carter estate

1992   *Phantom's Retreat*, red cedar, incomplete. Two large curved segments of the work upon which Dudley was carving just days before he died, served as benches in the Slough House Park while the artist-in-residence program was in effect. Removed when the artists vacated the park in the spring of 1998.

About the Authors

'Lyn Fleury Lambert
After a career in advertising and human resources, then raising two sons, 'Lyn acted as Dudley's "executive secretary" and, following his death in 1992, continued to serve as a source of information and material about Dudley Carter and his work. She has written promotional materials and given talks about Dudley. 'Lyn was born in Calgary, Canada, and now resides in Bellevue, Washington.

H. Mary Sikkema (1931–2015)
Mary was born in Hudsonville, Michigan, studied education at Hope College and Michigan State University, enjoyed a teaching career, served as a missionary in Ethiopia with her husband, and reared four children in Bellevue, Washington. She developed a passion for writing poetry, short stories, newspaper articles, and inspirational novels. Her articles have been published in several local newspapers.

Made in the USA
Middletown, DE
26 October 2022

13437678R00173